A REPUBLIC OF RIVERS

A REPUBLIC OF RIVERS

Three Centuries of Nature
Writing from Alaska
and the Yukon

Edited by
JOHN A. MURRAY

New York   Oxford
OXFORD UNIVERSITY PRESS
1990

Oxford University Press

Oxford   New York   Toronto
Delhi   Bombay   Calcutta   Madras   Karachi
Petaling Jaya   Singapore   Hong Kong   Tokyo
Nairobi   Dar es Salaam   Cape Town
Melbourne   Auckland

and associated companies in
Berlin   Ibadan

Copyright © 1990 by Oxford University Press, Inc.

Published by Oxford University Press, Inc.,
200 Madison Avenue, New York, New York 10016

Oxford is a registered trademark of Oxford University Press

Library of Congress Cataloging-in-Publication Data
A Republic of rivers :
three centuries of nature writing
from Alaska and the Yukon /
edited by John A. Murray.
p.   cm.   Includes bibliographical references.
ISBN 0–19–506102–0
1. Natural history—Alaska.
2. Natural history—Yukon Territory.
I. Murray, John A., 1954–   .
QH105.A4R46   1990   508.798—dc20
89–28906

9 8 7 6 5 4 3 2 1

Printed in the United States of America
on acid-free paper

This book is lovingly dedicated
to my wife Jane
and son Steve.

Preface

My first view of Alaska was from a jet aircraft en route from Seattle to Fairbanks. Somewhere north of the Queen Charlotte Islands, British Columbia, the pilot announced we were passing over Ketchikan, Alaska, a busy fishing and logging port just over the border from Canada. Down below, oil tankers, lumber freighters, and purse seiners inscribed ephemeral v's on the bright blue enamel of the sea. Hundreds of maritime islands, ranging in size from a pile of rocks just large enough to accommodate a colony of herring gulls to something on the order of Oahu, were scattered up and down the far northwestern coast of the Americas. Here the cedar totem poles of the Haida and Tlingit towered over deep cold bays where humpback whales sang their undeciphered epic sagas, and white-hooded eagles, mated for life, built sprawling nests in the Sitka spruce. Further to the north was Mount Saint Elias (18,008'), an appropriately sized cairn marking the international boundary with the Yukon Territory. Gold nuggets the size of river cobblestone once lured thousands beyond these mountains during the 1890s. Next came the cyclopean glaciers—Malaspina, the size of Rhode Island, Bering, Columbia, and others hardly noticed here that would be national parks anywhere else in the world. While we were flying low over the rugged Chugach Mountains, my excitement grew, knowing that grizzlies and wolves, both extinct in the Rockies where I then lived, still freely roamed this wild land. To the south was the Kenai Peninsula, world renowned for the spawning salmon that redden its rivers each year, and for the bull moose whose antlers span a width greater than many people are tall.

An hour later—after a brief layover in Anchorage—the captain identified Denali (20,320') in the prominent massif to the west, a mountain as distinctive as Fuji or Blanc or Kilimanjaro. The entire wide-bodied cabin of young and old, native and non-native, resident and traveler gathered in silence at the starboard windows to behold the highest mountain north of the Andes. A young mother traveling alone pressed her infant son—previously crying uncontrollably—to the bulkhead port, and, much to everyone's surprise, the child grew calm and still, and then broke into a beaming smile. On the final approach to Fairbanks I saw not one light, not one road, not one dwelling in all the twilight boreal country over which we descended. Elsewhere, spring was well underway, but here the first family of white-fronted geese, the first cannonade of break-up, were still weeks away. At the last moment we turned east over the Chena River to line up with the runway and I had a brief but tantalizing view of a distant snow-covered range—the White Mountains—beckoning to the north. Over these gentle summits and passes—homeland of the Athabaskan Indians—was the formidable Brooks Range, parts of which were mapped and explored only in the 1930s by Robert Marshall. Beyond those crags was a greater wilderness still, a vast coastal plain—arctic foxes, barren-ground caribou, and snowy owls—and then at last the Arctic Ocean—polar bears, ringed seals, and Eskimo kayaks. Imagine, I thought, arriving at the foot of the Rocky Mountains just fifty years after the worn moccasins of Lewis and Clark spanned the continent. The far north—particularly north of the Yukon River—still offers a view of just such an untouched land, a true frontier, where, in the words of Stewart Udall, "the early-morning mantle of primeval America can be seen in its pristine glory, where one can gaze with wonder on the land as it was when the Indians first came."[1]

I returned to Alaska in late August of that year to begin teaching English at the University of Alaska. Fairbanks—a close-knit arctic community of 20,000 hardy folk—was now my home. Since moving here, my explorations of the region have proceeded on two levels: first, I have traveled widely through the Alaska and Polar Regions Collection of Rasmuson Library, an unsurpassed assemblage of circumpolar literature, learning along the way how little it is possible for one person to know; and, second, I have roamed the wilderness that extends in every direction around Fairbanks, although most often my excursions have led to Denali National Park, a much-cherished sanctuary. A lifetime of directed reading provided a foundation for this book, but it could not have assumed its present form without the resources made available to me at the University of Alaska, and without the long-term residence necessary to physically experience the Arctic in all four seasons, from the midnight sun of June to the northern lights of January.

Two decisions were made early on in the preparation of this anthology: first, to have a larger number of shorter selections, in order to feature as much as feasible the work of lesser known figures, and, second, to include to an extent the literature of the Yukon—a region united by a common river, language, and history with those lands to the west—along with the literature of Alaska. These two strategies have enabled me to assemble a significant collection of representative pieces

---

1. Stewart Udall, The Quiet Crisis (New York: Holt Rinehart and Winston, Inc., 1963), 15.

ranging over the past three centuries, from 1741 through 1989, a rich bounty of works that will I hope lead the reading public further afield than has been the case before. Each of these writers has attempted to capture something of the beauty of this still pristine land, to render in human terms the immutable spirit of the earth that elevates, in turn, all who honor her. To read any or all of these selections is to experience at once a liberation and a communion. That uplifting of the fatigued spirit is, as Margaret Murie so eloquently expressed it, "the great gift Alaska can give to the harassed world."[2]

Fairbanks   J.A.M.
November 1989

2. Margaret Murie, *Two in the Far North* (New York: Alfred A. Knopf, Inc., 1957), ii.

Acknowledgments

A book of this scope can only be undertaken with the assistance of a large number of individuals. It could not have been written without the help of the following people and institutions and the resources they made available. While acknowledging my gratitude, all errors of fact and judgment are my own.

To the English Department of the University of Alaska, Fairbanks, I would like to express my deepest thanks for bringing me to Alaska: John W. Morgan, Alice L. Harris, David A. Stark, Roy K. Bird, Joseph A. Dupras, Marie Lium, Michael J. Schuldiner, Russell E. Stratton, Russell D. Tabbert, Cynthia L. Walker, Eric Heyne, Janis Lull, Leroy Perkins, Peggy Shumaker, Frank Soos, and Doris Ann Bartlett. I would also like to thank the Dean of the College of Liberal Arts, Anne D. Shinkwin, and the Chancellor, Patrick J. O'Rourke.

I am particularly grateful to the following individuals at the Elmer E. Rasmuson Library at the University of Alaska, Fairbanks, for their assistance: Bruce Parham, Marge Naylor, Richard Veezy, Paul McCarthy, and Marvin W. Falk.

A special thanks to Dr. Richard A. Pierce, Professor of History at the University of Alaska, Fairbanks, and Editor of The Limestone Press in Kingston, Canada, for granting permission to reprint the translations from his early Alaska series, as well as for offering guidance in the selection of materials from the Russian-American period.

The authors and their publishers have been wonderfully helpful in the preparation of this book; no anthology can be successfully undertaken without such eager assistance, and I thank them all for their enthusiasm and cooperation.

A grant from the Alaska Humanities Forum and the National Endowment for the Humanities facilitated my study of Dr. Adolph Murie. A special use permit from the National Park Service made possible the close field study of grizzly bears in Denali National Park; an essay from that work-in-progress is included here. Ralph Tingey, George Wagner,

Rick McIntyre, Bill McDonald, Tom Griffith, Russ Berry, and Ralph Cunningham were particularly helpful.

I'm also grateful to Bill Sisler, vice president and executive editor of Oxford University Press, for his encouragement and support.

Finally, I would like to thank my wife Jane for her many kindnesses and especially for her patience with my absences over the past year as I prepared this book. Her love helped this book come into being.

Contents

Introduction, 3

Part I 1741–1866: Russian America and the Age of Exploration, 21

1. The Sea Cow, 25
   Georg Wilhelm Steller

2. The Bering Straits, 33
   James Cook

3. Observations on Unalashka, 39
   Carl Heinrich Merck

4. Prince William Sound, 43
   George Vancouver

5. Arrival at the Arctic Coast, 49
   Alexander Mackenzie

6. St. Lawrence Island, 53
   Otto Von Kotzebue

7. The Bering Straits, 57
   Adelbert Von Chamisso

8. The Pribilof Islands, 63
   Frederic Litke

9. Notes on the Copper River, 69
   Ferdinand Petrovich Wrangell

10. Notes on the Islands of the Unalashka District, 73
    Ivan Venianimov

11. Nulato, a Settlement on the Yukon, 79
    L. A. Zagoskin

12. Letter to Sir John Richardson, 85
    Alexander Hunter Murray

Part II 1867–1958: Territorial Alaska and the Age of Exploitation, 89

13. The Rapids of the Yukon, 93
    William Henry Dall

14. The Pribilof Islands, 97
    Elizabeth Beaman

15. The Alexander Archipelago, 103
    John Muir

16. On Crossing the Alaska Range, 109
    Henry T. Allen

17. The Grand Canon of the Yukon, 113
    Frederick Schwatka

18. The Gustavus Peninsula, 117
    John Burroughs

19. The Dominant Primordial Beast, 121
    Jack London

20. Gold Prospectors of the Susitna Valley, 127
    Robert Dunn

21. Taku Inlet, 131
    Ella Higginson

22. On the Sheep Ranges, 135
    Charles Sheldon

23. The Barren Grounds Grizzly Bear, 143
    Vilhjalmur Stefansson

24. Koyukon Riddles, 149
    Julius Jetté

25. The Ascent of Denali (Mount McKinley), 153
    Hudson Stuck

26. The Kuskokwim River, 159
    May Wynne Lamb

27. Eskimo Poems, 165
    Knud Rasmussen

28. The North Fork of the Koyukuk, 171
    Robert Marshall

29. The Wolves of Mount McKinley, 181
    Adolph Murie

**Part III   1959–1989: Alaskan Statehood and the Age of
Environmentalism, 187**

30. Other Days, 191
    John Haines

31. The Old Crow, 197
    Margaret Murie

32. Glacier Bay Journal, 205
    Dave Bohn

33. Sheenjek, 213
    Kenneth Brower

34. One Man's Wilderness, 221
    Richard Proenneke

35. The Alaskan Journal, 225
    Thomas Merton

36. On Building a Raft, 231
    David J. Cooper

37. Here I Am Yet!, 241
    Johnny Taku Jack

38. Lake Dwarves and Giant Rat, 247
    Anna Nelson Harry

39. An Expedition to the Pole, 253
    Annie Dillard

40. The Subsistence Cycle, 257
    Richard Nelson

41. Gather at the River, 263
    Edward Abbey

42. Yukon-Charley: The Shape of Wilderness, 269
    Barry Lopez

43. Cape Prince of Wales, Alaska: A Suite, 275
    John Morgan

44. This Tangled Brilliance, 283
    David Rains Wallace

45. Haida Hunters and Legend of the Two Fin Killer Whale, 289
    George Hamilton

46. Two Great Polar Bear Hunters, 293
    Aloysius Pikonganna

47. The Cormorant Hunters, 297
    Frank Ellana

48. Ragged Ear of Sable Pass, 301
    John A. Murray

Further Reading, 311

Index, 321

This map has numbers on it corresponding to the authors represented in the anthology, so that the reader can geographically locate each selection.

1. Georg Wilhelm Steller
2. James Cook
3. Carl Heinrich Merck
4. George Vancouver
5. Alexander MacKenzie
6. Otto Von Kotzebue
7. Adelbert Von Chamisso
8. Frederick Litke

9. Ferdinand Wrangell
10. Ivan Venianimov
11. L. A. Zagoskin
12. Alexander Murray
13. William Henry Dall
14. Elizabeth Beaman
15. John Muir
16. Henry T. Allen

17. Frederick Schwatka
18. John Burroughs
19. Jack London
20. Robert Dunn
21. Ella Higginson
22. Charles Sheldon
23. Vilhjalmur Stefansson
24. Julius Jetté

25. Hudson Stuck
26. May Wynne Lamb
27. Knud Rasmussen
28. Robert Marshall
29. Adolph Murie
30. John Haines
31. Margaret Murie
32. Dave Bohn

33. Kenneth Brower
34. Richard Proenneke
35. Thomas Merton
36. David J. Cooper
37. Johnny Taku Jack
38. Anna Nelson Harry
39. Annie Dillard
40. Richard Nelson

41. Edward Abbey
42. Barry Lopez
43. John Morgan
44. David Rains Wallace
45. George Hamilton
46. Aloysius Pikonganna
47. Frank Ellana
48. John A. Murray

A REPUBLIC OF RIVERS

My prayer is that Alaska will not lose the heart-nourishing friendliness of her youth—that her people will always care for one another, her towns remain friendly and not completely ruled by the dollar—and that her great wild places will remain great, and wild, and free, where wolf and caribou, wolverine and grizzly bear, and all the Arctic blossoms may live on in the delicate balance which supported them long before impetuous man appeared in the North. This is the great gift Alaska can give to the harassed world.

Margaret Murie
Two in the Far North

Introduction

The persistent *donnée* of Arctic-American literature is wild nature, and for good reason: the environment is a controlling reality at higher latitudes as it is not elsewhere. Here is a polar land that is sustained by as little as one-fourth of the sunlight available at the equator, that is completely or almost wholly dark for up to three months of the year, and that endures periods of prolonged cold unsurpassed in the hemisphere. Some interior locations receive less precipitation than continental deserts. Several of the southeastern islands of Alaska, on the other hand, absorb more annual rainfall than the Amazon. Permafrost, poorly developed soils, and compressed growing seasons make life in the boreal regions marginal for both plants and animals, and, despite popular myths of abundance, wildlife in these taiga and spruce forest ecosystems is scarce. Army Lieutenant Henry T. Allen, writing in 1887 after an extensive reconnaissance of the Alaskan interior, reported that, "It is a mistaken idea, that of supposing the interior of Alaska possessed of much large game. To show the scarcity of such, I will say that during our entire travel . . . over a route covering 18° of longitude, we did not see a single moose or caribou, and but one bear."[1] Similarly, the biologist-brothers Adolph and Olaus Murie, who undertook a six-month, one-thousand-mile dog-sled trip in arctic Alaska during the winter of 1922–1923, later recounted that, "During the entire winter we saw not a *single* [emphasis added] wolf track."[2] Elsewhere in the arctic north, actively extruding volcanoes, Richter force 7 or 8 earthquakes, and 100-foot tsunamis—not to mention brown bears and mosquitoes—further challenge human life. All these environmental extremes translate into austerity, and have resulted in a preoccupation with nature—whether in the traditional Athabaskan riddles translated by Father Jetté in 1913 or the latest contemporary non-native nature essays—that is reflected in the literature.

Within the larger general theme of nature, there is much individual variation, and some classic American themes will be found: the quest for self-reliance, for communion, and for accomplishment. Given the fact

3

that many of these texts are idiosyncratic—enriched by several themes—
any attempt at providing a neat thematic taxonomy would be reductive.
In fact, very often the more successful selections—particularly those
from the mid to late twentieth century—integrate a plurality of themes,
as is the case, for example, with the 1983 river narrative of Edward
Abbey "Gather at the River," which is concerned with surviving on a
wilderness trip despite a serious illness, establishing a self-renewing
nexus with what the author humorously calls "the secret of the essence
of the riddle of the Spirit of the Arctic,"[3] and producing a durable work
of literature. However, insofar as one subject ordinarily predominates, it
is reasonable—these distinctions notwithstanding—to discuss the
works broadly in terms of theme.

Self-reliance is a theme as old as the American experience, infusing
the earliest colonial works—from private journals to public jeremiads—
of New England, Thoreau's *Walden* (Boston, 1854), and, more recently,
Henry Beston's *The Outermost House* (Doubleday, 1928). "Whoso
would be a man," wrote Ralph Waldo Emerson in his classic 1841 essay
'Self-Reliance,' "must be a nonconformist."[4] Two practitioners of Emer-
sonian self-reliance represented in this volume are John Haines, whose
selection describes his late 1950s homestead on Alaska's Tanana River,
and Richard Proenneke, who built a cabin in 1968 at Lake Clark before
the new Alaskan national park was formed there in 1980. "Little by
little," John Haines observed, "I am learning the ways of the north. In the
darkness and cold that is coming, we will not go hungry."[5] Ten years
later, a 51-year-old Richard Proenneke arrived on the shores of a wilderness lake with little more than an axe in his hand. He was confronted
there with the ageless question: "What was I capable of that I didn't
know yet?"[6] Both John Haines and Richard Proenneke strove, and
continue to strive, to base their lives on the Stoic principle of *autarky*, or
self-sufficiency; both have discovered in the process the verity of Thoreau's axiom: "Simplicity, simplicity, simplicity!"[7] Other writings in
this collection that are pervaded by this theme of self-reliance include
Dave Bohn's 1965 account of wilderness hiking in Glacier Bay National
Monument, Kenneth Brower's 1968 trek across the Brooks Range, and
Dave Cooper's more recent 1977 crossing of what has since become Gates
of the Arctic National Park. In each case, the authors tested themselves in
regions far from civilization, and emerged forever changed.

The writings of several women represented in this anthology are
also directly concerned with self-reliance. Libby Beaman, in 1879 the
first non-native woman to live on the remote Pribilof Islands of Alaska's
Bering Sea, refused to return to the Lower 48 when asked to do so by her
husband's supervisor, and then wrote resolutely in her journal that, "It is
up to me to make the best of everything and to do so with good grace. We
will never survive the two years and keep our sanity unless I do."[8] May
Wynne Lamb, arriving from Kansas at a remote Eskimo village to teach
school in 1916, resolved that, "My mother's good red blood was in my

veins, and if she could be a guiding light in a homestead on the prairies, I could do the same in a native village."[9] For both women there were many challenges and setbacks, and May Wynne Lamb would eventually lose her husband, but both managed not only to tenaciously survive in the Arctic, but also to transform their personal sagas into enduring literary works. Margaret Murie's selection—based on a trip she made with Olaus in the early 1920s to the northern Yukon—provides another example of self-reliance, as she and her husband are forced to accept the Arctic on its own terms: "The moment I pulled my hands out of the [dish] water, they would be black with mosquitoes."[10] Not only must Mardy hold the camp, and very often the boat together, but she must also care for their infant child. Her journal tells of bears and rapids, mammoth-tusks and engine breakdowns, and illustrates the difficulties, and the joys, of life in the far north.

The quest for communion, for a resonant, transforming moment with pristine nature—the rejuvenation of the drained spirit—is also a distinctive theme in American literature, from the poetry of William Cullen Bryant to that of Theodore Roethke, and is evident here in an interesting variety of selections. Thomas Merton's 1968 Alaskan journals come to mind first, as the Cistercian monk perceives the power of mountains to spiritually uplift humankind, describing Mounts Drum and Wrangell as "sacred and majestic mountains, ominous, enormous, noble, and stirring."[11] Reverend Hudson Stuck, who led the first successful ascent of Mount McKinley in 1913, found on the mountaintop a Mosaic-like inspiration, and returned to his pastoral work reinvigorated and recommitted to serving his faith. At the summit he discovered "no pride of conquest, no trace of that exultation of victory some enjoy . . . no gloating over good fortune . . . Rather was the feeling that a privileged *communion* [emphasis added] with the high places of the earth had been granted . . . seeing all things as they spread out from the windows of heaven itself."[12]

Other writers represented in this volume—John Muir, John Burroughs, Robert Marshall, David Rains Wallace, John Morgan—have similarly sought and received a transformative contact with the wild Arctic. A word that appears in their work both early and late is *sublime,* whether in John Muir's 1879 description of Glacier Bay as "a picture of icy wildness unspeakably pure and sublime,"[13] or Robert Marshall's 1929 description of the "wild sublimity"[14] of the Gates of the Arctic. The notion of the sublime—of all that is lofty, grand, and exalted—derives from the classical age of Rome, specifically from Longinus, and enjoyed great popularity in the eighteenth century with Edmund Burke's *A Philosophical Enquiry into the Origin of Our Ideas of the Sublime and Beautiful* (London, 1757). It has particular relevance to the Arctic, and to literary expressions of the manner in which writers commune with the region—Annie Dillard has written specifically that the "Polar explorers . . . sought at the Poles something of the sublime. Simplicity and purity attracted them; they set out to perform clear tasks in uncontaminated lands. . . . They praised the land's spare quality as if it were a moral or a spiritual quality."[15] An epiphany was what they really desired, Annie Dillard intimates, and not so much the ambitious geographic or commercial goals they concocted—from the discovery of the Northwest Passage to the rescue of the 1845 Franklin Expedition to the attainment of the North Pole—to sell their elaborate missions to wealthy and skeptical investors. Dillard herself, traveling to Alaska's remote Barter Island, relates a vision of Blakean innocence. Looking out at the ice floes, Dillard writes that "I saw what newborn babies must see: nothing but senseless variations of light on the retinas."[16] Barry Lopez's communion, walking along the Yukon River, is simpler still: "I fumble at some prayer I have forgotten, utterly forgotten, how to perform."[17] He places some stones he has gathered "back in the river, as carefully as possible, and move inland to sleep."[18]

Of the three themes discussed here, none is more prevalent, in Arctic-American writing or in this anthology, than the last: the quest for accomplishment. Given the American preoccupation with material achievement, particularly insofar as it asserts the value of the New World over the Old World, it is perhaps not surprising that so many of these quintessentially American selections are infused with the spirit of hard-earned conquest: acquiring commercially or scientifically useful information, extracting natural resources, climbing mountains, killing bears, overcoming wild rivers. Whether for naturalists like Georg Steller and Carl Merck, or for exploration commanders like George Vancouver and Otto Von Kotzebue, the Arctic promised not only new adventures and new horizons, but also the possibility of worldly riches and fame on their return to civilization. Thus did Adelbert Von Chamisso, the naturalist for Otto Von Kotzebue's 1815–1818 expedition, write that Georg Steller is the one "whom Pallas [another naturalist] calls *immortal* [emphasis added]," and that while "other learned men and collectors" have explored Pacific Asia and northwestern America, "the names of Steller and Merck have retained all their lustre."[19] To become "immortal" and to have a name that retained its "lustre" over time—these, together with the desire for riches, lured the earliest explorers to the north as much as the quest for geographic certitudes and empirical truths.

This quest for accomplishment theme persists from the Age of Exploration (1741–1866) through the Age of Exploitation (1867–1958) and well into the contemporary Age of Environmentalism (1959–1989), although it has diminished somewhat in the recent past. Robert Dunn, an unsuccessful turn-of-the century climber of Mt. McKinley, sat in his base camp on the Susitna River and painted a vivid sketch of the nearby prospectors as a pathetic and greedy lot of outcasts, failing in a humorous irony that later authors like Robert Marshall would seize upon with relish, to see that he is camped right there with them. After pioneering explorer Charles Sheldon killed a sow grizzly and left its orphan cub to die—considered unsporting even in his own time[20]—he smoked his pipe and mused over "the strange and beautiful lights and shadows playing on the mountains encircling me" to the "wailing of the [orphaned bear cub] pealing wildly through the mists above;"[21] again, so intoxicated with his endeavors—his quest to achieve—that he failed to grasp the absurdity of the moment. Both William Dall and Frederick Schwatka describe their separate runnings of the Yukon rapids (1866 and 1883) anti-climatically, as if nature had somehow cheated them by not making the accomplishment more perilous. Each of these authors— and a myriad of others—were drawn to the north by the desire for immutable, transcendent achievement. The purely aesthetic experience that arises from deep communion with the land was to a great extent beyond many of them, as was the sense of fulfillment that derives from simply living in self-reliant harmony with the land, but they still produced a durable body of natural history writing that, in addition to having intrinsic literary value, also laid a deep foundation for the visionaries and iconoclasts—writers like Thomas Merton and Edward Abbey—who came later.

Several genres are common in nonfiction nature writing, and will be apparent in the literary ecosystem of nature writing gathered here: the official expedition narrative, the individual adventure narrative, the scientific report, the personal journal and memoir, and the familiar essay. Those selections falling into the first category, which were generated by governmentally commissioned or corporately financed expeditions, include virtually all of the writings in the Russian-American period except Alexander Murray's natural history letter to John Richardson, as well as those selections in the Territorial Alaska period by Henry Allen, Frederick Schwatka, John Muir, John Burroughs, Vilhjalmur Stefansson, and Knud Rasmussen. The earliest official expedition narratives—by James Cook, George Vancouver, Otto Von Kotzebue and others—are written for the most part under the lingering influence of the Enlightenment, and are characterized by a rational European perspective, an emphasis on fidelity to scientific principles known then, the use of scientific method, and a reflexive consideration of the practical benefit of any new discovery. In later expedition narratives—particularly those written by John Muir and John Burroughs on the 1899 Harriman Expedition, but also evident in the writings of Vilhjalmur Stefansson on the 1908 American Museum Expedition and Knud Rasmussen on the 1921–1924 Fifth Thule Expedition—the objective reportage of the Age of Reason is replaced by the more subjective viewpoint of the Post-Romantic Age and early Modern Age.

Although individuals and small groups later explored relatively unknown areas in Arctic-America, they did so without institutional support and their writings fall into the category of individual adventure narratives. These private chronicles—written by Ella Higginson, Robert

Dunn, Hudson Stuck, Robert Marshall, Dave Bohn, Kenneth Brower, David Cooper, and Edward Abbey—do not have the scientific focus of the official expedition narrative, are much less formal in structure, and are written in the more relaxed private voice, as when Edward Abbey writes humorously of expedition-force coffee "powerful enough to deconstipate a sand-impacted Egyptian [mummy],"[22] and records camp-side small talk with a conversational familiarity that would have been anathema in the formal record of the earlier official expedition narratives.

The scientific orientation of nature writing has increased over the twentieth century to the extent that many of the better-known nature writers have either been professional scientists who have mastered the craft of writing—Robert Marshall, Adolph Murie, Richard Nelson—or professional writers who have become self-educated scientists—Barry Lopez, Annie Dillard, Edward Abbey. Thus we have here two selections excised from scientific monographs that have all of the fine literary qualities found in the best nature writing. Adolph Murie—the "Father" of wolf ecology—writes with descriptive clarity and narrative skill of the East Fork wolf pack in his selection, putting aside the specialized language of the monograph to bring the non-specialist closer to the subject of his work. Similarly, Richard Nelson, a distinguished social scientist, provides a kind of "Roman Naturalist Calender" to the seasonal subsistence cycle of the Koyukon Indians of Huslia, Alaska, vividly giving the reader a sense of the rich interrelationship that exists between these people and the land. Most of the earlier naturalists of the Russian-American period published their work not as self-contained scientific monographs on a single subject, but as expedition narratives in conjunction with the commanding officer or separately. Some, though, like Georg Steller's posthumously published *Journal of a Voyage with Bering, 1741–1742* (St. Petersburg, 1774), were received both as works of natural history and as expedition narratives.

Anyone who has read Dorothy Wordsworth's *Dove Cottage Journal* will know that very often a personal journal or memoir can contain extraordinary observations of nature, and the journals included in this collection are no exception, whether from Libby Beaman, May Wynne Lamb, Margaret Murie, Thomas Merton, or Richard Proenneke. Very often the naturalistic details come quickly, as when Margaret Murie described the vast Old Crow country in a single splendid sentence: "The country is alternating high yellow sand banks or mud banks or bluffs, and on the opposite shore low willow-grown mud shores or cut banks topped with small spruces on the mossy tundra, wild roses and red and pink Indian paintbrush blooming everywhere, the vivid light green of goose grass near the water—the deep, quiet, brown water."[23] Other times the observations are not of wild nature, but rather of human nature, as when Libby Beaman wrote candidly of her difficulties in adjusting to life on the Pribilof Islands of the Bering Sea, where her home was not far from the seal killing ground. "You at the Government House," one man told her, "will be spared the sight of the killing because of a fortunate rise in the land. But you'll not be spared the smell."[24] Richard Proenneke's season in the Alaskan Wilderness was more solitary, but no less challenging, and he recorded his daily life with just as careful an attention to detail. After a successful hunt for camp meat, he wrote in his journal: "A satisfying day. The search for meat is over. I hate to see the big ram end like this, but I suppose he could have died a lot harder than he did." For many a pioneer—from Libby Beaman to Richard Proenneke—the journal became that one silent friend to whom the truth could always be told, that one imperishable vessel in a constantly changing life landscape into which the beauty of the passing seasons could be poured.

Since Thoreau, the familiar essay has held a special appeal for nature writers, as they have found in the freedom the genre provides a literary parallel to the liberating experiences encountered in wild nature. It was Samuel Johnson who called the essay a "loose sally of the mind."[25] Joseph Addison wrote that "Among my Daily papers, which I bestow on the Publick, there are some which are written with Regularity and Method, and others that run out into the *Wildness* [emphasis added] of those compositions, which go by the name of essays."[26] For Aldous Huxley the essay was "a free association artistically controlled."[27] Everywhere there are resonances with the open and organic processes of nature. It is just these qualities of the "antigenre"[28] as some have called it, that have made the familiar essay so attractive to nature writers. The genre is represented in this collection with contributions by Barry Lopez, Annie Dillard, David Rains Wallace, and the editor (the Lopez and Dillard selections are excerpted from longer essays; the Wallace and Murray selections are *in tota*). It is interesting to note, both in these four selections and elsewhere in the contemporary nature essay, the similarities between this prose genre and the Romantic nature lyric, a poem that the Romantic scholar M. H. Abrams once defined as that work which "present[s] a determinate speaker in a particularized, and usually a localized, outdoor setting, whom we overhear as he carries on, in a fluent vernacular which rises easily to a more formal speech, a sustained colloquy."[29] The Romantic nature lyric, Abrams continued, "begins with a description of the landscape" after which "an aspect or change of aspect in the landscape evokes a varied but integral process of memory, thought, anticipation, and feeling which remains closely intervolved with the outdoor scene."[30] As a result of this interaction, the narrator "achieves an insight, faces up to a tragic loss, comes to a moral decision, or resolves an emotional problem."[31] One thinks here immediately of the Barry Lopez essay, which, in its complete form, encounters not only the experience of floating down the Yukon River, but also the whole notion of wilderness and, most important here, the author's deepest interactions with the landscape; it ends with a resonance as resounding as the closing lines of a nature lyric like Wordsworth's "Tintern Abbey."

The enormous influence of Victorian natural science on the contemporary nature essay is often acknowledged, but it is also helpful to recall
that not only, as the scholar Thomas Lyons has written, are "many of the
values seen in nature writing . . . shared with Romanticism,"[32] but
also that some of the Romantic literary paradigms have been adapted as
well.

The genres of poetry and fiction are represented with the passage
from Jack London, the Eskimo poems translated by Knud Rasmussen,
Anna Harry's two allegories, the stories from King Island, and John
Morgan's poem. Although the primary component of northern bibliog-
raphies to date is non-fiction, it is likely that in the future writers will
turn increasingly to poetry and fiction, and part of the reason for this is
that there is such a rich tradition in non-fiction. The relationship
between travel literature and the novel and poetry had been well
documented in a number of scholarly studies,[33] and it is possible that
cross-fertilization of the sort that produced works as diverse as Voltaire's
Candide and Coleridge's "Kubla Khan" in European literature could
also occur with Arctic-American literature. In fact, it often seems in the
"literary food chain" that the higher-order genres of poetry and fiction
"feed" on or at least partially draw their sustenance from the lower-order
non-fiction genres. Nevertheless, there is already a strong tradition in
both of these genres, and they form an integral component of Arctic-
American nature writing, whether the world-renowned sagas of Jack
London or the incomparably beautiful Eskimo poetry translated by
Rasmussen.

Turning to alternative perspectives on nature, it is important to
acknowledge that for at least twelve thousand years, Alaska and the
Yukon have been continuously occupied by the descendents of Asian
immigrants, the oral traditions of whom predate the written literatures of
western civilization by many millennia. The human relationships to
nature described in these oral traditions are often radically different
from those produced by the most recent wave of European and American
immigrants. Inevitably, many of these Native American lyrics, personal
narratives, and fictional stories lose something of their original vitality
in translation, and are further diminished as they are read silently on the
printed page, instead of being heard, as intended, with the modulations
and the moods that can be expressed by the spoken word. Very often
these works are infused with a profound respect for the land, and
describe the interdependence of life forms. George Hamilton, for example, a Haida Indian, tells a story of two fishermen who are transformed
into killer whales, a fable suggesting implicitly the underlying physical
unity of the *kosmos*, in which all things, as in Ovid's tales of meta-
morphosis, eventually become something else. Anna Harry, in her
allegories of the Giant Rat and the Lake Dwarves, similarly plays with
natural forms in such a way as to subtly express larger concerns. The
King Islanders tell about hunting polar bears on the ice pack, and about

an even wilder nature in the outback of the human heart. The Koyukon riddles translated by Father Jetté describe an austere but beautiful subarctic world thoroughly dominated by the forces of nature. Johnny Jack relates the difficulties of maintaining a dignified life close to nature in a time of cultural upheaval for his people, the coastal Tlingit. In the Eskimo poems and songs collected and translated by Knud Rasmussen we have as perfect a collection of poetry as found anywhere on Earth. The ultimate value of these selections for non-native readers is that they challenge assumptions not only about culture and literature, but also about nature.

Readers familiar with the "land-as-woman" thesis of ecofeminists Annette Kolodny, Carolyn Merchant, Elizabeth Gray and others, which equates the oppression of nature with the oppression of women, will find a pattern here common elsewhere in American literature, as male writers describe a pristine landscape—often referred to or symbolized in feminine terms—as it is violated in the name of progress. In the very first selection, for example, eighteenth-century naturalist Georg Steller relates the slaughter of a sea cow—a species extinct shortly thereafter—by shipwrecked sailors in telling Freudian language as "the men in the yawl thrust large knives and bayonets in all parts of its body."[34] Later he provides an unusually graphic anatomical description of a dead female sea cow and notes that, "a male two days in a row came to its dead female on the shore and inquired about its condition . . . the [sea cows] remained constantly in one spot, no matter how many of them were wounded or killed."[35] From his journal, it is clear that Steller's fellow crewmen destroyed considerably more of these animals than was necessary to sustain them, particularly when it is considered that they were able to use their nets to fish the rich waters. Angry at nature for devastating their dreams of discovery and conquest, the surviving crew of the *St. Paul* vented their frustrations on the defenseless sea cows. "They are not in the least afraid of human beings,"[36] wrote Steller cheerfully of the doomed species.

It is informative to compare Steller's 1741 passage of violation with Barry Lopez's more respectful description in 1986 of a female polar bear captured by wildlife biologists:

> One of the females we darted went down near a jumble of shattered ice. . . . I looked at details of her fur and felt the thickness of her ears, as though examining a museum specimen. Uncomfortable with all this, I walked over to the pressure ridge and sat on a slab of broken sea ice. . . . As I sat there my companions rolled the unconscious bear over on her back and I saw a trace of pink in the white fur between her legs. . . . I looked away. I felt I had invaded her privacy. For the remainder of the day I could not rid myself of this image of vulnerability.[37]

While those who came earlier—Georg Steller with the sea cow killing fields, Charles Sheldon proudly carving up his female grizzly bear, Jack

London with his frozen universe of alienated and isolated men—saw nature as a female to be subdued, later writers—Barry Lopez, Edward Abbey, Richard Nelson, and others—have attempted to reintegrate civilization with nature. Barry Lopez describes himself respectfully bowing: "I took to bowing on these evening walks. I would bow slightly with my hands in my pockets, toward the birds and the evidence of life in their nests—because of their fecundity, unexpected in this remote region."[38] Earlier naturalists—from Georg Steller to Charles Sheldon—brought enough preserved specimens back with them to fill entire museums. All along, the writings of women—Libby Beaman, May Wynne Lamb, Ella Higginson, Margaret Murie, Anna Harry, Annie Dillard—have provided an often welcome counterpoint to the hierarchy expressed in male writing. "The marvels here [in Alaska]," wrote Ella Higginson in an understatement characteristically rich with implications, "are not the marvels of men."[39]

Most of what could be called the literary criticism of Arctic-American nature writing to date has been confined to the occasional remarks of the practitioners—Ella Higginson, Edward Abbey, Annie Dillard, John Haines, Barry Lopez—as they pursued other topics in their essays, articles, reviews, memoirs, and books. Ella Higginson, writing in 1908, made a candid admission about the literary task facing her and others:

> The spell of Alaska falls upon every lover of beauty who has voyaged along those far northern snow-pearled shores . . . or who has drifted down the mighty rivers of the interior which flow, bell-toned and lonely, to the sea. I know not how the spell is wrought; nor have I ever met one who could put the miracle of its working into words. *No writer has ever described Alaska; no one writer ever will; but each must do his share, according to the spell that the country casts upon him* [emphasis added].[40]

This sentiment is echoed by Edward Abbey in his 1983 essay "Gather at the River." Abbey, like Higginson, allows himself to be overwhelmed by the immensity of the Arctic, and, through the act of surrendering to his subject, finally begins to grasp it: "What can I say except confess that I have seen but little of the real North, and of that little understood less . . . no prose however royally purple, can bracket our world within the boundaries of mind."[41]

When asked to name the best book about the north, Edward Abbey replied: "*The Call of the Wild* . . . Jack London captures there the essence of the mythos of the wilderness."[42] Abbey called John Haines' *Winter News* (Wesleyan University Press, 1978) the best book of poetry to come from Alaska, because it was "about ordinary things, about the great weather, about daily living experience, as opposed to technical poetry, which is concerned mainly with prosody, with technique."[43] He also admitted to being fond of the poetry of Robert Service: "I love him."[44] Abbey stated that he had "started . . . but never finished" John McPhee's *Coming into the Country* (Farrar Straus, 1977) and describes its author as "a first-rate reporter."[45] When asked to name the best prose book about Alaska, Abbey replied: "*Going to Extremes*, by Joe McGinnis. A brilliant book. Mandatory for anyone who wants a sense of what contemporary life in Alaska is like. My opinion does not set well with the locals. No! they say, McGinnis writes only about the sensational. Alaska, is a sensational place, I reply . . . [and] he tells the truth."[46]

Annie Dillard, writing in 1982 on the literature of polar exploration—which in this volume would include most of the authors in the Russian-American Period as well as later figures such as Vilhjalmur Steffanson and Knud Rasmussen—admits to being impressed above all by their Stoicism:

> Reading their accounts of life *in extremis*, one is struck by their unending formality toward each other. . . . Even in the privacy of their journals and diaries, polar explorers maintain a fine reserve. One wonders, after reading a great many firsthand accounts, if polar explorers were not somehow chosen for the empty and solemn splendor of their prose styles—or even if some eminent Victorians, examining their own prose styles, realized, perhaps dismayed, that from the look of it they would have go to in for polar exploration.[47]

Annie Dillard believes these individuals went "partly in search of the sublime," motivated by ideas of "eternity" and "perfection" almost as if "they were some perfectly visible part of the landscape."[48] Many of them failed because "despite the purity of their conceptions, they manhauled their humanity to the poles."[49]

Alaskan poet John Haines has written several important critical essays on Alaskan literature, which were reprinted in *Living off the Country, Essays on Poetry and Place* (University of Michigan Press, 1981). Haines admits to being disappointed with the literature of Alaska: "If we wish to read about the North, not as sensation or bald news report, we must go to Scandinavian literature, to the Russians, or to some extent, to the Canadians."[50] He warns that "We see Alaska through cliches to save us from thinking,"[51] and asks "How long might it take a people living here to be at home in their landscape, and to produce from that experience . . . [a] literature of the first rank? Several hundred years? A few generations?"[52] Haines believes that "closeness is needed, long residence, intimacy of a sort that demands a certain daring and risk: a surrender, an abandonment, or just a sense of somehow being stuck with it."[53] He concludes that "An original literature is possible in Alaska . . . [but] There is an inevitable provinciality of a newly settled place, the self-protectiveness of unsure people . . . The Alaskan writer must learn to love with the knowledge that what he or she writes may be recognized by only a few people."[54] Haines, above all, is critical of those who come on "literary excursion[s] through the 'Great Land'" almost as "sightseer[s] in a strange land" and produce works flawed by "knowledge acquired for the moment,"[55] as opposed to those who call this place home and know about it well enough to write about it fluently. "To live by a large river," Haines has written, "is to be kept in the heart of things."[56] This form of intimacy Haines believes is essential to the writer's task in Alaska. No doubt this is true, but it is also true that some of the best writing in this collection was by those who visited Alaska and the Yukon for the shortest period—no doubt the intensity of the experience and the writer's natural gifts also have something to do with what kind of writing is produced by a particular person or period.

In his 1986 book *Arctic Dreams* (Scribner's) Barry Lopez writes insightfully about some of the issues and problems in Arctic-American writing. Much of the writing of the exploration period, and what in this book is called the exploitation period, Barry Lopez sees darkly, in a view that diverges somewhat from Annie Dillard's emphasis upon "sublimity," as a "legacy of desire."[57] Lopez writes: "In the journals and histories I read of these journeys I was drawn on by a sharp leaning in the human spirit: pure *desire* [emphasis added]—the complexities of human passion and *cupidity* [emphasis added] . . . Rarely was the goal anything as selfless as an increase in mankind's geographic knowledge."[58] Lopez sees the single greatest motivation as "the promise of financial reward."[59] A key passage summarizes his point of view: "The literature of arctic exploration is frequently offered as a record of resolute will before the menacing fortifications of the landscape. . . . It is better to contemplate the record of human longing to achieve something significant."[60]

Those who read through these selections in chronological order will observe some significant changes in literary style and the use of language. The prose of the Russian-American Period (1741–1866) is largely devoid of the usual figurative comforts as the royal explorers and their Linnaean naturalists coldly and methodically narrate each new discovery and disaster, as when Captain George Vancouver describes Prince William Sound—one of the most beautiful locations in all of Alaska—as "a branch of the ocean that requires the greatest circumspection to navigate; and although it diverges into many extensive arms, yet none of them can be considered as commodious."[61] The Latinate prose of the Age of Reason—some of the selections, like the Steller piece, were translated from Latin—was replaced in the nineteenth century by the densely textured, laboriously wrought prose of the Post-Romantics and early Moderns—John Muir, John Burroughs, Ella Higginson, Charles Sheldon, and others—who rendered natural scenes as elaborately as Albert Bierdstadt and Thomas Moran painted their vast landscape canvases of the American West. John Muir, for example, composed a sentence of some 118 words—too prodigious to cite here—simply to describe one part of one channel in the Alexander Archipelago, a region, which he depicted elsewhere as a "true fairyland,"[62] and "the very paradise of the poets, the abode of the blessed,"[63] where the Sitka spruces leaning from the islands are "like flowers leaning outward against the rim of a vase."[64] For much of the twentieth century, and largely in response to the purple prose excesses that preceded it, a school of photorealism—characterized by a minimalist approach—has prevailed in Arctic-American literature as it has elsewhere. The laconic prose of John Haines—notable for its controlled narrative voice, concision of expression, and paucity of metaphor and simile—exemplifies this style. More recently, there has been an influx of some of the old lyricism and subjectivity of the nineteenth century, best seen in the rambling conversational tone and freely descriptive approach evident in the Edward Abbey selection.

What is the significance of this regional literature of nature with respect to English literature and World literature? There are at least three reasons to consider Arctic-American nature writing—particularly that written in the last several decades—as having literary significance, and each bears examination. First, while acknowledging that much of Arctic-American literature through the middle of the twentieth century is similar to colonial and immigrant literatures elsewhere in the English-speaking world, from India to Australia to Africa, it is evident that something unusual has been happening—both around the world and in the north—in the more recent past (1959–1989), and that these changes are enhancing—rather than diminishing—the importance of this particular region and, consequently, of its writing. It has become apparent, with the widespread destruction of tropical wilderness and the deterioration of the environment in the middle latitudes, that an increased emphasis is being placed on Arctic America—with its large integrated system of parks and refuges—as the last secure repository of wild nature on Earth. This new focus is most visibly manifest in the number of major authors—Edward Abbey, Barry Lopez, Annie Dillard—who now visit and write about wild Alaska, as Ernest Hemingway, Theodore Roosevelt, and Isak Dinesen once traveled to wild Africa, and as, in another age, Samuel Johnson, James Boswell, and others undertook their walking tours of wild Scotland. The nature writing of Alaska and the Yukon is important, in the first instance, simply because the region has become important, a situation that has, in the years since Alaskan statehood, produced a thriving nature literature unsurpassed in the English-speaking world.

A second and related reason for the increased importance of this nature writing is that it is a dynamic component of a worldwide revolution in environmental consciousness, a movement of which British conservationist John McCormick has recently written in his book *Reclaiming Paradise: The Global Environmental Movement* (Indiana University Press, 1989): "Of all the conceptual revolutions of the twentieth century, few have wrought so universal or so fundamental a change in human values as the environmental revolution . . . in just a few decades, the assumptions of centuries have been over-turned."[65] That is an impressive claim, but one other noted thinkers agree with. Literary scholar Thomas Lyon, for example, has written similarly that "The nature essay . . . may be seen as reflecting a general human stirring over the past two or three centuries, a movement in thinking toward what may be *a great watershed* [emphasis added]."[66] This environmental revolution has been characterized by two radical shifts: first, in its attempt to resanctify nature—to bow respectfully, as Barry Lopez does, instead of brutally violate, as Georg Steller recorded—the movement has sought to reverse the process of secularization—the conquest of a demystified nature—that began in earnest with the Renaissance; and second, in its sheer exuberance and optimism—Professor Lyon writes of the overwhelming "affirmation"[67] found at the core of the movement and its nature writing—it has begun to reverse an urban pessimism that has pervaded Western Literature since the end of the Romantic Age.

Nature writers whose works include representations of Alaska and the Yukon are active members of this larger global community of thinkers and writers, and—particularly because of the earlier-mentioned emphasis being placed on the arctic region—are contributing in a substantial way to this historic transition. The extent of the change, in this anthology, is nowhere more evident than in comparing the commercially tainted natural histories of the Russian-American period—nature writing in the service of whomever commissioned it—with the unified, biocentric viewpoint of those—Richard Nelson, David Rains Wallace, Barry Lopez, Annie Dillard, and others—writing in the contemporary period. There is a view of cultural history known as *universalgeschichte* that stipulates, in the words of the French philosopher Blaise Pascal, that we can "consider the entire sequence of human beings, during the entire course of the ages, as a single man who lives perpetually on and learns something all of the time."[68] One can only hope that the western "universal" mind, returning to the arctic north generation after generation, continues to evolve, as it now seems to be, toward a mature land ethic such as is seen, ironically, in the *weltanschauung*, or world view of the native Eskimo and Athabaskan people.

Third, the nature literature of Arctic America is important simply for its own sake, as the highest expression of the thoughts, aspirations, feelings, and impressions of the residents and travelers of this wild and beautiful realm at the top of the world. At its finest, the nature writing of this region achieves the characteristics of universality that define excellence in any language and at any time, and enables us to share the lives of those who came before: to mourn with Frederick Litke over the senseless slaughter of sea mammals, to probe with Ade Murie the daily life of a wolf pack, to laugh sardonically with the Koyukon over the mystery of the universe.

It has not been possible to do justice to all the authors or the issues raised by their texts in this introductory essay; such a thorough discussion belongs, more properly, in another sort of book, and perhaps such a volume will be written, for a thoughtful critical commentary is needed. What has been attempted here is to provide the reader with a kind of annotated map—pointing out landmarks, noting history, indicating routes, warning of hazards, suggesting side-trips. A Republic of Rivers is intended, chiefly, to send readers, and writers, up to some new floors of the library, and into some new conversations in their formal or informal literary clubs, for a work of literature lives only so long as it is read and discussed. Alaska and the Yukon, and the writings they have inspired, provide a vision of the world as it was before "the Fall" of industrial civilization, and can teach us not how to return to a Rousseauian paradise that never really was, but rather how to live more rationally and more gently on the planet as it exists now. These pristine arctic refugia, and the writings of those who love them, symbolize the common hope of humanity for a better future, a distant horizon beyond which all people can live in harmony with the freedom of wild nature, for, like Antaeus, we become stronger as we remain close to the Earth, and can only be destroyed as we are separated from nature.

Notes

1. Henry T. Allen, Report of an Expedition to the Copper, Tanana, and Koyukuk Rivers in the Territory of Alaska in the Year 1885 (Washington, D.C.: Government Printing Office, 1887), 142.

2. Adolph Murie, The Wolves of Mount McKinley (1945; Washington, D.C.: Government Printing Office; Seattle: University of Washington Press, 1981), 14.

3. Edward Abbey, Beyond the Wall, Essays from the Outside (New York: Holt, Rinehart, and Winston, 1984), 202.

4. Ralph Waldo Emerson, "Self-Reliance," The Norton Anthology of American Literature, Volume One, edited by Hershel Parker (New York: Norton, 1985), 891.

5. John Haines, Of Traps and Snares (Port Townsend: Greywolf Press, 1977), 3.

6. Richard Proenneke, One Man's Wilderness, an Alaskan Odyssey (Anchorage: Alaska Northwest Publishing Company, 1973), 3.

7. Henry David Thoreau, Walden: Or, Life in the Woods (New York: Random House, 1950), 82.

8. Libby Beaman, the Sketches, Letters and Journal of Libby Beaman, Recorded in the Pribilof Islands 1879–1880 (Tulsa: Council Oak Books, 1987), 71.

9. May Wynne Lamb, Life in Alaska, The Reminiscences of a Kansas Woman, 1916–1919 (Lincoln: University of Nebraska Press, 1988), 12.

10. Margaret E. Murie, Two in the Far North (New York: Alfred A. Knopf, Inc., 1957), 230.

11. Thomas Merton, Thomas Merton in Alaska: The Alaskan Conferences, Journals and Letters (New York: New Directions, 1989), 20.

12. Hudson Stuck, *The Ascent of Denali (Mount McKinley), A Narrative of the First Complete Ascent of the Highest Peak in North America* (New York: Charles Scribner's Sons, 1914), 108–109.

13. John Muir, *Travels in Alaska* (1915; Boston: Houghton Mifflin; San Francisco, Sierra Club, 1988), 123.

14. Robert Marshall, *Alaska Wilderness, Exploring the Central Brooks Range* (Berkeley: University of California Press, 1956), 14.

15. Annie Dillard, *Teaching a Stone to Talk, Expeditions and Encounters* (New York: Harper & Row, 1988), 28.

16. Dillard, 43.

17. Barry Lopez, *Crossing Open Ground* (New York: Charles Scribner's Sons, 1988), 92.

18. Lopez, 92.

19. Otto Von Kotzebue, *A Voyage of Discovery into the South Sea and Beering's [sic] Straits for the Purpose of Exploring a North-east Passage Undertaken in the Years 1815–1818, Volume III 'Remarks and Opinions, of the Naturalist of the Expedition'* (London, 1821), 305.

20. In this same time period President Theodore Roosevelt, an avid big-game hunter, refused to shoot a yearling black bear cub in Mississippi, an incident that drew so much national attention that "Teddy Bears," still manufactured today, first made their appearance.

21. Charles Sheldon, *The Wilderness of the Upper Yukon, a Hunter's Exploration for Wild Sheep in Sub-Arctic Mountain* (New York: Charles Scribner's Sons, 1911), 30.

22. Abbey, 198.

23. Murie, 234.

24. Beaman, 67.

25. Samuel Johnson, *A Dictionary of the English Language* (London: 1755), 131.

26. Joseph Addison, *The Spectator in Five Volumes*, ed. Donald F. Bond (London: Oxford University Press, 1965), IV: 186.

27. Aldous Huxley. *Collected Essays* (New York: Harper & Row, 1960), vii.

28. Carl H. Klaus, "Essayists on the Essay," *Literary Nonfiction: Theory, Criticism, Pedagogy*, ed. Chris Anderson (Carbondale: Southern Illinois University Press, 1989), 160.

29. M. H. Abrams, "Structure and Style in the Greater Romantic Lyric," *Romanticism and Consciousness: Essays in Criticism*, ed. Harold Bloom (New York: W. W. Norton and Company, Inc., 1970), 201.

30. Abrams, 201.

31. Abrams, 201.

32. Thomas J. Lyon, *This Incomparable Lande, A Book of American Nature Writing* (Boston: Houghton Mifflin, 1989), 20.

33. See, for example, Percy G. Adams, *Travel Literature and the Evolution of the Novel* (Lexington: University Press of Kentucky, 1983) and John Livingston Lowes, *The Road to Xanadu* (London: Oxford University Press, 1927).

34. Georg Wilhelm Steller, *Journal of a Voyage with Bering, 1741–1742*, edited by O. W. Frost (Stanford: Stanford University Press, 1988), 159–160.

35. Steller, 162.

36. Steller, 162.

37. Barry Lopez, *Arctic Dreams: Imagination and Desire in a Northern Landscape* (New York: Charles Scribner's Sons, 1986), 105–106.

38. Lopez, xviii.

39. Ella Higginson, *Alaska, The Great Country* (New York: Macmillan, 1908), 2.

40. Higginson, 3.

41. Abbey, 203.

42. Abbey, 195.

43. Abbey, 195.

44. Abbey, 195.

45. Abbey, 195.

46. Abbey, 195.

47. Dillard, 22.

48. Dillard, 28–29.

49. Dillard, 29.

50. John Haines, *Living off the Country, Essays on Poetry and Place* (Ann Arbor: University of Michigan Press, 1981), 14.

51. Haines, 15.

52. Haines, 15.

53. Haines, 18.

54. Haines, 18.

55. Haines, 31–32.

56. Haines, 25.

57. Lopez, 277.

58. Lopez, 277.

59. Lopez, 279.

60. Lopez, 278.

61. George Vancouver, *Voyage of Discovery to the North Pacific Ocean and Round the World, Volume III* (London, 1798), 194.

62. Muir, 11.

63. Muir, 12.

64. Muir, 15.

65. John McCormick, *Reclaiming Paradise: The Global Environmental Movement* (Bloomington: Indiana University Press, 1989), vii.

66. Lyon, xv.

67. Lyon, 20.

68. Blaise Pascal, Preface to *Le Traité du Vide, Opuscules et Lettres*, ed. Louis Lafuma (Paris: Éditions Montaigne, 1955), 54.

PART I

1741–1866

Russian America and the Age of Exploration

My islands, you are my islands. The sky over them in the morning today is joyous. Just so is the morning of today. If I shall live henceforth, let them be just so in memory.

Lines from an Aleut song,
as recorded by Ivan Veniaminov in
Notes on the Islands of the Unalashka District

. . . how glad we all were when we finally caught sight of land [Alaska]. Everybody hastened to congratulate the Captain-Commander, to whom the fame of discovery would most redound. However, he not only reacted indifferently and without particular pleasure but in our very midst shrugged his shoulders while gazing at the land.

Georg Wilhelm Steller
Naturalist aboard the *St. Paul,*
commanded by Captain Vitus Bering,
July 16, 1741 (on discovering Alaska)

14,000 years (or more) before present, the first Asian immigrants arrive in Alaska. 1725, on his deathbed Peter the Great directs Vitus Bering, a Dane in the Russian Naval Service, to seek out the unknown coast of northern America beyond Siberia. July 16, 1741, Bering discovers Alaska. 1778, Captain Cook explores Alaska for Great Britain. 1789, Scotsman Alexander Mackenzie reaches the Arctic Sea by traveling down the river that now bears his name. 1790, the German naturalist Carl Merck travels to Unalashka and Kodiak, both strategic islands in the growing empire of Russian America. 1791, Captain Alexandro Malespina, an Italian naval officer serving Spain, explores the southern Alaskan coast, and that same year French vessels visit the coast en route to Canton, China, an important trading center. 1792, Captain George Vancouver navigates the Alaskan coast. 1805, Lewis and Clark descend the Columbia River and winter near the mouth, the first official United States exploration party to reach the northwest. 1816, Von Kotzebue arrives in the Sound that now bears his name. 1824, Venianimov, a Russian missionary, begins his work among the Aleuts. 1826, Captain Frederick Litke explores the Alaskan coast. 1843, Russian Lieutenant L. A. Zagoskin explores the Alaskan interior. 1845, Captain John Franklin disappears while searching for the Northwest Passage. 1847, Scotsman Alexander Murray, a Hudson Bay Company trader, establishes Fort Yukon. 1852, ice is shipped commercially from Sitka to San Francisco. 1858, the first United States whaler operates in the Bering Strait. 1861, gold is discovered near Wrangell. 1866, the Western Union Company explores a trans-Siberian telegraph route through Alaska.

1

The Sea Cow

GEORG WILHELM STELLER

The German naturalist Georg Wilhelm Steller (1709–
1746) accompanied Vitus Jonassen Bering, a Dane in
the Russian naval service, on the latter's historic 1741–
1742 expedition to discover the northwestern coast of America. Steller's
journal, published posthumously, records the perils of eighteenth-
century sea travel—thirty-two of the original seventy-eight crewmen
died, including Bering, and forty-six spent the winter of 1741–1742
shipwrecked on a barren island in what was later named the Bering Sea.
In this selection, the author describes his discovery of the now extinct
Steller's sea cow, a northern Pacific manatee that formerly inhabited the
Aleutian Islands. Hydrodamalis stelleri became extinct in 1786, although there was an unconfirmed sighting of a group of six near Cape
Navarin, Alaska in July 1962. The gentle sea cow, as Steller's account
vividly relates, was no match for the cruelties and wanton slaughter that
followed its discovery.

From *Journal of a Voyage with Bering, 1741–1742*, by Georg Wilhelm Steller, edited
and with an Introduction by O. W. Frost; reprinted with the permission of the publishers,
Stanford University Press, copyright © 1988 by the Board of Trustees of the Leland
Stanford Junior University.

On May 11 and the days following, not only did the snow begin to thaw mightily, but the continuous rains with winds originating in the southeast also caused such high water that the creeks overflowed, and we could scarcely hold out in our subterranean homes, which became filled with water from one to two feet high. This caused us, after the rain stopped, to leave our winter homes and to build summer ones above ground. Nevertheless, the winter ones were still visited after the water soaked into the ground.

However, the building of the ship was halted by the rain for several days. Afterwards it continued with even greater enthusiasm when, much to our surprise, we discovered that the ship could be readily dismantled, an outcome we had not at first anticipated because the ship was new and very solidly built, and we did not have the tools for pulling it apart. Work on the new ship also increased daily so that, along with hope, everybody's zeal for work increased tremendously.

When, toward the end of May, the planking had all been finished and set on the keel, we began no longer to doubt at all the possibility of our being able to travel from here to Kamchatka in August; and we were intent only on how to eliminate the troublesome transport of meat and have food at home by the capture of sea cows which were daily present before our very eyes in great numbers on the shore. That way the work would go even faster, considering that already the men lacked vigor, and their shoes and clothes were badly tattered from traversing the very difficult route cross-country to the south and over the mountains.

Therefore, on May 21, we made the first attempt, with a large manufactured iron hook to which was fastened a strong and long rope, to cut into this huge, powerful sea animal and to pull it ashore, but in vain because the hide of this animal was too tough and hard. We also did not fail to make several experiments and change the hook. But these attempts turned out even worse, and it happened that these animals escaped into the sea with the hooks and ropes.

Finally, the most extreme necessity forced us to think of the most expedient means, since the men for the reasons given above were no longer capable of continuing the former hunt. For this purpose, toward the end of June, the yawl, which in the fall had been badly wrecked on the rocks by the waves, was repaired. A harpooner and five other persons for rowing and steering took their places in it. They had a very long rope lying in it in proper order, in exactly the manner as in Greenland whaling, one end of which was fastened to the harpoon, with the other held on shore in the hands of the other forty men.

They rowed very quietly towards the animals, herds of which were foraging for food along the coast in the greatest security. As soon as the harpooner had struck one of them, the men on shore started to pull it to the beach while those in the yawl rowed toward it and by their agitation exhausted it even more. As soon as it had been somewhat enfeebled, the men in the yawl thrust large knives and bayonets in all parts of its body until, quite weak through the large quantities of blood gushing high like a fountain from its wounds, it was pulled ashore at high tide and made fast.

As soon as the tide had receded and it was stranded on the dry beach, we cut off meat and fat everywhere in large pieces, which with great pleasure we carried to our dwellings. A part we stored in barrels. Another part, especially the fat, we hung up on racks. And at long last, we found ourselves suddenly spared all trouble about food and capable of continuing the construction of the new ship by doubling the workers.

This sea animal, which was first seen by the Spaniards in America and with many intermingled inaccuracies first described by the Spanish physician Hernandez and after him by Carolus Clusius and others, they called manatee. The English call it either the sea cow, like the Dutch, or, like Dampier, *Mannetes,* from the Spanish language. This sea animal is found on both the eastern and the western side of America and has been observed by Dampier (and this is very strange) with fur seals and sea lions in the southern hemisphere as well as by me and others in the northern.

The largest of these animals are four to five fathoms long [a fathom is six feet or 1.83 meters] and three and a half fathoms thick around the region of the navel where they are the thickest. Down to the navel it is comparable to a land animal; from there to the tail, to a fish.

The head of the skeleton is not in the least distinguishable from the head of a horse, but when it is still covered with skin and flesh, it somewhat resembles the buffalo's head, especially as concerns the lips.

In place of teeth, it has in its mouth two broad bones, one of which is affixed above to the palate, the other on the inside of the lower jaw. Both are furnished with many crooked furrows and raised ridges with which it crunches seaweed as its customary food.

The lips are furnished with many strong bristles, of which those on the lower jaw are so thick that they resemble the feather quills of chickens and clearly show by their interior hollowness the actual nature of hairs generally, which are likewise hollow.

The eyes of this animal, without eyelids, are no larger than sheep's eyes.

The ears are so small and concealed that they can hardly be found and recognized among the many grooves and wrinkles of the hide until and before the hide is cut off, when the ear ducts because of its polished blackness catches one's eye; yet it is hardly spacious enough to accommodate a pea. Of the outer ear, not the slightest traces are to be found.

The head is joined to the rest of the body by a short and indistinguishable neck.

Below, on the chest, there are two strange things to be seen. First, the feet, consisting of two joints, have outermost ends rather like a horse's hoof. Underneath, these are furnished with many short and densely set bristles like a scrub brush, and I am not prepared to say whether to call them hands or feet, for the reason that, besides the birds, there is no single two-footed animal. With these forefeet, it swims ahead, beats the seaweed off the rocks on the bottom, and when, lying on its back, it gets ready for the Venus game, one embraces the other with these as if with arms.

The second curiosity is found under these forefeet, namely, the breasts, provided with black, wrinkled, two-inch-long teats, at whose outermost ends innumerable milk ducts open. Brushed against rather hard, they give off a great quantity of milk, which in taste, fat content, and sweetness excells the milk of land animals, but is otherwise not different.

Also, the back of this animal is formed almost like that of an ox. The middlemost backbone sticks up raised. Next to it on both sides is a flat hollow the length of the back. The sides are round lengthwise.

The belly is plump and very expanded, and at all times so completely stuffed that at the slightest wound the entrails at once protrude with much hissing. Proportionally, it is like the belly of a frog.

From the genitals, the body suddenly diminishes very markedly in its circumference. The tail itself becomes thinner and thinner toward the flipper, but immediately before the flipper it is still on the average two feet wide. By the way, excepting the tail flipper, this animal has no fin, neither on the back nor on the sides, wherein it is again different from the whale and other sea animals. The tail flipper is parallel with the sides of the animal, as with the whale and the porpoise.

The male organ is like an ox's as concerns length and position; but in its shape and nature like a horse's, nearly a fathom long and with a sheath fastened under the naval. The female genitals are directly above the anus, nearly oblong, square, and at the upper part, provided with a strong, sinewy clitoris one and a half inches long.

Like cattle on land, these animals live in herds together in the sea, males and females usually going with one another, pushing the offspring before them all around the shore. These animals are busy with nothing but their food. The back and half the belly are constantly seen outside the water, and they munch along just like land animals with a slow, steady movement forward. With their feet they scrape the seaweed from the rocks, and they masticate incessantly. Yet the structure of the stomach taught me that they do not ruminate, as I at first supposed. During eating they move the head and neck like an ox; when a few minutes have elapsed, they heave the head out of the water and draw fresh air by clearing their throats like horses. When the tide recedes, they go from the shore into the sea, but with the rising tide they go back again to the beach, often so close that we could reach and hit them with poles from the beach.

They are not in the least afraid of human beings, nor do they seem to hear too faintly, as Hernandez asserts contrary to experience.

I could not observe indications of an admirable intellect, as Hernandez declares, but they have indeed an extraordinary love for one another, which extends so far that when one of them was cut into, all the others were intent on rescuing it and keeping it from being pulled ashore by closing a circle around it. Others tried to overturn the yawl. Some placed themselves on the rope or tried to draw the harpoon out of its body, in which indeed they were successful several times. We also observed that a male two days in a row came to its dead female on the shore and inquired about its condition.

Nevertheless, they remained constantly in one spot, no matter how many of them were wounded or killed.

They play the Venus game in June with lots of lengthy diversionary tactics. The female flees—slowly—ahead of the male with constant detours, and the male pursues her incessantly. But when the female tires of this mock flight and the vain enticements, she lies on her back, and the male completes intercourse in the human way.

When they want to rest on the water, they lie on their backs in a quiet spot near a cove and let themselves float slowly here and there in that position.

These islands are found at all times of the year everywhere around this island in vast numbers such that the entire coast of Kamchatka could continually supply itself plentifully from them with both fat and meat.

The hide of this animal has a dual nature. The outer hide is black or blackish brown, an inch thick, and with a consistency almost like a cork, around the head full of grooves, wrinkles, and holes. It consists of nothing but perpendicular strands that lie hard upon one another as in a crosscut Spanish reed or cane. The individual bulbs of the strands are round at the bottom, and therefore the upper layer can be easily separated from the true hide, but in the hide itself lie the cavities of the bulbs, giving it the look of the surface of a thimble. It is my opinion that the outer hide is thus a composition of many hairs in a continuous body of crusts, and I found these crusts just this way in the whale.

The inner hide is somewhat thicker than an oxhide, very strong and white in color. Underneath this, a layer of fat surrounds the entire body of the animal. It is a lobe of fat four fingers thick. Then the flesh follows.

The weight of this animal, with hide, flesh, meat, bones, and entrails, I estimate at 200 puds or 80 short hundred weight [about 8,000 pounds].

The fat of this animal is not oily or flabby but rather hard and glandular, snow-white, and, when it has been lying several days in the sun, as pleasantly yellow as the best Dutch Butter. The boiled fat itself excells in sweetness and taste the best beef fat, is in color and fluidity like fresh olive oil, in taste like sweet almond oil, and of exceptionally good smell and nourishment. We drank it by the cupful without feeling the slightest nausea. In addition, it has the virtue of acting as a very gentle laxative and diuretic when taken somewhat frequently; therefore, I consider it a very good remedy for chronic constipation as well as gallstones and urine blockage.

The tail consists of nothing but fat, and it is much more agreeable than that in other parts of the body. The fat of the calves quite resembles the meat of young pigs, but the meat itself resembles the meat of young calves, and it swells up so that it doubles its colume and is boiled entirely within a half-hour.

The meat of the old animals is indistinguishable from beef and differs from the meat of all land and sea animals in the remarkable characteristic that even in the hottest summer months it keeps in the open air without becoming rancid for two whole weeks and even longer, despite its being so defiled by blowflies that it is covered with worms everywhere. I attribute the reason to the diet of plants and to the saltpeter usually mixed in them, from which the meat itself also gets a much redder color than the meat of land and carnivorous sea animals.

It was evident that all who ate it felt that they increased notably in vigor and health. This was noticeable especially in some sailors who had relapses and had been unable to recuperate up until now. With this, all doubts were now ended about what kind of provisions we should go to sea with; and by means of sea animals it pleased God to strengthen us human beings who had suffered shipwreck through the sea.

As concerns the inner structure of these wonderful creatures, I refer curious readers to my detailed description of this animal [Stellar refers to his work *De bestiis marinis*], but here note only briefly (1) that the heart is divided into two parts and thus, contrary to the usual heart, is double, and that the pericardium does not surround it directly, but from a special cavity; (2) that the lungs, enclosed in a firm, sinewy membrane, are situated at the back, as in birds; therefore, it can hold out longer under water without breathing; (3) that it has no gall bladder, but only a wide gall duct, like horses; (4) that the stomach has a similarity with the stomach of a horse, just like the entrails; (5) that the kidneys, like those of calves and bears, are composed of very many small kidneys, each of which has its distinct ureter, pelvis, little arteries, and papillae, and that they are two and a half feet long and weigh thirty pounds.

From the head of this animal, the Spaniards customarily take out a bone, hard as stone, and sell it to the druggists and apothecaries under the false name of a stone, calling it *lapis manati*. I sought in vain in so many animals that I therefore have the idea that it is a product of the climate or that this is a distinct species of the animal, especially since the inquisitive Mr. Dampier mentions two species near the island of St. Ferdinand.

Moreover, I was not a little astonished that despite asking scrupulously about all the animals on Kamchatka, I heard nothing about this one before my return from the voyage, whereas on my return I received information that this animal is known from around Cape Kronotski to Avacha Bay and is sometimes thrown ashore dead. Lacking a special name, they have given it the name "kelp-eater."

2

The Bering Straits

JAMES COOK

James Cook (1728–1779) was born the son of a farm laborer and worked his way up through the British naval ranks from common seaman to Ship's Captain. In 1768 he was given command of the Endeavor and subsequently conducted an historic three-year exploration of the Pacific. On August 19, 1771, he was promoted from lieutenant to commander and entrusted with the command of the Resolution, a 460-ton vessel. Cook was promoted to full captain in 1775 and departed from England on July 12, 1776, for another expedition to the Pacific aboard the Endeavor. Two years later, in 1778, Cook explored the Alaskan coast and in September sailed north of 63° north latitude into the Bering Straits, a feat recorded here. In February 1779 he was killed by angry natives in the Hawaiian Islands following a dispute over some stolen goods. Cook's Inlet, an important bay for commercial fishing and oil drilling near Anchorage, Alaska, is named for Captain Cook.

The Pulitzer-Prize winning historian William Goetzmann has written of Cook that his "Pacific voyages were . . . models of rigorous, exact exploration as he rediscovered, in the name of science, the oceanic world." They represented, again in Goetzmann's words, "the epitome of Baconian or Lockean empirical observations conducted over a huge portion of the world." Finally, and perhaps most important, Goetzmann points out that "Cook's journals, maps, collections and drawings . . . forced savants back in the centers of learning to rethink fundamental premises about natural history and the richly varied peoples of the globe."[1] Such was the significance of Cook's great voyages into what was then the vast unknown of the Pacific Ocean, no area of which was more alien than the Arctic.

1. William Goetzmann, *New Lands, New Men: America and the Second Great Age of Discovery* (New York: Viking, 1986), 51–52.

From *Voyage to the Pacific Ocean in the Years 1776–1780*. London, 1782.

On the 5th we lost sight of the main continent of Asia, which we left the day before.

On the 6th we saw land from W.N.W. to E.N.E. very woody, and covered with snow in the valleys. Here we found the continent of America and the Asiatic shore not above 6 leagues distant [a league was a unit of distance varying from about 2.4 to 4.6 statute miles], lat. 63 deg. 58 min. long. 192 deg. 10 min.

On the 7th, there came two canoes from the shore, with four Indians in them, though we were full four leagues distant. We hove too for their coming up; but when along side, they had little or nothing to part with, except some dried fish. They were invited on board, but could not be persuaded to enter. The Captain made them presents of some trifles, with which they departed well pleased. They were cloathed in skins after the manner of all the inhabitants of the western coasts of America, among whom we found no remarkable distinction of dress or colour.

On the 8th we steered E. ¹/₂ N. passing several bays and fine harbours all day, found the country pleasant, and the coast delightful. Here we found a strong current to set to the S.E. at the rate of 5 knots an hour.

On the 9th the land opened all round, from one shore to the other, and we found ourselves in the middle of a deep bay, but very shallow, sometimes 3, but never above 5¹/₂ fathoms water. We saw the bay to run as far as the eye could carry, but impossible to proceed, as in many places the water shallowed under three fathom. We sent the boats out to sound, at the same time land appeared from S.E. to E. like two islands, which we afterwards found to join to the land.

On the 10th, having a stiff breeze, we ran right across the mouth of the bay, for the N.W. shore, and just before night the Resolution narrowly escaped running upon a rock. We were now again in Bhering's [sic] Straits.

On the 11th we came to anchor in 6 fathom water, the eastermost point of the bay bearing N.E. by E. distance 8 miles very high land. In the night we saw several fires, but no Indians came off to us.

On the 12th, in the morning, the boats from both ships were sent on shore, where they saw some houses of a wretched construction; a small sledge, and several other articles belonging to the Indians; but none of the natives. About ten they returned with a load of wood, which they found drifted on the beach, but no water; the wood had drifted from the southward, for we saw no trees but black spruce. We then stretched over to the other shore, and the boats were again sent out, and about nine in the evening returned, loaded with wood, which the men were obliged to carry through the water on their shoulders, as the boats could not come within half a mile of land for breakers. This was a grievous talk, as many of them had but just recovered their late illness. This day several natives came from S.S.E. in large canoes, having great quantities of salmon dried and fresh, which they exchanged for blue and red beads, needles, pins, knives or scissors, or any European trinkets that were offered them, but what they valued most was *tobacco*. For this they would exchange their bows and arrows, their warlike instruments, and whatever else they valued most; but of this commodity, as has already been noticed, we had but little to spare. We were again obliged to change our station, and stretch to the other shore, where a safe anchorage was discovered, near which we could wood and water with the greatest ease. Here our great cutter was sent out, properly provided with a compass, and six days provision to survey the bay, in order to determine whether that land, which the Russians have laid down as Heleneski, joins to the American continent, or whether there might not be a passage to some other sea intervene.

On the 13th, while the cutters were on this service, the boats were busy in wooding and watering, and before the return of the former, the latter had got more than 20 tons of water on board the Discovery, and near double that quantity on board the Resolution, with a proportionable quantity of wood. The men had then leave to go ashore, by turns, to gather berries, which they now found ripe, and in great abundance, such as raspberries, blue berries, black and red currants, huckle berries, with various other sorts, all in full perfection. A party was likewise sent out to cut spruce, to brew into beer for both ships. Of this liquor, however, the men were not very fond in this cold climate, especially when they were given to understand that their grog was to be stopped, and this beer substituted in the room of it. This occasioned great murmuring, and it was found necessary to give it alternately, spruce one day and grog another.

On these excursions, the parties were always well armed and had marines to attend them, and their orders were never to go out of hearing of the ships guns, but to repair instantly on board on the proper signals. These precautions, however, seemed unnecessary, as they never met with any molestation from the natives, who were not numerous upon the coast.

On the 17th, the party that were sent out to survey the bay returned, after a diligent examination of two days and two nights. Their report was, that it extended within land above 40 leagues, that they coasted it round, sounding as they went, that they found the soundings regular from 5 to 3½ fathom; that it had no communication with any other sea, not any current that indicated a passage to any other continent whatever.

This report being confirmed by the officers who commanded the cutters from both ships, the boats were all taken on board and secured, and

On the 18th we weighed and sailed, retracing the coast we had before explored, without making any material discovery.

On the 25th we met with a dreadful tempest of wind, rain and hail, or rather ice, between two and three inches square, by which several of our men who were obliged to keep the deck, were severely wounded. In this long run, we passed several remarkable promontories and islands. . . .

3

Observations on Unalashka

CARL HEINRICH MERCK

The German naturalist Dr. Carl Heinrich Merck (1761–1799) was born into a family prominent for its pharmacists and physicians and, following his father's footsteps, Merck studied medicine in Germany and in Russia, passing medical examinations at St. Petersburg in 1785. After a long trek through Siberia, Merck finally reached Unalashka in the Aleutians aboard the Slava Rossii on June 1, 1790. Some 162 folio pages of his 1788–1792 journal survive, written primarily in Latin as was the custom. Historian Richard A. Pierce has written of Merck that he was "a scholar of the 18th century standard, educated in the tradition of the encyclopedists" and "competent—for his times—not only in enthnography but in geology, ornithology, icythology, botany and zoology."[1] In this selection Merck provides some of the Aleut names for marine fauna, describes the topography of Unalashka with some specific geological references, and takes time to note "a beautiful waterfall." From such humble origins did modern physical science—and contemporary nature writing—derive.

1. Richard A Pierce, Siberia and Northwestern America 1788–1792, The Journal of Carl Heinrich Merck, Naturalist with the Russian Scientific Expedition Led by Captains Joseph Billings and Gavrill Sarychev (Kingston: The Limestone Press, 1980), xvi.

5th of June 1790. About ten versts [a verst was .66193 statute mile or 1.06 kilometers] toward the sea from the narrow strait, which divides this island [Spirkin] from Unalaska, there is the mouth of a little river which flows from a small valley into the bay. There are also many brooks which rush down between the mountains. In one of them the gravel had an ocher color. Close that arm which connects up with the sea, the rock is of the kind numbered 97 [reference to a rock sample numbered 97]. Up to that point we proceeded on foot. In lower layers the rock is 98. There is also black iron ore.

During the night of the 6th there was a slow rain. During the day at first overcast with some misting. Toward afternoon and on toward the evening the sun brightened up the weather.

During low tide I found a kind of sea anemone attached to the rocks in a rock crevice on the shore. It is deep red.

A crab is called *Illghakuk* in Unalaska. Seaweed, *umyak*. That black bugshell, which the Aleuts eat, they call *Kasshigok*. Sea sponge, *Tshamchok*. Jellyfish, *Kitshiklak*, and *Uyalik*. There is a kind of gorgonia which they occasionally haul up from the depth with a fishing rod. They call it *Kunyuk*.

The octopus is *Amhuk*. Sea urchin, *Agohnak*, plentiful everywhere here. Sea shell, *Tschalak*.

The coral moss which grows on the rocks is dirty-yellowish brown. On the beach it is almost white. There is a small crab in the seaweed. It is dark blood-red, and whitish underneath. Each of the joints has a white dot. The feelers are yellowish-grey; the pincers not too black, then dark-red. The outer point in back is whitish.

In the afternoon we arrived on the other side. Most of the mountains slope up gradually with hills along their sides. Their tops are sometimes rounded; more seldom broader or unevenly blunted and rocky on top. In some places a mountain consists of several peaks, each higher than the next. There are also folded mountains, their ridges forming peaks and indentations. The highest mountains are pointed with jagged sides. Those hills are either rocky all around or only one side; some are only valleys which run down their sides. And there are springs with good cold water, which become the sources of brooks. Sometimes they form small waterfalls as they foam down the mountain side. The rocks of these hills are uneven but low. They consist of vertical, undefinable pieces which become narrower along their sides toward the top. Different ones of the higher mountains do all have such rock formations close to the top. Sometimes these rocks resemble remnants of old ruins. The elevation of these mountains ranges from 80 to 150 faden [German measurement equalling 6.99 feet or 21.336 decimeters]. (The north sides of these mountains are still covered with much snow in higher reaches. A mountain peak, *Kauga*. A valley, *Tshanganak*.) Some of the mountains extend with their corners into the bay, where they form cliffs and small islands. And these alternate with coves along the shore.

Along a few mountains along the right shoreline I found evidence of spontaneous combustion of sulfur gravel. The surface of the rock is more even. In some places it is layered like shale and somewhat uneven. It is dark yellow, sometimes light yellow with iron content, 117 [reference to a rock sample numbered 117]. In a cover on the left bank there is firm rocksalt attached to the surface. 99 is one kind of rock on the left shore. 101 are some boulders on the right side in front. 102 sits on top of them. 103 is the kind of rock at the place where the burnt gravel is. 104 is found close by that place.

Toward evening we sailed past a beautiful waterfall. The water comes as a little river from the mountain, and then it falls almost vertically into the cove. See sketch 33, after a drawing made by Mr. Sarychev.

The night of the 7th was star-clear and cold. Where the water stood still, there it was covered with a thin layer of ice. The day was fair with sunshine.

At noon we went with Mr. Sarychev to a dwelling place [Illiuliuk] which lies north-west of the Kapitanskaia Harbor. In our party were a hunter and several young Aleuts who rowed the boat and acted as our guides. Mr. Krebs had to remain on board ship to put in order the items we had collected.

The path starts from a small cove. It leads upward along a small river, which rushes down to the bay. The way climbs gradually along the base of the mountains. Then we crossed a low mountain from where the path descends through some valleys to the few huts. They are situated on a grassy plain near the shore of a separate part of the bay which is hidden by several islands. . . . Along the way there was a grassy valley where the bottom of a pool of standing water was covered with a rind (layer) of ocher. Springs trickle from the mountains in several brooks, which come together in a small river. This river enters the harbor west of the dwelling place. Fish enter this river. There were willow bushes here and there on the lower parts of the mountains. Their buds were beginning to unfold. On the way when we were closer to the harbor we saw a volcano at a distance in a west to southern direction. It was completely covered with snow. At its peak the mountain was ringed with some knolls. A white column of smoke. 100 versts from the shore at the harbor.

4

Prince William Sound

GEORGE VANCOUVER

George Vancouver (1758–1798) entered the British navy at thirteen as a common seaman on board Captain Cook's Resolution on Cook's second voyage. In 1780 Vancouver was promoted to lieutenant and in 1790 he was made a full commander. His 1790–1795 expedition explored regions of the North Pacific first reconnoitered by Cook. Vancouver successfully sailed around and mapped the sizeable island off the coast of British Columbia that is now named for him. He also conducted important surveys of the Canadian coast south to Puget Sound. In this passage from his journal (first published in 1798), Vancouver describes Alaska's Prince William Sound as seen from aboard his vessel Discovery. Most interesting from the standpoint of natural history is Vancouver's observation that "the visible effects of the axe and saw" were already (1794) noticeable along the coast and that "during the surveying excursions not a single sea otter, and but very few whales or seals" were seen. He also notes that wild fowl were "not met with in that plenty" observed in earlier English expeditions. Prince William Sound was the location of the United States' worst oil spill disaster in March 1989, as 11 million gallons of crude oil poured from the Exxon Valdez, destroying large portions of the same region through which Vancouver sailed in 1794.

From *Voyage of Discovery to the North Pacific Ocean in the Years 1790–1792.* London, 1798.

Friday, May 16, 1794

The weather was delightfully serene and pleasant, and the morning of the 16th was ushered in by a sight we little expected in these seas. A numerous fleet of skin canoes, each carrying two men only, were about the *Discovery*, and, with those that at the same time visited the *Chatham*, it was computed there could not be less than four hundred Indians present. They were almost all men grown, so that the tribe to which they belonged must consequently be a very considerable one. They instantly and very willingly entered into trade, and bartered away their hunting and fishing implements, lines and thread, extremely neat and well made from the sinews of animals; with bags ingeniously decorated with needle work, wrought on the thin membrane of the whales intestines; these articles, with some fish, and some well executed models of canoes with all their appendages, constituted the articles of commerce with these people, as well as with our Indian friends in Cook's inlet; for excepting those furs given to me by *Chatidooltz's* party, not an article of this description had been offered for sale, or even seen in the possession of the natives, as forming a part of their apparel, as was the case in my former visit to this country. The clothing of these Americans now chiefly consisted of garments made from the skins of birds or quadrupeds, of not the least value. This humble fashion had most likely been introduced by their Russian friends, for the sake of increasing the number of the skins of the sea otter, foxes, martin, ermine, and of such other animals as come under the denomination of furs, which they find to be worth the trouble of exporting.

These good people, like all the others we had lately seen, conducted themselves with great propriety; and as the wind was very light, they continued with us until near noon, when they all retired to a bay or harbour we were then abreast of. . . . The coast we sailed along this day is in most parts very mountainous, and descends rather quickly into the ocean, excepting in those places where it is broken into vallies, some of which are extensive, and gradually incline to the water side. These in some instances were still buried in ice and snow, within a few yards of the wash of the sea; whilst here and there some of the loftiest of the pine trees just shewed their heads through this frigid surface.

We could not avoid remarking, that the whole of this exterior coast seemed to wear a much more wintry aspect than the countries bordering on those more northern inland waters we had so recently quitted. . . .

Friday, June 20, 1794

. . . The minute examination we were empowered to make of Prince
William sound, not only brought us acquainted with its utmost limits in
every direction, but proved it to be a branch of the ocean that requires the
greatest circumspection to navigate; and although it diverges into many
extensive arms, yet none of them can be considered as commodious
harbours, on account of the rocks and shoals that obstruct the approach
to them, or of the very great depth of water at or about their entrances. Of
the former, innumerable have been discovered, and there is great reason
to suppose that many others may have existence, of which we gained no
knowledge. By what may be collected from our inquiries, Snug-corner
cover, and the passage to it from the ocean, seem to be the least liable to
these objections of all places of shelter which the sound affords. The
place of our anchorage in port Chalmers, can only be considered as a
small cove in a rugged rocky coast; so very difficult of access or egress,
that our utmost vigilance in sounding was unequal to warn us of the rock
on which the ship grounded, and which is situated N. 72 W. from the
north point of the harbour, distant one mile; and N. 6 E. from the woody
islet, at about the same distance. . . . In the neighborhood of port
Chalmers, the country as high up the sides of the mountains as vegetation extended, was in most places free from snow before we quitted that
anchorage, and afforded us an opportunity of forming some judgement
on the nature of the soil; which, from the diversity of surface in plains,
and spaces clear of trees, presented a pleasing verdant appearance to the
eye; but on a more attentive examination it proved to be in most place an
intire moras, composed of a very poor black moorish earth, formed
apparently of decayed vegetables, not sufficiently decomposed to produce any thing but a variety of coarse mosses, a short spiry grass, a few
cranberry, and some other plants of a dwarfish stunted growth; some of
these morasses compose the sides of the hills, and although these had
considerable inclination, yet they had the property of retaining the water
to a very deceitful and unpleasant degree; exhibiting an apparently dry,
verdant surface, which when walked upon sunk to nearly half leg deep
in water. The soil from whence the forests have sprung is of similar
materials, and not reduced to a more perfect mould; but this generally
covers a rocky foundation, from whence pine trees seem to derive great
nourishment, as very large ones had frequently been found growing from
out of the naked rock. Those about this harbour did not grow with the
same luxuriance as at the place from whence our fore-yard had been
procured, about 5 leagues to the south-west, but composed rather a
dwarfish forest; which, although producing many of the common berry
bushes, cannot be considered as much interrupted with underwood. The
shores are in general low, and as has been already observed, very
swampy in many places, on which the sea appears to be making more

rapid incroachments than I ever before saw, or heard of. Many trees had been cut down since these regions had been first visited by Europeans; this was evident by the visible effects of the axe and saw. . . . It was remarked, that during the surveying excursions not a single sea otter, and but very few whales or seals had been seen; and that the wild fowl were not met with in that plenty during Mr. Whidbey's, as in Mr. Johnstone's, expedition.

5

Arrival at the Arctic Coast

ALEXANDER MACKENZIE

Alexander Mackenzie (1755?–1820) was born near In-
verness, Scotland, around 1755 and by 1784 had some-
how made his way to Michigan, where he found employ-
ment as a trader and explorer for the North-west Fur Company, an early
rival of the Hudson's Bay Company. In his own words:

> I was led, at an early period of life, by commercial views, to the country
> North-West of Lake Superior, in North America, and being endowed by
> Nature with an inquisitive mind and enterprising spirit . . . I not only
> contemplated the practicability [sic] of penetrating across the conti-
> nent of America, but was confident in the qualifications, as I was
> animated by the desire, to undertake the perilous enterprize.

Beginning at Fort Chepewyan, this industrious young Scotsman made
his way to the Great Slave Lake in what is today the Canadian Northwest
Territories, and then traveled down the river that now bears his name to
the Arctic Coast. In July 1789, as France exploded in violent revolution,
Alexander Mackenzie was making a different sort of history at the
furthest reaches of the known world. In this passage Mackenzie de-
scribes his arrival near the outlet of the river on what is today called
Mackenzie Bay. Of equivalent importance historically was his arrival
on June 22, 1793, at the Pacific Ocean, a feat that fulfilled his youthful
dream of being the first person to cross the North American continent.
He was knighted on February 10, 1802.

From Voyage from Montreal over the Continent of North America to the Frozen and
Pacific Oceans, in the Years 1780–1793. London, 1801.

Sunday, July 12, 1789

It rained with violence throughout the night, and till two in the morning; the weather continuing very cold. We proceeded on the same meandering course as yesterday, the wind North-North-West, and the country so naked that scarce a shrub was to be seen. At ten in the morning, we landed where there were four huts, exactly the same as those which have been so lately described. The adjacent land is high and covered with short grass and flowers, though the earth was not thawed above four inches from the surface; beneath which was a solid body of ice. This beautiful appearance, however, was strangely contrasted with the ice and snow that are seen in the vallies. The soil, where there is any, is a yellow clay mixed with stones. These huts appear to have been inhabited during the last winter; and we had reason to think, that some of the natives had been lately there, as the beach was covered with the track of their feet. Many of the runners and bars of their sledges were laid together, near the houses, in a manner that seemed to denote the return of the proprietors. There were also pieces of netting made of sinews, and some bark of the willow. The thread of the former was plaited, and no ordinary portion of time must have been employed in manufacturing so great a length of cord. A square stone-kettle, with a flat bottom, also occupied our attention, which was capable of containing two gallons; and we were puzzled as to the means these people must have employed to have chiselled it out of a solid rock into its present form. To these articles may be added, small pieces of flint fixed into handles of wood, which, probably, serve as knives; several wooden dishes; the stern and part of a large canoe; pieces of very thick leather, which we conjectured to be the covering of a canoe; several bones of large fish, and two heads; but we could not determine the animal to which they belonged, though we conjectured that it must be the sea-horse.

When we had satisfied our curiosity we re-embarked, but we were at a loss what course to steer, as our guide seemed to be as ignorant of this country as ourselves. Though the current was very strong, we appeared to have come to the entrance of the lake. The stream set to the West, and we went with it to an high point, at the distance of about eight miles, which we conjectured to be an island; but, on approaching it, we perceived it to be connected with the shore by a low neck of land. I now took an observation which gave 69.1 North latitude. From the point that has been just mentioned, we continued the same course for the Westernmost point of an high island, and the Westernmost land in sight, at the distance of fifteen miles.

The lake was quite open to us to the Westward, and out of the channel of the river there was not more than four feet water, and in some places the depth did not exceed one foot. From the shallowness of the water it was impossible to coast to the Westward. At five o'clock we arrived at the island, and during the last fifteen miles, five feet was the deepest water. The lake now appeared to be covered with ice, for about two leagues distance, and no land ahead, so that we were prevented from proceeding in this direction by the ice, and the shallowness of the water along the shore.

We landed at the boundary of our voyage in this direction, and as soon as the tents were pitched I ordered the nets to be set. When I proceeded with the English chief to the highest part of the island, from which we discovered the solid ice, extended from the South-West by compass to the Eastward. As far as the eye could reach to the south-Westward, we could dimly perceive a chain of mountains, stretching further to the North than the edge of the ice, at the distance of upwards of twenty leagues. To the eastward we saw many islands, and in our progress we met with a considerable number of white partridges [probably ptarmigan], now become brown. There were also flocks of very beautiful plovers, and I found the nest of one of them with four eggs. White owls, likewise, were among the inhabitants of the place: but the dead, as well as the living, demanded our attention, for we came to the grave of one of the natives, by which lay a bow, a paddle, and a spear. The Indians informed me that they landed on a small island, about four leagues from hence, where they had seen the tracks of two men, that were quite fresh; they had also found a secret store of train oil, and several bones of white bears were scattered about the place where it was hid. The wind was now so high that it was impracticable for us to visit the nets.

My people could not, at this time, refrain from expressions of real concern, that they were obliged to return without reaching the sea: indeed the hope of attaining this object encouraged them to bear, without repining, the hardships of our unremitting voyage. For some time past their spirits were animated by the expectation that another day would bring them to the Mer d'ouest: and even in our present situation they declared their readiness to follow me wherever I should be pleased to lead them. We saw several large white gulls, and other birds, whose back, and upper feathers of the wing are brown; and whose belly, and under feathers of the wing are white.

6

St. Lawrence Island

OTTO VON KOTZEBUE

Otto Von Kotzebue (1787–1846) accompanied Admiral A. J. Von Krusenstern on his circumnavigation of the world in 1803–1806, and subsequently commanded two other voyages around the world in 1815–1817 and 1823–1826. It was on his second voyage that he explored the northwestern coast of Alaska in 1816 in an unsuccessful attempt to find the "Holy Grail" of arctic exploration—the northwest passage. He named Kotzebue Sound for himself, a large bay 35 miles wide by 80 miles long north of the Seward Peninsula in extreme northwestern Alaska. In this passage from his journal, Kotzebue relates his exploration of Saint Lawrence Island, which is located in the north Bering Sea between Siberia and Alaska. Of particular interest are his descriptions of the natives, who offer him "a wooden trough of whale blubber" on which to dine and who are then fascinated by his telescope and are "seized with the most extravagant joy" upon viewing distant objects through it. Sometimes the observations of these early travelers vis-à-vis human nature are just as interesting as their notes on wild nature.

From *Voyage of Discovery into the South Sea and Behring* [sic] *Straits, for the Purpose of Exploring a Northeast Passage, in 1815–1818.* Weimar and London, 1821.

June 27th

The fog continued undiminished: my patience was put to a hard trial. I had several times observed, that when the barometer stands high, there is the finest weather on shore; while, about a mile from the coast, the thickest fog prevails. I therefore resolved to steer directly up to the shore, and the attempt succeeded. The lead showing ten fathoms' water, soon announced that it was near at hand: the thick fog dispersed, the sun shone, the weather was serene, and a ridge of high mountains, covered with snow, appeared before us. . . . We observed people and tents on the shore; and the wish of becoming acquainted with the inhabitants of this island, who had never been visited by any navigator, and also to give our naturalists an opportunity by examining this unknown country, induced me to pay it a visit. Two of our four-oared boats were directly put into the water, and we set out, well armed with pistols, sabres, and guns. As the consequences might have proved dangerous, if we had cast anchor in this open bay, the *Rurick* remained under sail, and Lieutenant Schischmareff took the command. The wind blew faintly from the S.W.; the *Rurick* was obliged to stand off a little from the shore, and was soon enveloped in fog. At a small distance from the shore, we were met by a baydare (boat) with ten islanders, who approached us without fear, calling aloud to us, and making the most singular motions, holding fox-skins in the air, with which they eagerly beckoned us. We easily perceived their arms hidden in their baydare, and therefore observed the greatest caution. After some salutations, according to their custom, which consisted in stroking themselves several times with both their hands, from the face to the belly, their first word was Tobacco! . . . I continued my way to the shore, which seemed to frighten them very much, as they ran anxiously to and fro, and some, probably only women, fled into the mountains. Some of them came up to us bravely enough; but their fear, which they in vain strove to hide under the mask of friendship, was visible. At everything we did they laughed without bounds; but as soon as any of our motions excited the least suspicion of hostility, they assumed a fierce look; they prepared themselves partly for flight and partly for resistance. Their friendship, however, returned when they perceived their error, and this sudden change from laughing to serious-ness, gave their faces, which were smeared with train-oil, an extremely comical appearance. . . . While our naturalists were strolling about the mountains, I entertained myself with my new acquaintance, who, as soon as they learnt that I was the commander, invited me to their tent. A filthy piece of leather was spread on the floor for me to sit on; and then they came up to me one after the other—each of them embraced me, rubbed his nose hard against mine, and ended his caresses by spitting in his hands and wiping them several times over my face. Though these signs of friendship were not very agreeable to me, I bore all patiently. To suppress their further tenderness, I distributed some tobacco, which they received with much pleasure, and were going to repeat all their caresses again. I hastily took some knives, scissars [sic], and beads, and thus happily prevented a second attack. An almost still greater misery awaited me; when, in order to refresh me, they brought forth a wooden trough of whale blubber (a great delicacy among all the northern inhabitants of the sea coasts), and I bravely took some of it, sickening and dangerous as this food is to an European stomach. This, and some other presents, which I afterwards made them, sealed the bond of our friendly acquaintance. . . . Nothing attracted their attention so much as my telescope; and when I showed them its properties, and they really saw quite distant objects close before their eyes, they were seized with the most extravagant joy. At two o'clock in the afternoon, we arrived safe at our ship. We were all satisfied; the naturalist with his collected treasures, the artist with his likenesses of several islanders, and I with my discovery.

7

The Bering Straits

ADELBERT VON CHAMISSO

Adelbert Von Chamisso was the chief naturalist on Otto Von Kotzebue's 1815–1818 "Voyage of Discovery" that explored the south and north Pacific. Von Chamisso reveals himself here to be as meticulous an observer as Georg Steller. He notes, for example, that as they sailed northward aboard the Rurick, terrestrial fauna and flora diminished as marine life increased ("the sea becomes more and more peopled"). The secret of human survival on the coasts of the circumpolar north is that, paradoxically, the seas offer a rich bounty of food resources that can sustain not only isolated settlements but also an entire widespread culture. Even though there are some modern aspects to Von Chamisso's narrative—as with Steller earlier—references still occur to folklore (Marco Polo's journal) and fables (the legend of the polypus) that betray its chronology. Von Chamisso is not quite as unsophisticated as the Roman naturalist Pliny the Elder, who based entire books on folklore, superstition, and fable, but he is not quite to the level of Charles Darwin and others, who in a few short years would radically transform natural history forever. Still, Von Chamisso gives a credible description of some of the terrestrial and marine mammals of arctic Alaska, from his correct assessment of the grizzly bear as a species "which appears to be [emphasis added] the European brown bear" to his placement of "the white-headed American eagle" on Unalashka, which has some biological significance. Of final interest are the series of questions found in his narrative, which indicate how little was really known about the world in a time that is not so very remote from our own.

From *Voyage of Discovery into the South Sea and Behring [sic] Straits, for the Purpose of Exploring a Northeast Passage, in 1815–1818.* Weimar and London, 1821.

Steller, whom Pallas calls immortal, first developed, under Beering [sic], the natural history of this country and these seas; and Merk [sic], under Billing, honourably followed his example. Other learned men and collectors have explored Kamtschatka more at their ease, and Oonalashka has been visited. The names of Steller and Merk have retained all their lustre. Of their botanical collections much has remained unpublished, particularly in the herbaries of Lamberti, Willdenow, and Görenki. Pallas, in the *Zoographia Rossica*, as far as it went (to the middle of the fishes) has collected every thing relating to zoology. With due respect to our predecessors, we shall make but a few observations on the Fauna of these seas and coasts.

The large mammalia have gone over from the American continent to Oonemak. There we find the rein-deer, a wolf, and a bear, which appears to be the European brown bear. The black bear (*Ursus Americanus, gala genisque ferrugineis*), the valuable skin of which is sought for furs, is first met, together with the brown bear, on the remote north-west coast. There is, besides, at Oonalashka, the black fox, and several small *Glires*, among which the *Mus oeconomus* is distinguished, which stores under the snow, for winter stock, the roots of the *Polygonum viviparum*, of the *Surana* (*Silium Kamtschaticum*) and other plants. The other mammalia belong to the Fauna of the sea.

As, on the one hand, in proportion as you go further in the land towards the north, the woods become less lofty, the vegetation gradually decreases, animals become scarcer, and, lastly (as at Nova Zembla,) the rein-deer and the *Glires* vanish with the last plants, and only birds of prey prowl about the icy streams for their food; so, on the other hand, the sea becomes more and more peopled. The *Algae*, gigantic species of *Tang*, form inundated woods round the rocky coasts, such as are not met with in the torrid zone. (The sea *Tang*, which serves the Manilla galleons as a mark of the vicinity of land on the coast of California, might, perhaps, mark the extreme progress of this formation to the limits of the Monsoon. To this is added the *Fucus buccinalis*, which occurs at the Cape of Good Hope.) But the waters swarm with animal life, though all acquatic animals seem to remain in a lower scale than their relatives of the same class on land. The *Medusae* and *Zoophytes, Moluscae* and *Crustaceae*, innumerable species of fish, in incredibly crowded shoals, the gigantic swimming mammalia, whales, physeters, dolphins, morse and seals fill the sea and its strand, and countless flights of water-fowls rock themselves on the bosom of the ocean, and, in the twilight, resemble floating islands.

The sea-otter does not seem to penetrate to the northward beyond the chain of the Aleutian islands, and begins to become scarce after it has caused the destruction of the native tribes. The sea-lion and the sea-bear appear to keep in about the same limits; other seals, more resembling the *Phoca vitulina*, are found more frequently to the north. Countless herds of morse are met with in Beering's Straits, and the teeth of these animals seem to form a considerable branch of trade with the natives of St. Lawrence Island. We heard only corrupted traditions at Oonalashka, which seemed to refer to the *Manatus borealis* [Steller's sea cow]. A *Physter*, a sea-wolf, six different species of whale, *Delphinus orca*, and two other dolphins, are found round the Aleutian islands; and, besides this, the *Delphinus leucas*, in the north of Beering's Straits, as we infer from several accounts.

On the coast of Beering's Straits are found several species of *Viverra* and *Canis*, among which the black fox has chiefly excited our rapacity. The very common *Arctomys cytillus*, the skin of which produces an elegant fur, is distinguished among the *Glires*. The rein-deer, which belongs to both coasts, seems to be wanting in St. Lawrence Island. The dog, every where in the north the first companion to man, and his useful draught animal, is wanting only on the Aleutian islands, where it was formerly introduced and increased, but was extirpated by the masters of the country, because it pursued the fox, whose skin was their surest source of riches.

Many land-birds have spread over to Oonalashka from the nearest coast, of which the white-headed American eagle is predominant. With respect to the albatrosses, *Diomedea exulans*, we have to correct a very common error, which has gained credit under the authority of Pallas. The albatross does not visit the north as a transitory guest from the southern hemisphere, merely to appease its hunger for a short time, and then to return at the breeding season to its southern home. The albatross builds its nests of feathers on the highest summits of the Aleutian islands, namely, on Umnack and Tschatirech Sobpotschnie ostroff (the Island of the Four Peaks). It lays two very large eggs, of a blueish colour, and hatches in the summer season. The black variety mentioned by authors is the young one. The Aleutians ascend these summits towards August, and take the eggs from the nest; they also throw darts, made for the purpose, at the sitting birds, and are particularly eager after their fat, with which they abound at this season.

Not a single animal of the class of *Amphibiae* appears either at Oonalashka or the Aleutian islands.

Among the insects, the beetle is predominant; and among these the *Carabus*, of which Dr. Eschscholtz counted sixteen kinds, many of which are not hitherto described. Several water-beetles animate the lakes and standing water. It might perhaps be in vain to look for them more to the north.

The common northern large Maja (*Lithodes artica*, Lat.) is distinguished among the crabs, and is particularly excellent for food.

We refer to Pallas and other authors with respect to the fish, on the constant and innumerable swarms of which the subsistence of the people of the north, and of their domestic animals (Inclined to make comparisons, we observe that Marco Polo mentions, in the 46th chapter of the third book, of the country of Aden (in the torrid zone) that even the horses, oxen, and camels, all eat fish, as no herb appears about the soil, on account of the extreme heat. The cattle rather eat dried than fresh fish), with the exception of the rein-deer depends. . . . Among the *Molluscae*, the cuttle-fish (*Sepia octopus?*) which is the most remarkable, grows to a size, that really renders it dangerous to the small baydares of the natives, as it is able to over-turn them, and justifies, in some degree, the fable of the polypus, which is said to entwine ships in its arms, and draw them to the bottom. . . . The muscle [sic], which among us is generally eaten, is here a most dangerous food, which is only taken in case of necessity. It is said to operate, at times, as a most decisive poison; and we were assured that people had often died in consequence of eating it. . . . The fishermen frequently draw up with their lines, from the bottom of the sea, large twigs, six feet long, which, from their near resemblance, they consider to be the beard of a gigantic animal, and which appeared to us to be the skeleton of a sea-pen (*Pennatula*).

To the north of Beering's [sic] Strait, lies before us the still unexplored field of the last important problems in geography; and we are called upon to give our opinion on them at a time when several expeditions are fitting out to examine into the facts, and our voice expires unheard. We proceed with hesitation to this task.

Are Asia and America separated? and is the sea into which you penetrate through Beering's Strait to the north, the great Icy Sea itself? Or, is this basin a Bay of the Southern Ocean, bounded and surrounded by the coast of the two uniting quarters of the globe in the north?

Can a north-west passage be possible, from the waters of Hudson's and Baffin's Bay, along the north coast of America to Beering's Strait?

Can it be possible to come into Beering's Strait from the Atlantic Ocean, northwards of Spitzbergen, and even over the north pole itself? and is there an open navigable polar sea, or a polar glacier of firm solid ice?

A man, whose name inspires us with the greatest respect, who is equally distinguished by learning and sound criticism, who was himself a companion of Cook in his second and third voyage, who has repeatedly navigated the South Polar Ocean, and the sea of the north of Beering's Strait, James Burney (A Memoir on the Geography of the North-Eastern part of Asia, and on the question whether Asia and America are contiguous, or are separated by the Sea. By Captain James Burney.—Philosophical Transactions, 1818, refuted in the Quarterly Review, June 1818. A Chronological History of the North-Eastern Voyages of Discovery, by Captain James Burney, F.R.S. London, 1819), is inclined to suppose that Asia and America are united, and parts of one and the same continent.

We confess that Captain Burney has not gained us over to his opinion.

8

The Pribilof Islands

FREDERIC LITKE

The 1835 Voyage Autour du Monde ("*Voyage Around the World*") chronicles the world travels of Captain-Lieutenant Frederic Litke (1797–1882) in Alaska and elsewhere aboard the sixty-two manned Russian corvette Seniavin. The official mission of the Seniavin was, according to imperial order, primarily geographic and scientific—Litke and his naturalist Dr. Mertens assiduously collected diverse specimens, including 100 amphibians, 300 fish, 150 crustaceans, 700 insects, 300 birds, as well as human skulls, an unspecified number of sea shells, 2,500 plants, 350 rocks and minerals, and numerous ethnographic artifacts. Litke's most important scientific achievements were the identification of several new species of seal, the collection of some rare species of bat, and the gathering of measurements on the Earth's magnetic field that were significant for the age.

In this selection, Litke provides one of the first critiques of government-sanctioned natural resource exploitation. Litke calls the extravagant hunting of otters, seals, and blue foxes on the Pribilof Islands an "unreasonable destruction of these animals" because more animals were being harvested than could be naturally replaced. Today the practice of managing a wildlife population for continual use in perpetuity is known as sustained-yield management. Writing in 1835, however, Litke was many years ahead of his time, and sounds almost like a contemporary animal-rights activist in passages like this: "There is something revolting in this cold blooded carnage of thousands of defenseless animals." Libby Beaman, visiting the Islands in 1879 and 1880, would have similar observations; eventually the U. S. Government provided adequate legal protection for these mammals.

The inhabitants [of the Pribilof Islands] occupy themselves in hunting fur seals, sea lions, foxes and birds, in treating the skins and in gathering wood from the seashore for fuel. With the exception of the last named which goes on all year, all the other tasks begin in May and end in November. The natives pass the rest of the year in complete idleness, which is as harmful physically as it is morally. The most industrious of the Aleuts spend time carving various trifles, chessmen, etc. Several of the islanders understand chess very well.

The vast number of otters, sea lions and fur seals, especially the latter, that were found on the discovery of these islands, is unbelievable. These animals were then so placid that all one had to do to kill them was to go along the shore armed with a large club and strike down whichever one was wanted. It was so easy, in fact, that, it is said that the prom-yshlenniks [hunters, fishermen, and laborers in the Russian colonies] had the habit of playing chess with an otter as the prize, and they played on condition that the loser would kill, on the shore or in the shallows, whichever otter the winner chose. Eventually the hunters tired of such an easy prey. Also, the expedition of Pribylov alone took, during the first two years, more than 2,000 otters, 40,000 seals and 6,000 blue foxes; this excludes what other expeditions there took.

However, this abundance did not last for long, owing to the unrea-sonable destruction of these animals. I say "unreasonable" because not only were more animals destroyed than could be replaced by natural increase but more were destroyed than even the destroyers themselves could cope with, timewise. In 1803, at Unalashka, where all the products of hunting are accumulated, some 800,000 furs of seals which had been treated in haste and badly dried, spoiled to such a point that it was found necessary to burn or dump in the sea more than 700,000 skins, also to prevent the prices going down at Kiakhta. Were not 700,000 pointless murders?

According to most accurate calculations, more than 3 million skins of fur seals were taken from the Little Islands from the time of their discovery until 1828, that is to say, over a period of forty-two years. It is hard to understand how this whole race of animals was not completely wiped out after such destruction.

But the products of hunting diminished rapidly. Soon there was not a single otter left; and the fur seals became rarer and rarer, year by year. This is why when the Little Islands, together with the Unalashka section, were brought under the general administration of the colonies, the first thing Baranov did was to suspend all hunting in these islands for two years. It was later decided to leave, in turn, some of the herds in peace, but in spite of that, the number of animals killed decreased all the time. In 1811, 80 thousand skins were obtained from the Little Islands; in 1816, 3 thousand; in 1821, 50 thousand, and in 1827, 30 thousand of which 20 to 25 thousand came from Saint Paul and 5 to 8 thousand from Saint George. It is clear that this source was threatened with complete exhaustion. An outline of the way in which this hunting is carried out will explain the reason for its deterioration.

The hunters divide the fur seals into five grades, according to age and sex. First—males over four years of age; second—males from three to four years of age; third—males two years old; fourth—males under two years of age, and fifth—females.

The fur seals arrive at the islands from the south towards the middle of April and always settle in the same place as previously, according to what the old natives tell. The males arrive first; then the females arrive, about mid-May. As they approach, the male, by howling, calls his females to him and they come and range themselves around him while he climbs up on top of a rock from which he can see his whole family and can watch that no other males come and interfere. A strong male will have from 200 to 300 females; the old and feeble, one or two. The young males are in awe of the strongest ones and always keep at a distance from them, surrounded themselves by only a small number of females.

The females do not leave the shore until they have had their young. Usually they give birth to one pup only, very rarely two. Then in June they begin to mate again. The jealousy and spitefulness of the males at this time is beyond all description. Too bad for the feeble one who intentionally or inadvertently strays near a family strange to him. The male jumps upon him and within a few seconds will kill him with fierce blows from his flippers. Should it happen that they are of equal strength, the fight will last a long time, with bits of flesh flying through the air from both sides; often one of them will remain on that spot. It is to this jealousy that one attributes the persistence of the male in not going into the water during all this time, for if once he leaves his troop of females, they will go off and join in with other bands. Since they stay thus for almost two months without food, they become very emaciated and extremely weak.

The young ones suckle from their mothers up to the autumn and have no other nourishment at all during this time. Up until the month of June, they crawl among the stones and never go into the water. In June they begin to paddle on the seashore among the rocks. When the little one has grown a bit, the mother seizes him by her teeth, throws him into the water and swims around him while he struggles about and endeavors to get back to the shore. As soon as he comes out of the water, the mother seizes him again and plunges him back into the water yet again, and so it goes on until he has learned to swim. At the end of two months, these young ones can swim perfectly. They stay on land during the night; in the morning they go into the sea and swim until midday; then they come back on shore to rest and return to the sea about 4 o'clock. At the end of September, or in October, their education is completely finished and it is then that the hunting season starts.

The hunters form a human chain along the shore and cut off any possible retreat of the animals to the sea. They then push them all, without distinction, inland. Then they separate the first and third class males as well as the females and drive them back to the sea. As to the young ones which they intend to kill, they chase them as far as to the settlement—a distance of two or three leagues [any of various units of distance from about 2.4 to 4.6 miles]—but without hurrying them and letting them rest often, for without this precaution the animals could die of exhaustion, especially at a hot and windless time. Once they arrive at the settlement, the hunters kill the animals by blows. On the Island of Saint Paul herds of 3,000 to 4,000 seals can be driven inland in this way, and on the Island of Saint George herds of 500 to 2,000.

There is something revolting in this cold blooded carnage of thousands of defenseless animals. The hunters themselves, hardened as they are to this form of murder, confess that often they can hardly raise their clubs to strike this innocent creature which, lying on its back with its paws in the air and crying plaintively like a baby, seems to be imploring mercy.

It is necessary to take the precaution of separating the big males from those which are to be killed in order to ensure their multiplication, but is this precaution adequate? If all the young ones are exterminated, from where will come more large males? Experienced hunters have observed that the fur seals live up to fifteen to twenty years, in which case, under these conditions, there would not be one left in twenty years. Is it not astonishing that this species was not completely exterminated during the first twenty years when no one had yet thought about taking any kind of precaution? Now it has been decided, as previously mentioned, to leave some of the herds in peace, in turn, but this would not seem to be enough protection since their numbers continue to diminish all the time.

9

Notes on the Copper River

FERDINAND PETROVICH WRANGELL

Baron Ferdinand Petrovich von Wrangell (1796–1870) was one of the most important figures of Russian America. A German born in Estonia, he entered the Russian navy at an early age and sailed as a midshipman, lieutenant, and commander from Siberia to America. In 1828 he arrived in New Archangel (known today as Sitka) as an officer of the Russian-American Company, and almost immediately changed the way the business was operated in several respects, including the cessation of overhunting furbearers and the modernization of relations with Alaskan natives. Later in life he traveled widely, returned to Russia, and was a founder of the Russian Geographic Society. In 1856 Wrangell was promoted to admiral and he remained a trusted governmental aide whose advice was sought even after he retired in 1864. In this chapter from his book Russian America, which was first published in German in 1839, Wrangell provides a detailed description of the Copper River, which drains south from the Wrangell Mountains of southern Alaska into the Gulf of Alaska, as well as the Nuchek River and the surrounding coastal country. The gornyi baran to which Wrangell refers to as a mountain sheep may instead be the mountain goat, which has the straight horns mentioned in the description. His location of the hummingbird (probably the Rufous Hummingbird, Selasphorus rufus) in the region south of Sitka is entirely accurate.

The river, which is called the Mednaia (Copper) River in the colonies, but the Atna by the tribe living downstream, is a separate river system originating in high mountains. [These mountains] extend on one side toward the east from Mount St. Elias to the northeast and on the other [west] side, also in a northeasterly direction, farther than Cook's inlet and the sources of the rivers which flow into the Bering Sea (and are indeed in the river basin of the rivers Kvikpak and Kuskokvim) from those which run into the ocean with the river Atna. The higher, north-eastern tributaries of this river lie in a region unvisited by any wild tribe known to us, and therefore I could not obtain any information about them. The Kolosh, Kenai and Kolchan [Indian tribes of coastal Alaska] unanimously maintain that they have never heard of any river exceeding the Atna in length and breadth. Its five branches discharge into the sea, and in its course the river builds up great sandbanks which stretch far out to sea, particularly on the Nuchek side. The river has found a way through the Yakutat Mountains [these mountains are adjacent to Mount St. Elias], which extend to the coast and whose canyons contain eternal ice; it undermines these masses of ice, which break off in great chunks and are hurled with a mighty roar into the river, so that many fish are tossed onto the river bank; ice sometimes piles up in places where the river narrows, causing local floods and making any journey by boat into those regions dangerous if not impossible. Mountain canyons filled with ice 20 fathoms thick are found on the river itself and are about one and a half versts across; in some places, the ice has been covered by earth and on this grow moss, berries and alder. An iceberg in midstream, covered in green and ripe berries, is not an uncommon sight. Above [perhaps below], where rapids have formed, where the river has broken through the glaciers of the Yakutat Mountains, the ice ends and one enters a region exposed to sea winds and fog. These winds and fog are principally confined to the coastal strip of the river's lower waters. Apart from the Ugalentsky, no natives live here, and even they come only to the eastern mouth of the river during the summer, to catch fish.

During the whole journey [down the Nuchek River], one is aware of the mountains on both sides of the river; the banks are rocky and covered with silver fir, poplars, sand willows and birches. Several varieties of ocean fish are driven into the river and in the upper part of the rapids one can easily catch red fish (*Salmo lycaodon*) and *Salmo orientalis*, which are also found as far as the native dwellings across the Chechitna to the north. Farther to the north one comes upon a fairly extensive plateau between the mountains on both sides of the Atna. On the left side, in sight of the odinochka, is a dome-shaped mountain which throws out perpetual fire and whose summit is crowned with eternal snow; it is not connected to the chain of mountains, but stands alone. This part of the country is shaken by strong earth tremors several times a year.

After several small rivers and streams have joined the Atna from both sides, the river divides into two main branches, apparently about 1 3/4 degrees north of the odinochka. The right branch springs from a fairly large lake, called Mantilbana by the Kenai, five winters days' journey from its junction with the left branch, which runs through the mountains with such speed that it is not possible to sail up it, neither by using a tow-rope, nor by using a pole in place of a rudder. The natives on the river Atna have in their territory Lake Mantilbana as well as the river which runs from it, as far as the sea; on the other hand, the eastern branch belongs to the Kolchan (as the Atna call them) or to the Galtsan (in the language of the Kenai)—i.e. foreigners or guests. A small stream joins the river Atna from the west, below the Chechitna; it comes from a lake where there is an easy portage to Chugach Bay. In winter, the natives can reach the north end of Cook's Inlet in ten days, since they travel straight across bogs, lakes and mountains.

In the country belonging to this river system there are fox, beaver, muskrat, evrashka (*Spermophilus*), pine-marten, porcupines, marmot, wolves, wolverine, black bear, reindeer and elk. These last are very seldom found farther west than Cook's Inlet and the lowland through which run the waters of Chugach Bay and Cook's Inlet. Bison and musk ox (*Bos bison* and *Bos* (*Ovibus*) *moschatus*) are not found in the Atna district and it appears that they do not cross the mountains from which the great river flows to the sea. The mountain sheep, as it is called here *gornyi baran*, with straight ram's horns and long white wool, beneath which lies a most beautiful down, lives in the mountains along the sea coast and also comes as far as the Kolosh coast and the mountains which border Chugach Bay; another kind called the *iaman* here, lives in the same coastal mountains, but farther west than Chugach Bay and on both sides of Cook's Inlet. It is noteworthy that hummingbirds can be seen in the Kolosh Archipelago south of Sitkha in the springtime when the raspberry is in flower; they also visit Nuchek but are not to be seen farther west and north. Apart from Sitkha, swallows are not seen in our settlements, with the exception of Nuchek, where they regularly appear towards May 23rd and leave about August 15th.

10

Notes on the Islands of the Unalashka District

IVAN VENIANIMOV

Ivan Venianimov (1797–1879), a Russian missionary born in Siberia and educated in a seminary at Irkutsk, figures prominently in the Russian-American period. He arrived in Unalashka with his family in 1824 and immediately set to work learning about the Aleut language and culture, and developing plans to help the native people. He traveled widely in the Russian colony and as far south as California, writing several important works, the most influential of which was Notes on the Islands of the Unalashka District (St. Petersburg, 1840). After the sale of Russian America to the United States, Venianimov returned to Russia, where, in recognition of his extraordinary service, the Emperor appointed him to one of the most important posts in the Russian Orthodox Church. In this selection from his celebrated study of the Aleuts and Unalashka, Venianimov proves himself to be quite knowledgeable about the natural history of the sea otter, noting various aspects of sea otter ecology, including the use of hauling grounds, the employment of rocks to break open shells, and the general reclusiveness of the species. Of particular interest to the contemporary reader is his concern, evident also in the earlier selection by Frederic Litke, about the welfare of the animal as a resource. He argues, as does Litke, for restraint in the otter harvest: "it is not natural for any kind of animal, left at liberty, to decrease or become extinct by itself."

The *sea otter* is the best animal of its kind in all respects. Its fur is the most valuable of all furred animals of the world. The shape of its body is beautiful. The abilities of its body are incomparably superior to all the other amphibians. It is extremely smart, wary, even intelligent, so that the Aleuts formerly thought that sea otters were of human origin. The shape of sea otter bodies to some extent gives credence to that idea. Its head is almost completely round, the chest as flat as that of a human. The front paws strongly resemble hands and [the sea otter] uses them expertly and freely. For instance, having brought up a mollusk from the bottom of the sea, it breaks it with a rock. The usual position of a sea otter in the sea is on its back, which is rounded as are the backs of other animals. It can swim in that position. The females are very fond of their young. They always carry the very young children on their chests. In case of danger a mother does not abandon her child in the water but carries it and defends it until it becomes impossible to do so. Many of the aged Aleuts say that sea otter females fuss over their children almost exactly as women do, and that occasionally they have heard the mothers [singing] lullabys until [the children fell asleep].

Sea otters cannot or, it is better to say, do not want to live where people disturb them. One has only to briefly visit a sea otter hauling ground [rookery] and leave the smallest indication of one's visit and at once the sea otters begin to look for another refuge for themselves. Therefore, the Aleuts, when hunting sea otters, observe strict precautions to the point that when yet several half-score versts out to sea, they do not permit even spitting into the water.

Formerly, the sea otters were found everywhere and often hauled out on shore in large herds, especially on one of the Pribylov Islands. Nowadays, they are not found there at all. There is not a single spot in the entire Unalashka District where sea otters haul out. [The translator notes that the disappearance of sea otters in the Pribylovs may have been related to severe winters and that sea otters persisted in the region into the American period of the late nineteenth century.] They are found now only far off shore, in shallow places, especially where kelp is plentiful. They haul out on shore only during severe winds, in winter, and only in places inaccessible to man. It does happen that they come close to shore in summer but only at dawn seeking food. By day, in good weather and on the places safest for them, there is not even a single sea otter to be found on shore.

In the Atkha district there are certain places where sea otters are found and where they breed but in the local district there are no such places at all. Between the local, Kuril, Atkha and California sea otters, there is a great difference in fur. So, if the sea otters, like all other amphibian animals, breed on land, then the question is, where do the sea otters breed which are found in the water around the shores of the Unalashka district? [The location of sea mammal wintering and breeding grounds was an important and highly debated question of the time.] If [they breed] in the water, then why are they found predominantly off the southern shores, in the sea there, while formerly they were more numerous in the northern sea? This circumstance permits us to hypothesize that in the south sea [the Pacific] there are islands, or rocks as yet unknown to us. The Aleuts designate as [the breeding place] of the sea otters found off Umnak an island to the south of and close to Unalashka, which has already been mentioned above (in Section Three of the First Part). But from whence come the sea otters to Sannakh? And especially in winter, when it is stormy? It is quite probable that they come from the same places as the fur seals and sea lions, that is, from the places as yet unknown.

Because of their great value and small numbers, sea otters by now constitute almost a rarity. The time was when they were hunted by the thousands but now only by the hundreds. [The translator notes that thousands is an exaggeration.] In many places, where formerly there was a multitude of sea otters, already for several years now none have been observed.

The cause of this is quite obvious. It must be said, however, that in many places sea otters disappeared, not because they were hunted out, but because, as was said earlier, they do not like to live where they are disturbed. The sea otters are as much exterminated as they are frightened away. Annual disturbance [hunt] forces them to depart for other safer places.

Consequently, in order not to lose the sea otters completely, our own benefit requires us to take measures not to drive the sea otters away and, at the same time, to profit from them as much as is possible.

But what measures can be taken for this?

One of the best measures for this, in my opinion, is *not to hunt at each sea otter place each year* but to go to each place no more than after three or, at the least, after two years, in order after having disturbed the sea otters one summer, to give them time to recover again and become calm in the following years. I speak of *"being disturbed"* because there is no instance in which, of a considerable number of sea otters, some of these animals did not escape the hunters even if only a few. On the contrary, very often it happens that from a whole enormous herd and with the very best circumstances for hunters, they got no more than 10 sea otters.

Of course, when such a measure is implemented, the number of sea otters [taken] will decrease; but then, they will never be exterminated. Consequently, the profits will be always assured. . . . In the contrary case, that is, if this measure is not instituted, it is very possible that after ten or twenty years there will not be a single sea otter anywhere in the entire district, and not because they would be exterminated but because of constant and uninterrupted disturbance and attacks everywhere, they will leave for other, safer places. . . . This measure, even if one assumes that it will not bring projected benefit for sea otter industry (which is not a reasonable assumption), in the very least it will not have an adverse effect on sea otter breeding. True, in the early years the sea otter take will be less—but then one should bear in mind that the price of the pelts will go up proportionately, the fewer sea otters are taken.

It cannot be that there will be no benefit from my proposed measure because it is not natural for any kind of animal, left at liberty, to decrease or become extinct by itself under the same conditions.

The measures I am proposing for the sea otter industry should have a beneficial effect on the increase or, in the very least, an extension of the existence of sea otter species. [The translator notes that "rotation of sea otter hunting grounds was instituted much earlier than his sojourn in the Aleutians and after the decades 1810–1820 was practised consistently." Despite these measures, sea otter populations continued to dwindle.]

**11**

Nulato, a Settlement on the Yukon

L. A. ZAGOSKIN

Lieutenant L. A. Zagoskin (1808–1890) was sent by the Russian government to explore the western coast and interior of Alaska from 1842–1844. The expedition represented a significant investment for the Russians—total cost for the two-year, four-month period was over 6,000 rubles—but the benefits were substantial as Zagoskin explored both the Kvihpak (Yukon) and Kuskokwim drainages. Nulato, described in this selection, was and still is a small native community on the Yukon River downstream from the confluence with the Koyukuk River, a major river that drains south from the interior Brooks Range. Zagoskin notes that both the black and grizzly bear are found in the region, that "there are not many wolves here," and that the Nulato River is rich with otters and has good numbers of beavers. Some of his observations anticipate the findings on boreal ecology and native cultures made by anthropologist Richard Nelson (see "The Subsistence Cycle"), who worked north of this area in Huslia during the 1970s. Particularly touching is Zagoskin's description of the plentiful song birds of the boreal forests. Even to those unfamiliar with the species cited from their Latin appellations, his words are evocative: "Some are expressing the spring's songs, others songs of shelter, and others songs to their little ones. Everything is in love, everything is in a hurry to enjoy the short summer of the north." In lines like this, Zagoskin's nearly forgotten narrative calls to mind that great masterpiece of Russian nature writing Nature's Diary (Moscow, 1925), written by Mikhail Prishvin (1873–1954), which shines with a similar joie de vivre.

From Travels on Foot, and Description of the Russian Possessions in America, from 1842–1844. St. Petersburg, 1847. Undated and anonymous English translation in manuscript form in Alaska and Polar Regions Collection, University of Alaska, Fairbanks.

July 30, 1844

The Nulato village lay on latitude of 64° 42′ 11″ and longitude to the west from Greenwich is 157° 58′ 18″. The location of the village is on the right beach of Kvihpak River ½ of a mile up from the bank of the river. The plain land which lies between the river and Tiakintit Cliff is probably made by the action of running water. The border of this land is fifteen or eighteen feet high above the river, and in some ways represents a rampart, which in some places is five sagen wide. The level land has many small lakes and basins in which the heaping water from melted snow is held all summer. All the banks of Nulato River are not more than ten feet high. As a result of this in the spring time the overflowing water comes to the settlement from the firm land, before the Kvihpak is overflowing its channel.

The low plain earth of this country is probably the result of very poor growing forest whose trees are withered and trunks are crooked, on account of it the natives use the timber from the opposite side of this bank.

The soil around the settlement is clayish slime, about one foot thick, but the level land is covered by many scattered hillocks of orgillous forms. On one of these kinds of hillocks we fixed a bed for a garden which was about twenty-five sagen square and on May 20th we planted some radishes and turnips which came out very well. . . . The source of the Nulato River runs from the northwest top of the mountain and has many mountain streams, which divide the basin of the Kvihpak from the seashore of Norton Bay. Eight miles from its mouth it forms into quite a large creek. We have been by boat and by walking up to this place. In the month of June way high in the mountain one of our hunters killed one deer [Zagoskin refers to the barren-ground caribou here and elsewhere as either deer or reindeer], but by the words of natives, the reindeer were seen in the fall way down on the tundra or close to Nulato.

There are two kinds of bears here; black and brown, which once in awhile come down to fish and very often destroy the tottering barabaras where natives keep their winter supplies and leave them without food.

There are not many wolves here.

The natives here are not very zealous for catching foxes or beavers.

The Nulato river gives a preference of many beavers. In the spring by her mouth we caught four beavers. Tatlek during his three trips caught sixteen, the two natives from the Unna-ka river in four days at hunting caught twenty-eight.

The river is rich with otters. The natives hunt them with arrows. During the winter time the otters are trapped by a particular trap, "the spruce muzzle," but this hunting does not require any difficult work and is disposed only to the old aged men or the shamans.

These two northern rivers are so unlike. The Kvihpak is magnificent running by our settlement and almost a mile wide, with original rolling water which came from Nulato bar; in lengthways of right banks shows up a stretch of rocky beach, at the same time in the middle of the river is seen the long shallow sand bank, and during the flood waters they compress the Kvihpak waters in two streams, each of them not more than two hundred sagen wide. . . . The shore from the Nulato to the mouth of the Unna-ka at some places is covered by slime, others by stones and talc. The sharp pointed cliffs had many hardened layers of clays and in falling earth were layers of stratum. . . . The shore of the Kvihpak at some places is elevated by the beautiful poplar; willow, osier and alder bush particularly grow in marshes and in the bank spits. The other leaf trees are not more thick than four inches in diameter and grow in dry tundra; the mountain ash grows in the valley; the snow-drop grows from five feet high to the small sprays, and spreads all over between the bushes of black-currant and wild rose. The juniper grows in low bushes close to the Tliakintit Cliff.

The natives for winter supply themselves with the cranberries, cloudberry, and blueberries; the rubus arcticus has a very pleasant taste and is picked up only by the small children; the red and black currants are left for the bears only.

All sorts of mushrooms are growing on the hills; cibarius, red tops, birch-mushrooms, agarics, reddish-yellow chanterill, we dried and salted them for winter, they were used by us when we were short of fish, the natives never eat them.

I told before that in the good search for deer we could easy provide ourselves with meat, and even if the successful hunting were not very often, we could have it once in awhile for refreshment.

Just the same for the game birds of grouse and ptarmigans (*Tetroa canadensis, tetroa umbillus*) which were the only hunting game. From the four periods of the year, the geese and ducks show up between the seventeenth or twenty-second of April, and by the fifteenth of May all of them fly to the north. The swans fly over the beach and never stop here. The crane on their flight sometimes stop for a rest on the tundra by Tliakintit Cliff. . . . I must remark here a few words about singing birds. In the deep days of winter around Nulato in open places among the ice were seen a *Cinelus canadensis* (here is a remark for somebody, that the meat of northern magpie is quite delicious). In the forest jungle now and then show up a *Picus arcticus* (Swainson) and *Corythus enucleator;* the last ones are seen in the first part of March on the blooming bushes of willow by the river banks.

Together with the *Corythus* come big flocks of *Fringilla Sinaria* (Jay).

From the month of May the forest is inspired by different kinds of singing and hollering birds. The *Turdus minor* are whistling all the night long; *Sylvia wilsonie* or *Mulcipapa pussila Wilson* (Audubon) may be seen with her golden feathers from sun beams, or *Sylvicola Coronata* is fluttering from one bush to another and twittering some noise; the *Loxia lencoptera* from the tops of spruce is spreading her quavering song; the *Alcedo alcyon* is jumping from one block of ice to another. Some are expressing the spring's songs, others songs of shelter, and others songs to their little ones. Everything is in love, everything is in a hurry to enjoy the short summer of the north.

12

Letter to Sir John Richardson

ALEXANDER HUNTER MURRAY

Alexander Hunter Murray (1818–1874) was born in Kilmun, Scotland, in 1818. Like so many Scotsmen of his generation, he emigrated to the United States, shortly finding work with the American Fur Company. He traveled widely as their representative in Louisiana, Texas, and Belize. In 1846 Murray left the American Fur Company and went to work for the Hudson's Bay Company as a senior clerk, Mackenzie River District. In 1847 Murray made a permanent place for himself in Arctic history by founding Fort Yukon near the confluence of the Porcupine River and the Yukon River. This fort enabled the British to control the fur trade of interior Alaska and the Yukon, even in an area considered then to be under the jurisdiction of the Russians. Murray retired from the Hudson's Bay Company in 1867 and spent the last seven years of his life in a cottage on the Red River in Canada. As late as 1910, one of his descendents, Alexander Campbell Murray, was still in the service of the Hudson's Bay Company in northern British Columbia. The elder Murray's Journal of the Yukon, 1847–1848 provides important insights into the early history of the upper Yukon basin. It is clear in this letter Murray wrote to Dr. John Richardson, one of the more prominent naturalists of the age, that, in addition to being a shrewd businessman and tireless explorer, Alexander Hunter Murray was also a close observer of nature who was well familiar with the taxonomy and terminology of the age. Additionally, some of the sketches that Murray drew to illustrate his journal were eventually reproduced in one of John Richardson's books, Arctic Searching Expedition.

From *Journal of the Yukon 1847–1848*. Ottawa: Government Printing Bureau, 1910.

May, 1850—from Fort Yukon

. . . Of the two kinds of swan, only the largest sort (*Cygnus buccinator*) are seen here; they pass on to the northward of the Porcupine river, to breed among the lakes. Bustards [Canada geese] are plentiful, and breed everywhere, from Council Bluffs on the Missouri to the vicinity of the Polar sea. On the ramparts of Porcupine river they frequently build high up among the rocks, where one would suppose only hawks and ravens would have their nests. How they take their young down is unknown to me, but they must be carried somehow. Ravens and large gulls are very destructive to young geese. With respect to the breeding quarters of the laughing geese (*Anser albifrons*), I am able to inform you correctly, having myself seen a few of their nests; and, since the receipt of your letter, made further inquiry among the northern Indians. Their nests are built on the edges of swamps and lakes, throughout most of the country north of the Porcupine, where the ground is marshy. It is only near the most northerly bends of that river that they are seen in the breeding season, and these are male birds. They pass to their breeding places in the beginning of June, and make their nests among long grass or small bushes, where they are not easily seen. They are shy birds when hatching; and, when any one comes near the nest, manage to escape unperceived, and then show themselves at a distance, and manoeuvre [sic] like grouse to lead the intruder away from the place. Notwithstanding our ruthless habit of collecting eggs of all kinds to vary our diet, I have often felt for a laughing goose, whose anxiety for the safety of its eggs was frequently the means of revealing to us the situation of its nests. When the bird was swimming some hundreds of yards off, immediately that any person in walking round the lake came near its treasure, the poor bird, began to make short, impatient turns in the water, resuming her calm demeanour if the intruder passed the nest without seeing it. As soon as the eggs are taken, the goose rises out of the water and flies close to the head of the captor, uttering a frightened and pitiful cry. These geese are more numerous in the valley of the Yukon than any other kind, and the numbers that pass northwards there are perhaps equal to that of all the other species together. The Gens du large (*Neyetse-kutchin*) who visit the north coast regularly to traffic with the Eskimos, say that they have never seen any flying northwards over the sea in that quarter. White geese (Snow geese, *Chen myperboreus*) are also passengers here, and there are likewise black geese, which I presume you have never seen. A few of them pass down Peel's river, but they are more abundant on the Yukon. They are very handsome birds, considerably smaller than the white geese, and have a dark brown or brownish black colour, with a white ring round the neck, the head and bill having the shape of that of the bustard. The black geese are the least numerous and the latest that arrive here. They fly in large flocks with remarkable velocity, and generally pass on without remaining, as the others do, some days to feed. When they alight, it is always in the water; and if they wish to land, they swim ashore. They are very fat, and their flesh has an oily and rather disagreeable taste. Bustards, laughing geese, ducks, and large gulls make their appearance here from the 27th to the 29th of April. Snow geese and black geese about the 15th or 16th of May, when the other kinds become plentiful. They have mostly passed by the end of the month, though some, especially the bustards, are seen in June. The white geese and black geese breed only on the shores of the Arctic Sea. They return in September and early in October, flying high, and seldom halting.

PART II

1867–1958
Territorial Alaska and the Age of Exploitation

The resources of the new territory [of Alaska] having now been pointed out, it only remains for the irresistible energy of American citizens to hasten their development. Time alone can prove their ultimate value.

William H. Dall
Alaska and Its Resources

It is a very remarkable fact that a region under a civilized government for more than a century should remain so completely unknown as the vast territory drained by the Copper, Tanana, and Koyukuk Rivers.

Henry T. Allen
Report of an Expedition to the Copper, Tanana, and Koyukuk Rivers in the Territory of Alaska

March 30, 1867, Alaska is sold to the United States by Russia for 7.2 million dollars. 1870, the Alaska Commercial Company is awarded the fur seal contract for the Pribilof Islands. 1872, 30,000 gold prospectors arrive in Wrangell. 1879, John Muir visits Alaska for the first time. 1879, Libby Beamann is the first American woman in the Pribilof Islands. 1883, Frederick Schwatka explores the southeast coast and the Yukon region. 1884, the first red salmon cannery opens in Bristol Bay. 1885, U. S. Army Lieutenant Henry Allen explores the Copper, Tanana, and Koyukuk Rivers. 1886, gold is discovered near Dawson City. 1890, the first oil claims are made near Anchorage. 1897, the first halibut is shipped south from Juneau. 1897, Jack London visits Alaska. 1898, Skagway booms as gold seekers cross Chilkoot Pass. 1899, the Harriman Expedition explores Alaska. 1900, the first oil well is drilled in Cook Inlet. 1902, gold is discovered near Fairbanks and mining continues in earnest in what is now the Yukon-Charley National Preserve. 1904, Robert Service moves to Dawson City from San Francisco. 1905, a telegraph line is run from Valdez to Fairbanks. 1907, the Chugach National Forest is established. 1908, the Tongass National Forest is established. 1910, the first ascent of Mount McKinley by the Sourdough Expedition fails to reach the south peak. 1910, Sitka National Park is formed. 1913, Hudson Stuck climbs Mt. McKinley. 1918, Katmai National Monument is set aside. 1925, Glacier Bay National Monument is established. 1929, Robert Marshall explores the Brooks Range. 1935, Will Rogers and Wiley Post die in a plane crash near Barrow. 1939–1941, Adolph Murie becomes the father of modern wolf ecology as he intensely studies the wolves of Mt. McKinley National Park. 1942, Kluane National Park is formed in the Yukon. 1942, Japan occupies Attu and Kiska Islands. 1954, the Ketchikan pulp mill is complete. 1957, Atlantic Richfield discovers oil at Swanson River on the Kenai peninsula.

13

The Rapids of the Yukon

WILLIAM HENRY DALL

William Henry Dall (1845–1927) grew up in Boston and attended Harvard but never graduated. In 1866 he accompanied the historic Western Union Telegraphy Company expedition to Alaska, which sought to find an overland route for a transcontinental telegraph line to Europe. This objective proved impossible to achieve, but Dall later produced an important book as a result of his adventures in the north, Alaska and Its Resources (Lee and Shepard, 1870). From 1871–1884 Dall served in the U. S. Coastal Survey. In 1880 he was named honorary curator of molluscs in the U. S. National Museum, and later held the Chair of Invertebrate Paleontology at the Wagner Institute of Science in Philadelphia. In 1897 Dall was named to the National Academy of Science and from 1899–1915 he was the honorary curator of the Bishop Museum in Hawaii. One of the accomplishments of the Western Union Telegraph expedition was the determination that the Yukon River was essentially navigable for most of its length. In the passage included here, Dall describes their ascent of the Rapids of the Yukon, a fabled obstacle which, despite many grave warnings ("The Russians had predicted that we should not be able to ascend them"), is quickly overcome by the Americans.

From *Alaska and Its Resources*. Boston, 1870.

Monday, June 10

We entered, about three o'clock in the afternoon, between high bluffs and hills rising perhaps fifteen hundred feet above the river, which here was exceedingly deep and rapid and not more than half a mile wide. The bends were abrupt, and the absence of sunlight and the extreme quiet produced a feeling as if we had been travelling underground. The appropriate and expressive English name for these bluffs is "the Ramparts."

We were approaching the so-called Rapids of the Yukon, of which we had heard so many stories. The Russians had predicted that we should not be able to ascend them. The Indians joined in this expression of opinion, and had no end of stories about the velocity of the current and the difficulty experienced in ascending them. We all felt a little anxious, but were confident of overcoming the supposed difficulty in some way. We met some Indians and obtained a little fresh meat. About midnight we arrived at the Rapids. The river is very narrow here, and the rocky hills rise sharply from the water. The rocks are metamorphic quartzites, and a dike or belt of hard granitic rock crosses the river. The fall is about twelve feet in half a mile. The rapid current has worn the granite away on either side, forming two good channels, but in the middle is an island of granite, over which the river rushes in a sheet of foam during high water. There are several smaller "rips" along the shore, especially near the left bank, but nothing to interrupt steamer navigation, except the very rapid current.

Several Indians attempted to ascend in their small canoes. We saw them reach a point just below the island, and by dint of the hardest paddling keep stationary there a few minutes; when, their strength being exhausted, away went the canoes down stream like arrows.

We joined our tracking-line with several rawhide lines belonging to the Indians, and by keeping close to the rocks succeeded in tracking over the worst part without much difficulty. Taking our seats again, we had a hard pull to pass one jutting rock, and our troubles were over. We then enjoyed a well-earned cup of tea, and took a parting glance at the Rapids from above. From this point only a broad patch of foam in the middle of the river indicated their existence.

Friday, June 14

Passed a very small stream called by the Indians *Tatsun-ikhtun,* or "Caught-in-the-rocks." I found a fossil skull of the musk ox (*Ovibos moschatus*) on the beach. Wild roses, snowballs, and gold-thread were in blossom on the hillsides, and the fragrant juniper scented the air. A fine bluff, with a rocky face like a great staircase, marked the mouth of the Tseetoht River on the right bank. After this the river begins to widen, and numerous small islands occur.

Tuesday, June 18

One of the few who accompanied us followed a cow-moose in the water until tired out, when he killed her with his knife, and with some difficulty we towed her ashore. We occasionally saw a black bear or a Canada lynx on the bank. For several days we kept steadily on, little of interest occurring. It was noticed that the trees began to grow smaller and more sparse as we ascended the river. The sun hardly dipped below the horizon at midnight, and his noontide rays scorched like a furnace. The mosquitoes were like smoke in the air. . . . Both banks had become very low and flat; the region had a dreary appearance. Only five snow-covered peaks, supposed to be part of the Romantzoff range, rose above the level of the plains. These are the only mountains near the Yukon, in Russian America north of the Alaskan range, which bear snow throughout the year.

The plain here described reaches to the shores of the Arctic Ocean, broken only by a few ranges of low mountains near the coast, of which the Romantzoff are the highest. To the eastward it rises almost imperceptibly, attaining its highest elevation between the headwaters of the Porcupine and the left bank of the Mackenzie. This table-land, somewhat broken and rocky, as seen abutting on the Mackenzie River has the appearance of high hills. These are the "mountains" of Richardson. There are no true mountains north of the Yukon, except the Romantzoff. Nothing of less than five thousand feet in height has a right to the title of mountain; but in the careless speech of the Hudson Bay trappers and traders anything more than two hundred feet high is a "mountain."

14

The Pribilof Islands

ELIZABETH BEAMAN

Elizabeth Dubois Beaman (1844–1932) was the first non-native American woman to live on the remote Pribilof Islands of Alaska's Bering Sea. She arrived on the islands in 1879 with her husband, John Warren Beaman, a U. S. government official. At that time the Alaska Commercial Company operated the profitable fur seal industry in the region. Her writings were published posthumously in 1987 as Libby: The Sketches, Letters, and Journal of Libby Beaman, Recorded in the Pribilof Islands 1879–1880 (Council Oak Books). These narratives are remarkable not only for their literary quality, but also for the insights they provide—as interior monologues—into the private life of the author's mind. Like all good literary works, the writings are highly quotable, whether in her philosophical observations, her satiric commentaries on existence, her vivid descriptions, or her recordings of interesting bits and pieces of dialogue. "Though I've been the rebel of our set," Libby Beaman states, "about the silly, outmoded customs and manners we have to keep—I've not gone mannish like Cousin Fanny Chase. I prefer to win my rebellion while remaining entirely feminine (p. 18)." Of her virtues she writes "Why, because I am a woman, must I hide them? . . . I am not intent on outdoing men. I am only trying to prove that women can do the things they can do and should be permitted to do them (p. 19)." In this selection the author describes her view of the remote island at the edge of the known world that was to be her home for the next two years. There is some first-rate natural description here, as is the case throughout the Beaman journals.

"Journal Entry: May 27, 1879" from Libby: The Sketches, Letters, and Journal of Libby Beaman by Libby S. Beaman. 1879 text reprinted by permission of Council Oak Books and copyright © 1987 by Betty John (granddaughter).

May 27

We've had a rough and turbulent three days, all of us seasick and frightened. At first there were the terrifying mountain islands to sail between, with their jagged, black precipices coming down into the waters and their glaciers breaking away and falling into the sea in great roaring avalanches of rock and ice, so near at times as to rock the ship. We were like a bit of chaff in a whirlpool. There were sudden storms, tidal swells that all but dashed us against those perpendicular cliffs, and shallows where least expected; most treacherous of all were the currents and countercurrents forced between the close islands, apparently of warm and cold origin, for the fogs they formed have been the most hazardous.

The greatest warm current, the Japan Stream, squeezed itself between Attu and Kamchatka after having swerved in under Alaska and back westward under the Aleutian Chain. Where it hit the bitterly cold waters of the Bering Sea, dense fogs and turbulent storms formed, making this the most dangerous stretch of all the trip to navigate. We were sailing through banks of fog that opened and closed, and though we'd begun to get a faint odor of land, no land was yet in sight. Birds, too, came out to greet us. They wheeled about our mainmast by the thousands—all kinds: terns and auklets, gannets and gulls, and many others I did not recognize. They were noisy greeters, at times deafening. We could not hear each other speak. We did not speak. We were too full to speak. Our destination was so near.

"Land ho!" the watch called down. "Land ho!"

So near, dear Lord, so near, and yet we are not there, not really there until our feet are on the land. We ride at anchor, straining at the anchor buoy about a mile from the Village of St. Paul. A dense fog lies over us, lies over the Bering Sea.

The captain said that it is sometimes days (once two weeks) before he can land. "Not this time, fortunately. The sea is calming," he said when he saw how disappointed I was that we could not go in immediately. "We did at least find the anchorage, and that is something I've also spent days hunting for it. By tomorrow the sea will be calm enough, I think, to send in the lighter, the first time with only crew aboard because there's still so much loose ice in the harbor. They'll have to chart a course and tell us whether it's safe enough for passengers to follow."

"You mean the ship doesn't go in to the wharf?" I asked, aghast at the thought of having to climb down the side of this heaving vessel into a tiny boat bobbing at its side.

"She can't. Water's too shallow. This is the shallowest water I dare draw, and it's the only safe anchorage for the island. Unfortunately there are no sheltered bays up here. We always take our chances with fog, storms, and changes—volcanic changes, that is—in the shallows. I hope for your sake, Mrs. Beaman, that the day will be calm and clear tomorrow."

I do too. The hours of waiting are longer than any I've had to wait before. The sea is still too rough for me to write legibly. But let me try. We've little else to do during these disappointing hours. We did catch a glimpse of our future home before the fog blanket descended. It was in those same few clear minutes that Captain Erskine performed the miracle of finding and anchoring us at the buoy. Miracle it is, indeed, when one thinks of how he manages to find these tiny pin dots on that map I once traced of the Alaskan Purchase. Navigation is still an incomprehensible science to me. For one thing, neither Captain Erskine nor the ship's mate has once been able to take an astral fix because of cloudy skies at night; not even a solar fix has been taken since we saw the Orca. They've navigated entirely on calculations, the careful computations on their charts, accurate timing, compass readings (which because of the closeness to the North Pole are erratic), and by recording every degree of every single turn of the wheel, as well as sounding constantly with the lead line and straining their ears for the sounds of seals and breaking surf.

"When I smell seals," our captain jokes, "I know I've come in too far. I arrive by smell."

We know otherwise. We say a private prayer.

Speaking of smells, the cold winds from land come toward us laden with earth odors, seaweed rotting, animal debris, fish and rotting fish, and, above all, seals. *Pahknoot*, the Aleuts call odors. "You are getting the pahknoot of the Pribilofs," one gentleman informed me. "Something you will have to live with. It never goes away."

"How horrible," I said.

"Lady, you haven't smelled anything yet. Wait 'til you're right in it."

A few days ago, when we came through the straits, we were all asked to look out for pirate ships. They linger about the narrows where the great herds of migrating seals have to squeeze through from the Pacific into the Bering. There pirates can do their pelagic killing with the greatest of ease. Our government has been trying to stop this illicit trade that has decimated the seal herds considerably through the years. But this time we saw no pirates. In fact, the straits were so violent rough, I thought we'd never see another day.

"There's always plenty of excitement if we catch any pirates at it. We're permitted to use guns and we have, often," Captain Erskine said.

"The storm is enough excitement for me," I admitted. I was thankful that we didn't have to go to war with anyone over the seals, though I could see that the men were itching for a good fight. There were other excitements they watched for—treacherous icebergs, and we saw many—but no polar bears, which would have interested me more. We did see whales—which also linger at the narrows because seal meat is a favorite meat—and sharks, as well as other ships. In all this great waste of frigid waters, anything makes one feel less small, less lost.

I wanted to know if it was my imagination or if the water of the Bering was greener than that of the Pacific. And if it was greener, was that because it was shallower or colder or what? To me, it appeared to be a brilliant green.

"It's sweeter," a fellow passenger answered. And in response to my raised eyebrows, he explained, "Seawater is always less salty, so it refracts light differently. That is why seawater is greener than ocean water."

I suppose the main reason we all stayed on deck today, in spite of the chill and the stormy sea, is because we wanted to watch landfall, and fortunately, we had our brief glimpse of it—a bleak, cold, inhospitable-looking mass of rock, here at the other end of the earth.

We came in from the south, ignoring St. George, which would have been the nearer island but is too stormy to approach at this time of year. The *St. Paul* visits it only twice a year and then merely to load pelts, of which none is ready now anyway. St. George lies about thirty miles southeast but seldom can be seen. It appears, I am told, still more formidable and inhospitable upon approach. St. Paul has bleak, sharp contours relieved by soft, rounded, worn down hills. Inland there are snowcapped peaks and deep violet shadows ending sharply in pinkish sand dunes, vast, vivid patches of grass, and rocky shores where great chunks of greenish ice are piled in mountainous heaps. Low beaches sweep inland to high bluffs of perpendicular rocks with flat plateaux on top. Some cliffs drop directly into the sea with shelves of rock at their bases, undercut by waves and tides. On these and on the beaches are thousands and thousands and thousands of male seals. From the ship, they appear to be black bobs restlessly swaying or moving back and forth between the water and the land. The sight is incredible. I had heard descriptions, but my wildest imaginings had not prepared me for such a sight.

These teeming, restless, barking, roaring hordes, then, are to dominate our lives.

"The groupings are called 'rookeries,'" John said, reiterating some of the lore he had gathered on the way up. "Don't ask me why, unless from a distance they resemble the hordes of noisy rooks we have at home." In that brief moment of seeing them, they presented a dramatic, fascinating sight.

Our approach, even from a mile away, had stirred up another overwhelming sight. Millions of seabirds wheeled into the sky from every nook and cranny of the cliffs. We could hear, and still do, their screams and squawkings above the surf pounding over the ice and against the rocks. The birds drown out the barking of the seals.

The village of St. Paul, visible for only a few minutes before the fog closed in, presented a pretty picture. It is built up a steep slope away from the harbor, where the small boats of skin called *bidarkahs* and the bidarrahs are pulled up on the little wharf. Low hills surround the village, and one hill drops in a sheer cliff just to the south of the buildings. It drops 300 feet straight down to a narrow shelf where there are seals, the smallest rookery on the island, I am told, Nah Speel. Government House, our home-to-be, sits high on the central slope overlooking the roofs of the other houses. But it is not Government House that dominates the scene. The vivid blue onion dome of the Orthodox church gives cohesion and charm to the scene and gathers unto itself the neat white frame buildings of the Alaska Commercial Company and the eighty white frame houses of the eighty Aleut families it serves.

To the left of the village, I could make out a long spit of sand, seal inhabited and parallel to the shore, enclosing a narrow lagoon which extended inland and seemed to broaden out beyond my vision. "That's Lagoon Rookery and its lagoon," one man said. "It does broaden out into a saltwater lake inland. That vast stretch of green grass between it and the first houses is the killing ground. That is where we drive the seals to be killed."

"How awfull!" I said. "Right under the villagers' eyes!"

"Right under their noses would be more correct," he countered. "You at Government House will be spared the sight of the killing because of a fortunate rise in the land. But you'll not be spared the smell. St. Paul is a smelly place in which to have to live."

"So I've already discovered," I said. "Even out here, the pahknoot of the island is strong."

15

The Alexander Archipelago

JOHN MUIR

Scottish-born John Muir (1838–1914) was the great pop-
ularizer of the conservation legacy of Henry David
Thoreau. The Father of both Yosemite National Park
and the Sierra Club, Muir was also active in movements to establish
other parks in the west, including Sequoia National Park and Grand
Canyon National Park, and was involved in many of the salient issues of
the day, such as the damming of Hetch Hetchy Valley.

In this selection Muir describes the Alexander Archipelago in
southeastern Alaska, a region through which he passed in his first
(1879) trip. The prose is vintage Victorian rhapsody, as the author calls
the wilderness a "true fairyland" and "the very paradise of the poets,
the abode of the blessed." Metaphors and similes gild almost every
paragraph. Exposed rocks in the ocean are, in a wavering reach, "mere
dots punctuating grand, outswelling sentences of islands." In a stronger
image, the spruces on the small islands are "like flowers leaning
outward against the rim of a vase." To appreciate how much the prose of
nature writing has changed in the past 100 years, it is instructive to read
David Rains Wallace's essay "This Tangled Brilliance" side by side
with Muir's "The Alexander Archipelago."

From *Travels in Alaska*. Boston: Houghton Mifflin, 1915.

To the lover of pure wildness Alaska is one of the most wonderful countries in the world. No excursion that I know of may be made into any other American wilderness where so marvelous an abundance of noble, newborn scenery is so charmingly brought to view as on the trip through the Alexander Archipelago to Fort Wrangell and Sitka. Gazing from the deck of the steamer, one is borne smoothly over calm blue waters, through the midst of countless forest-clad islands. The ordinary discomforts of a sea voyage are not felt, for nearly all the whole long way is on inland waters that are about as waveless as rivers and lakes. So numerous are the islands that they seem to have been sown broadcast; long tapering vistas between the largest of them open in every direction.

Day after day in the fine weather we enjoyed, we seemed to float in true fairyland, each succeeding view seeming more and more beautiful, the one we chanced to have before us the most surprisingly beautiful of all. Never before this had I been embosomed in scenery so hopelessly beyond description. To sketch picturesque bits, definitely bounded, is comparatively easy—a lake in the woods, a glacier meadow, or a cascade in its dell; or even a grand master view of mountains beheld from some commanding outlook after climbing from height to height above the forests. These may be attempted, and more or less telling pictures made of them; but in these coast landscapes there is such indefinite, on-leading expansiveness, such a multitude of features without apparent redundance, their lines graduating delicately into one another in endless succession, while the whole is so fine, so tender, so ethereal, that all penwork seems hopelessly unavailing. Tracing shining ways through fiord and sound, past forests and waterfalls, islands and mountains and far azure headlands, it seems as if surely we must at length reach the very paradise of the poets, the abode of the blessed.

Some idea of the wealth of this scenery may be gained from the fact that the coast-line of Alaska is about twenty-six thousand miles long, more than twice as long as all the rest of the United States. The islands of the Alexander Archipelago, with the straits, channels, canals, sounds, passages, and fiords, form an intricate web of land and water embroidery sixty or seventy miles wide, fringing the lofty icy chain of coast mountains from Puget Sound to Cook Inlet; and, with infinite variety, the general pattern is harmonious throughout its whole extent of nearly a thousand miles. Here you glide into a narrow channel hemmed in by mountain walls, forested down to the water's edge, where there is no distant view, and your attention is concentrated on the objects close about you—the crowded spires of the spruces and hemlocks rising higher and higher on the steep green slopes; stripes of paler green where winter avalanches have cleared away the trees, allowing grasses and willows to spring up; zigzags of cascades appearing and disappearing among the bushes and trees; short, steep glens with brawling streams hidden beneath alder and dogwood, seen only where they emerge on the brown algae of the shore; and retreating hollows, with lingering snow-banks marking the fountains of ancient glaciers. The steamer is often so near the shore that you may distinctly see the cones clustered on the tops of the trees, and the ferns and bushes at their feet.

But new scenes are brought to view with magical rapidity. Rounding some bossy cape, the eye is called away into far-reaching vistas, bounded on either hand by headlands in charming array, one dipping gracefully beyond another and growing fainter and more ethereal in the distance. The tranquil channel stretching river-like between, may be stirred here and there by the silvery plashing of upspring salmon, or by flocks of white gulls floating like water-lilies among the sun spangles; while mellow, tempered sunshine is streaming over all, blending sky, land, and water in pale, misty blue. Then, while you are dreamily gazing into the depths of this leafy ocean lane, the little steamer, seeming hardly larger than a duck, turning into some passage not visible until the moment of entering it, glides into a wide expanse—a sound filled with islands, sprinkled and clustered in forms and compositions such as nature alone can invent; some of them so small the trees growing on them seem like single handfuls culled from the neighboring woods and set in the water to keep them fresh, while here and there at wide intervals you may notice bare rocks just above the water, mere dots punctuating grand, out-welling sentences of islands.

The variety we find, both as to the contours and the collocation of the islands, is due chiefly to differences in the structure and composition of their rocks, and the unequal glacial denudation different portions of the coast were subjected to. This influence must have been especially heavy toward the end of the glacial period, when the main ice-sheet began to break up into separate glaciers. Moreover, the mountains of the larger islands nourished local glaciers, some of them of considerable size, which sculptured their summits and sides, forming in some cases wide cirques with canons or valleys leading down from them into the channels and sounds. These causes have produced much of the bewildering variety of which nature is so fond, but none the less will the studious observer see the underlying harmony—the general trend of the islands in the direction of the flow of the main ice-mantle from the mountains of the Coast Range, more or less varied by subordinate foothill ridges and mountains. Furthermore, all the islands, great and small, as well as the headlands and promontories of the mainland, are seen to have a rounded, over-rubbed appearance produced by the over-sweeping ice-flood during the period of greatest glacial abundance.

The canals, channels, straits, passages, sounds, etc., are subordinate to the same glacial conditions in their forms, trends, and extent as those which determined the forms, trends, and distribution of the land-masses, their basins being the parts of the pre-glacial margin of the continent, eroded to varying depths below sea-level, and into which, of course, the ocean waters flowed as the ice was melted out of them. Had the general glacial denudation been much less, these ocean ways over which we are sailing would have been valleys and canons and lakes; and the islands rounded hills and ridges, landscapes with undulating features like those found above sea-level wherever the rocks and glacial conditions are similar. In general, the island-bound channels are like rivers, not only in separate reaches as seen from the deck of a vessel, but continuously so for hundreds of miles in the case of the longest of them. The tide-currents, the fresh driftwood, the inflowing streams, and the luxuriant foliage of the out-leaning trees on the shores make this resemblance all the more complete. The largest islands look like part of the mainland in any view to be had of them from the ship, but far the greater number are small, and appreciable as islands, scores of them being less than a mile long. These the eye easily takes in and revels in their beauty with ever fresh delight. In their relations to each other the individual members of a group have evidently been derived from the same general rock-mass, yet they never seem broken or abridged in any way as to their contour lines, however abruptly they may dip their sides. Viewed one by one, they seem detached beauties, like extracts from a poem, while, from the completeness of their lines and the way that their trees are arranged, each seems a finished stanza in itself. Contemplating the arrangement of the trees on these small islands, a distinct impression is produced of their having been sorted and harmonized as to size like a well-balanced bouquet. On some of the smaller tufted islets a group of tapering spruces is planted in the middle, and two smaller groups that evidently correspond with each other are planted on the ends at about equal distances from the central group; or the whole appears as one group with marked fringing trees that match each other spreading around the sides, like flowers leaning outward against the rim of a vase. These harmonious tree relations are so constant that they evidently are the result of design, as much so as the arrangement of the feathers of birds or the scales of fishes.

Thus perfectly beautiful are these blessed evergreen islands, and their beauty is the beauty of youth, for though the freshness of their verdure must be ascribed to the bland moisture with which they are bathed from warm ocean-currents, the very existence of the islands, their features, finish, and peculiar distribution, are all immediately referable to ice-action during the great glacial winter just now drawing to a close.

 **16**

On Crossing the
Alaska Range

HENRY T. ALLEN

Lieutenant Henry Tureman Allen (1859–1930) led one of the last official U. S. Army expeditions of note in Alaska, exploring the Copper River north over the Alaska Range into the Tanana River drainage. The Pulitzer-Prize winning historian William Goetzmann has called Allen's report "a classic in the literature of Alaskan exploration" and a "model example of the old-style all-purpose reconnaisance."[1] In this passage from the Report of an Expedition to the Copper, Tanana, and Koyukuk Rivers in the Territory of Alaska, in the Year 1885 (Washington) Henry Allen describes the exciting moment when the expedition accomplished what had never been done before—the crossing of the divide between the Copper and the Tanana River: "From this [location] the most grateful sight it has ever been my fortune to witness was presented."

1. William Goetzmann. New Lands, New Men: America and the Second Great Age of Discovery. New York: Viking, 1986, 430.

From Report of an Expedition to the Copper, Tanana, and Koyukuk Rivers in the Territory of Alaska in the Year 1885. Washington, D.C.: Government Printing Office, 1887.

About noon of June 5, 1885, after engaging natives, taking observations for position and arranging the packs of all, including those of the dogs, we left the settlement, and soon began the ascent of the mountains, which were free of snow excepting the highest points and the ravines. The upper or northerly end of Lake Suslota was yet covered with ice and snow. As we slowly ascended the rather gradual slope, the Copper River basin appeared before our eyes, a beautiful sight. Looking south the lofty mountains on the east bank, the flat country on the west, with numerous small lakes, hedged in with evergreen timber; the river itself, with numerous channels, made an impression long to be retained. On our left, while ascending, was visible the small tributary emptying into Suslota. Up it is a trail used by the natives in going to Lake Metasta, the source of Slana River.

After having reached an elevation of 1,000 feet above Suslota, in traveling about 3 miles, we found in our front a continuation of mountains, the highest of which was 1,000 feet above us, but which looked insignificant when compared with the lofty white masses to our south and east. . . . After a march of about 7 miles we were near the foot of Mount "Tebay," pyramidal in shape and on a brook which feeds Lake Suslota. To our great surprise and delight the long looked for salmon were endeavoring to ascend it. In some of the little channels the ice prevented further progress, in other places there was so little water that the fish, in endeavoring to push their way up on their sides, actually shoved themselves out of the brook onto the land. These were the advance guard that had doubtless passed through Suslota after our start in the morning. We had no difficulty in taking all we needed, nor was there any hesitancy about one and all eating until completely satisfied— an unusual occurrence.

We had about three days' supply of meat on hand, which was about all we could carry, under the circumstances. I know this seems rather incredible, but not more so than the fact that any one of the party could easily eat 4 pounds of meat at a sitting. One of the party ate three salmon, including the heads of all and the roe of one from the time of going into camp until retiring. This camp (No. 1) was the only place between Nuchek and the Yukon River where it would have been possible to lie over and obtain food in sufficient quantity to satisfy our hunger; yet I did not deem it prudent to attempt to recuperate our strength on fish diet alone.

With one day's ration of salmon, and our moose meat we left camp No. 1 and traveled NE. 1/2 N., 5 miles, passing the little lake to which the salmon were making in order to deposit their spawn. I asked our natives whether these fish ever descended. They replied in the negative, thus in measure corroborating the same views held by some of the natives of the Yukon.

One and a half miles further brought us to a water-shed between the Tanana and Copper, where, for the first time, was sighted the long sought Tanana waters. . . . [From Camp No. 3 Allen's detachment finally reaches the pass]. At 1:30 a.m., after the steepest ascent made by the expedition, we were on a very short and narrow "divide," 4,500 feet above the sea-level, with bold, barren bluffs on each side. From this the most grateful sight it has ever been my fortune to witness was presented. The sun was rising, but not in the east, in fact just two points east of north. We had nearly reached the "land of the midnight sun," to find in our front the "promised land." The views in advance and in rear were both grand; the former showed the extensive Tanana Valley with numerous lakes, and the low unbroken range of mountains between the Tanana and Yukon Rivers. On this pass, with both white and yellow buttercups around me and snow within a few feet, I sat proud of the grand sight which no visitor save an Atnatana or Tananatana [Indian] had ever seen. Fatigue and hunger were for the time forgotten in the great joy at finding our greatest obstacles overcome. As many as twenty lakes were visible, some of which were north of the Tanana, more than 20 miles away. . . . Had we ascended the craggy, rocky peak on our right, which obstructed the eastern view, we could probably have traced the Tanana many miles towards its source, but the greatest of all obstacles to exploration, hunger, prevented. The northern declivity was extremely abrupt, and our descent lay along a gorge similar to the one ascended, excepting the absence of ice and snow. A mile down this gorge, at the first obtainable timber, we halted and cooked the last Leibig's extract of beef, that we had so carefully preserved for just such a contingency.

At 5 a.m. we went into Camp 4, barely able to stand. . . . We had crossed the Alaskan Mountains [the Alaska Range], represented in this section on all charts that attempt vertical delineations as very rugged and lofty, which is hardly the case. Not four weeks before our landing at San Francisco, a scout sent into Alaska the year preceding us had returned and reported that a crossing from the Copper to the Tanana would be utterly impossible; that a fair idea of the nature of the country could be obtained by placing one Mount Hood on another. His information was obtained from natives, and is not more inaccurate than is frequently obtained from the same source. The traders of the Yukon, who are supposed to be more familiar with the general topography of the interior than any other white men, believed the crossing to be next to impossible, and were more than surprised when we reached the Yukon River.

17

The Grand Canon
of the Yukon

FREDERICK SCHWATKA

Frederick Schwatka (1849–1892) was one of the most remarkable figures of his century: army officer, attorney, medical doctor, best-selling author, and arctic explorer. Born in Galena, Illinois, Schwatka graduated from West Point in 1871, was admitted to the Nebraska Bar in 1875, and received a medical degree from Bellevue Hospital Medical College in New York in 1876. Obsessed with the lost 1845 Franklin expedition, he undertook an expedition into the Arctic in 1879–1880 and actually located some graves. This was hailed in his time as one of the great triumphs of arctic exploration. Schwatka later resigned his military commission and spent the rest of his short life traveling and writing. He died of a drug overdose at the age of forty-three in Portland, Oregon, after a long illness.

In 1883, Schwatka floated the entire length of the Yukon River in a homemade raft. This was the first comprehensive survey of the river that was to figure so prominently in regional history after gold was discovered in the Yukon. His book Along Alaska's Great River (Hill, 1885) was an immediate success, and helped to focus increased attention on the far north. In this selection from that work Schwatka describes his harrowing descent of the rapids of the Grand Canon of the Yukon.

From Report of a Military Reconnaissance in Alaska, Made in 1883. Washington, 1885.

On the morning of July 1st, we approached the great rapids of the Grand Canon of the Yukon. Just as I had expected, our Tahkheesh guide in his cottonwood canoe was *non est*, until we were within sight of the upper end of the canon and its boiling waters, and tearing along at six or seven miles an hour, when we caught sight of him frantically gesticulating to us that the rapids were in sight, which was plainly evident, even to us. He probably thought that our ponderous raft was as manageable in the seething current as his own light craft, or he never would have allowed us to get so near. In the twinkling of an eye we got ashore the first line that came to hand, and there was barely time to make both ends fast, one on the raft and the other to a convenient tree on the bank, before the spinning raft came suddenly to the end of her tether with a snappish twang that made the little rope sing like a musical string. Why that little quarter-inch manilla did not part seems a mystery, even yet—it was a mere government flagstaff lanyard that we had brought along for packing purposes, etc.—but it held on as if it knew the importance of its task, and with the swift water pouring in a sheet of foam over the stern of the shackled raft, she slowly swung into an eddy under the lee of a gravel bar where she was soon securely fastened, whereupon we prepared to make an inspection of our chief impediment. . . .

The Yukon River, which had previously been about three hundred or three hundred and fifty yards in width, gradually contracts as it nears the upper gate of the canon and at the point where the stream enters it in a high white-capped wave of rolling water, I do not believe its width exceeds one-tenth of that distance. The walls of the canon are perpendicular columns of basalt, not unlike a diminutive Fingal's cave in appearance, and nearly a mile in length, the center of this mile stretch being broken into a huge basin of about twice the usual width of the stream in the canon, and which is full of seething whirlpools and eddies where nothing but a fish could live for a minute. On the western rim of this basin it seems as though one might descend to the water's edge with a little Alpine work. Through this narrow chute of corrugated rock the wild waters of the great river rush in a perfect mass of milk-like foam, with a reverberation that is audible for a considerable distance, the roar being intensified by the rocky walls which act like so many sounding boards. Huge spruce trees in somber files overshadow the dark canon, and it resembles a deep black thoroughfare paved with the whitest of marble. . . . So swift is it, so great the volume of water, and so contracted the channel, that half its water ascends the sloping banks, runs over them for nearly a score of yards, and then falls into the narrow chute below, making a veritable horseshoe funnel of boiling cascades, not much wider than the length of our raft, and as high as the end of her mast. Through this funnel of foam the waves ran three or four feet high, and this fact, added to the boiling that often forced up columns of waters like small geysers quite a considerable distance into the air, made matters very uninviting for navigation in any sort of craft.

Every thing being in readiness, our inspection made, and our resolution formed, in the forenoon of the second of July, we prepared to "shoot" the raft through the rapids of the grand canon, and at 11:25 bow and stern lines were cast loose and after a few minutes' hard work at shoving the craft out of the little eddy where she lay, the poor vessel resisting as if she knew all that was ahead of her and was loth to go, she finally swung clear of the point and like a racer at the start made almost a leap forward and the die was cast. A moment's hesitation at the canon's brink, and quick as a flash the whirling craft plunged into the foam, and before twenty yards were made had collided with the western wall of columnar rock with a shock as loud as a blast, tearing off the inner side log and throwing the outer one far into the stream. The raft swung around this as upon a hinge, just as if it had been a straw in a gale of wind, and again resumed its rapid career. In the whirlpool basin of the canon the craft, for a brief second or two, seemed actually buried out of sight in the foam. Had there been a dozen giants on board they could have had no more influence in directing her course than as many spiders. It was a very simple matter to trust the rude vessel entirely to fate, and work out its own salvation. I was more afraid of the four miles of shallow rapids below after the canon, but she only received a dozen or a score of smart bumps that started a log here and there, but tore none from the structure, and nothing remained ahead of her but the cascades. These reached, in a few minutes the craft was caught at the bow by the first high wave in the funnel-like chute and lifted into the air until it stood almost at an angle of thirty degrees, when it went through the cascades like a charge of fixed bayonets, and almost as swiftly as a flash of light, burying its nose in the foam beyond as it subsided. Those on board of the raft now got hold of a line from their friends on shore, and after breaking it several times they finally brought the craft alongside the bank and commenced repairing the damage with a light heart, for our greatest obstacle was now at our backs.

**18**

The Gustavus Peninsula

JOHN BURROUGHS

In 1899 Union Pacific magnate Edward Harriman asked John Burroughs (1837–1921), John Muir, George Bird Grinnel, Edward Curtis, William Healy Dall, and dozens of other luminaries to join him on an extended oceanic exploration of Alaska. Burroughs, well known as a naturalist of the Catskill Mountains and the Hudson River Valley of New York, agreed to go on what was to be the last of the great nineteenth-century ocean adventures, a scientific voyage roughly comparable to the modern cruises of Jacques Cousteau aboard the Calypso. Under the considerable influence of John Muir, at that time an international authority on glaciers, Burroughs describes here the revegetation of regions exposed by retreating glaciers. The area they explored that day later became Glacier Bay National Monument, partly as a result of the attention brought to it by Muir on an earlier (1879) trip and by the 1899 Harriman expedition. Today it is known as Glacier Bay National Park, and is still a place to witness, as Burroughs relates, the "terrible labor throes" of the glaciers as sections of ice calve from them into the sea. It is interesting to note, finally, that Burroughs, who disliked nothing more than the personification of nature—he later attacked Ernest Thompson Seton as a "nature faker" for his animal stories—humanizes the landscape in this passage with references like "terrible labor throes" and "the workshops and laboratories of the elder gods."

From *Alaska, the Harriman Expedition, 1899*. New York: Doubleday, Page, 1901.

Gustavus Peninsula seems to be a recent deposit of the glaciers and our experts thought it not much over a century old. The botanists here found a good illustration of the successive steps nature takes in foresting or reforesting the land—how she creeps before she walks. The first shrub is a small creeping willow that looks like a kind of 'pusley' [sic]. Then comes a larger willow, less creeping; then two or more other species that become quite large upright bushes; then follow the alders and with them various herbaceous plants and grasses, till finally the spruce comes in and takes possession of the land. Our collectors found the first generation of trees, none of them over forty years old. Far up the mountain side at a height of about 2,000 feet they came to the limit of the younger growth and struck a well-defined line of much older trees, showing that within probably a hundred years an ice sheet 2,000 or more feet thick, an older and larger Muir [Glacier], had swept down the valley and destroyed the forests.

In the meantime the rest of us spent the days on and in the vicinity of the glacier, walking, sketching, painting, photographing, dredging, mountain climbing, as our several tastes prompted.

We were in the midst of strange scenes, hard to render in words, the miles upon miles of moraines upon either hand, gray, loosely piled, scooped, plowed, channeled, sifted, from 50 to 200 feet high; the sparkling sea water dotted with blue bergs and loose drift ice, the towering masses of almost naked rock, smoothed, carved, rounded, granite-ribbed and snow-crowned that looked down upon us from both sides of the inlet, and the cleft, toppling, staggering front of the great glacier in its terrible labor throes stretching before us from shore to shore.

We saw the world-shaping forces at work; we scrambled over plains they had built but yesterday. We saw them transport enormous rocks, and tons on tons of soil and debris from the distant mountains; we saw the remains of extensive forests they had engulfed probably within the century, and were now uncovering again; we saw their turbid rushing streams loaded with newly ground rocks and soil-making material; we saw the beginnings of vegetation in the tracks of the retreating glacier; our dredges brought up the first forms of sea life along the shore; we witnessed the formation of the low mounds and ridges and bowl-shaped depressions that so often diversify our landscapes—all the while with the muffled thunder of the falling bergs in our ears.

We were really in one of the workshops and laboratories of the elder gods, but only in the glaciers' front was there present evidence that they were still at work. I wanted to see them opening crevasses in the ice, dropping the soil and rocks they had transported, polishing the mountains, or blocking the streams, but I could not. They seemed to knock off work when we were watching them. One day I climbed up to the shoulder of a huge granite ridge on the west, against which the glacier pressed and over which it broke. Huge masses of ice had recently toppled over, a great fragment of rock hung on the very edge, ready to be deposited upon the ridge, windrows of soil and gravel and boulders were clinging to the margin of the ice, but while I stayed not a pebble moved, all was silence and inertia. And I could look down between the glacier and the polished mountain side; they were not in contact; the hand of the sculptor was raised as it were, but he did not strike while I was around; in front of me upon the glacier for many miles was a perfect wilderness of crevasses, the ice was ridged and contorted like an angry sea, but not a sound, not a movement anywhere.

19

The Dominant Primordial Beast

JACK LONDON

Jack London (1876–1916) arrived in the far north in 1897, eagerly sought his fortunes along with thousands of other prospectors, and then returned to his home town of San Francisco less than one year later, financially ruined and suffering from scurvy. In 1900 his collection of short stories The Son of Wolf (Houghton Mifflin) was published. The book met with immediate success, and several other volumes quickly followed, including his best-selling masterpiece The Call of the Wild (Houghton Mifflin, 1903). A compulsive worker and America's first millionaire-author, London wrote a thousand words a day and produced nearly fifty books by the time of his death in 1916. The frozen, hostile kosmos that London encountered in the Yukon and Alaska provided a perfect vehicle for his dark vision of life as a Darwinian struggle in a deterministic universe.

In this selection, from the third chapter of Call of the Wild, the dog Buck, abducted in California and brought to work as a sled dog in the Yukon, vanquishes his dreaded rival in the pack, Spitz. At no other point in the novel is the author's philosophy of life as a brutal battle of competitors more evident: "Buck stood and looked on, the successful champion, the dominant primordial best who had made his kill and found it good."

From The Call of the Wild. New York: Macmillan, 1904.

There is an ecstasy that marks the summit of life, and beyond which life cannot rise. And such is the paradox of living, this ecstasy comes when one is most alive, and it comes as a complete forgetfulness that one is alive. This ecstasy, this forgetfulness of living, comes to the artist, caught up and out of himself in a sheet of flame; it comes to the soldier, war-mad on a stricken field and refusing quarter; and it came to Buck, leading the pack, sounding the old wolf cry, straining after the food that was alive and that fled swiftly before him through the moonlight. He was sounding the deeps of his nature, and of the parts of his nature that were deeper than he, going back into the womb of Time. He was mastered by the sheer surging of life, the tidal wave of being, the perfect joy of each separate muscle, joint, and sinew in that it was everything that was not death, that it was aglow and rampant, expressing itself in movement, flying exultantly under the stars and over the face of dead matter that did not move.

But Spitz, cold and calculating even in his supreme moods, left the pack and cut across a narrow neck of land where the creek made a long bend around. Buck did not know of this, and as he rounded the bend, the frost wraith of a rabbit still flitting before him, he saw another and larger frost wraith leap from the over-hanging bank into the immediate path of the rabbit. It was Spitz. The rabbit could not turn, and as the white teeth broke its back in midair it shrieked as loudly as a stricken man may shriek. At the sound of this, the cry of Life plunging down from Life's apex in the grip of Death, the full pack at Buck's heels raised a hell's chorus of delight.

Buck did not cry out. He did not check himself, but drove in upon Spitz, shoulder to shoulder, so hard that he missed the throat. They rolled over and over in the powdery snow. Spitz gained his feet almost as though he had not been overthrown, slashing Buck down the shoulder and leaping clear. Twice his teeth clipped together, like the steel jaws of a trap, as he backed away for better footing, with lean and lifting lips that writhed and snarled.

In a flash Buck knew it. The time had come. It was to the death. As they circled about, snarling, ears laid back, keenly watchful for the advantage, the scene came to Buck with a sense of familiarity. He seemed to remember it all—the white woods, and earth, and moonlight, and the thrill of battle. Over the whiteness and silence brooded a ghostly calm. There was not the faintest whisper of air—nothing moved, not a leaf quivered, the visible breaths of the dogs rising slowly and lingering in the frosty air. They had made short work of the snowshoe rabbit, these dogs that were ill-tamed wolves; and they were now drawn up in an expectant circle. They, too, were silent, their eyes only gleaming and their breaths drifting slowly upward. To Buck it was nothing new or strange, this scene of old time. It was as though it had always been, the wonted way of things.

Spitz was a practiced fighter. From Spitzbergen through the Arctic, and across Canada and the Barrens, he had held his own with all manner of dogs and achieved mastery over them. Bitter rage was his, but never blind rage. In passion to rend and destroy, he never forgot that his enemy was in like passion to rend and destroy. He never rushed till he was prepared to receive a rush; never attacked till he had first defended that attack.

In vain Buck strove to sink his teeth in the neck of the big white dog. Wherever his fangs struck for the softer flesh, they were countered by the fangs of Spitz. Fang clashed fang, and lips were cut and bleeding, but Buck could not penetrate his enemy's guard. Then he warmed up and enveloped Spitz in a whirlwind of rushes. Time and time again he tried for the snow-white throat, where life bubbled near to the surface, and each time and every time Spitz slashed him and got away. Then Buck took to rushing, as though for the throat, when, suddenly drawing back his head and curving in from the side, he would drive his shoulder at the shoulder of Spitz, as a ram by which to overthrow him. But instead, Buck's shoulder was slashed down each time as Spitz leaped lightly away.

Spitz was untouched, while Buck was streaming with blood and panting hard. The fight was growing desperate. And all the while the silent and wolfish circle waited to finish off whichever dog went down. As Buck grew winded, Spitz took to rushing, and he kept him staggering for footing. Once Buck went over, and the whole circle of sixty dogs started up; but he recovered himself, almost in midair, and the circle sank down again and waited.

But Buck possessed a quality that made for greatness—imagination. He fought by instinct, but he could fight by head as well. He rushed, as though attempting the old shoulder trick, but at the last instant swept low to the snow and in. His teeth closed on Spitz's left foreleg. There was a crunch of breaking bone, and the white dog faced him on three legs. Thrice he tried to knock him over, then repeated the trick and broke the right foreleg. Despite the pain and helplessness, Spitz struggled madly to keep up. He saw the silent circle, with gleaming eyes, lolling tongues, and silvery breaths drifting upward, closing in upon him as he had seen similar circles close in upon beaten antagonists in the past. Only this time he was the one who was beaten.

There was no hope for him. Buck was inexorable. Mercy was a thing reserved for gentler climes. He maneuvered for the final rush. The circle had tightened till he could feel the breaths of the huskies on his flanks.

He could see them, beyond Spitz and to either side, half-crouching for the spring, their eyes fixed upon him. A pause seemed to fall. Every animal was motionless as though turned to stone. Only Spitz quivered and bristled as he staggered back and forth, snarling with horrible menace, as though to frighten off impending death. Then Buck sprang in and out; but while he was in, shoulder had at last squarely met shoulder. The dark circle became a dot on the moon-flooded snow as Spitz disappeared from view. Buck stood and looked on, the successful champion, the dominant primordial beast who had made his kill and found it good.

 **20**

Gold Prospectors of the Susitna Valley

ROBERT DUNN

No collection of Arctic-American literature would be
truly representative without a selection derived from
the rich mining history of the region. Here Robert Dunn
(1877–1955), in a passage from his climbing classic The Shameless
Diary of an Explorer (Outing, 1907), describes a group of prospectors
camped near his expedition's bivouac on the Susitna River. No one has
ever captured better, or in a briefer space, the tragedy and the comedy of
the common prospector. Dunn, by the way, failed to reach the summit of
Mount McKinley on this trip.

From The Shameless Diary of an Explorer. New York: Macmillan, 1907.

Nearly all the cabins are occupied. Prospectors are coming into this valley for the first time. No strike has been made, none, but it's the last valley in Alaska still untouched. They have spent the late summer boating up their years' supplies from the head of the Inlet. Some have dogs, some hope to get them from somewhere before winter. They are the bedrock Alaskan article, the men to be first on the claims if an Eldorado is struck. They start their stampede the winter before, not in the spring, which is the tenderfoot way. Each has just waked from failure—in a rush camp, or looking for daily wages in Valdez. Again they take up the old, relentless, dream-trail to riches through the desolate and uncertain North. Human beings, at least, men after my heart! In Arizona, Oregon, South Africa, the Philippines, each has more than once risked his poor all, and lost, always lost. But now the Eldorado is at hand, in this Susitna valley, here in the place. They may hand-sled their outfits up the river in March, making many double trips; but to what point each is still undecided. There's plenty of time yet to think.

They handle the few rocks I have picked up, asking the simple, penetrating questions of men who have learned geology only in the field, and with one idea, placer gold. They talk of porphyry, bull granite, and gravel wash. They trace wise, slow fingers across our sketch maps, asking advice where they should go, like children. But if we have not seen such and such a schist on this or that creek, with bedrock so deep, it settles *that* Eldorado. Climbing McKinley does not interest them at all.

A tall, gaunt man has just come from prospecting in Luzon. He is cursing that country with great ingenuity. It's worthless, apparently, because you cannot grow oats there; corn, either, which he took out to settle the fate of the tropics with. There the natives are so thick and starved they search the mountains at night with candles for lizards to eat, till the hills seem alive with fire-flies.

Silently we look up to Mount Susitna, rising clear and lone over the glossy river and the unknown wilderness, which is bright with uncertain auroras.

 **21**

Taku Inlet

ELLA HIGGINSON

Ella Higginson (1862–1940) authored nine books, including From the Land of the Snow-Pearls: Tales from Puget Sound (Macmillan, 1897), When the Birds Go North Again (Macmillan, 1898), and Mariella, of Out-West (Macmillan, 1902). It was in Alaska, the Great Country (Macmillan, 1908) that her talent reached its fullest expression. The work presents a history of Alaska in alternating chapters with personal accounts of her four trips to the region. As with Mary Austin's The Land of Little Rain (Houghton Mifflin, 1903), a book to which it can be favorably compared, Ella Higginson's Alaska, the Great Country focuses more on the land than on the people. In both cases modern readers may be distracted by the purple prose that was stylish at the turn of the century. "I have often stood at mid-night," Higginson writes, "and watched the amethyst lights on the mountains darken to violet, purple, black—while the peaks themselves stood white and still, softly outlined against the sky (p. 269)." But these are small quibbles, and the poetry in the prose is really one of the book's virtues, as when Higginson describes the ocean mists of Queen Charlotte Sound as rolling "upon the surface like thistle-down along the country lane—here one instant, vanished the next (p. 18)."

In this selection the author writes of a captive bear "chained on the hurricane deck of a steamer" with a "look of almost human longing and rebellion in his small eyes," an evocative passage that has always reminded this reader of Isak Dinesen's magnificent description of the caged giraffes on the German steamer at Mombassa in her book Out of Africa (Random House, 1938). In each case, a woman sympathizes deeply with a wild animal that has lost its freedom, and in so doing comments implicitly on other forms of human subjugation as well.

From *Alaska, the Great Country*. New York: Macmillan, 1908.

There is no air so indescribably, thrillingly sweet as the air of a glacier on a fair day. It seems to palpitate with a fragrance that ravishes the senses. I saw a great, recently captured bear, chained on the hurricane deck of a steamer, stand with his nose stretched out toward the glacier, his nostrils quivering and a look of almost human longing and rebellion in his small eyes. The feeling of pain and pity with which a humane person always beholds a chained wild animal is accented in these wide and noble spaces swimming from snow mountain to snow mountain, where the very watchword of the silence seems to be "Freedom." The chained bear recognized the scent of the glacier and remembered that he had once been free.

In front of the glacier stretched miles of sapphire, sun-lit sea, set with sparkling, opaline-tinted icebergs. Now and then one broke and fell apart before our eyes, sending up a funnel-shaped spray of color—rose, pale green, or azure.

At every blast of the steamer's whistle great masses of ice came thundering headlong into the sea—to emerge presently, icebergs. Canoeists approach glaciers closely at their peril, never knowing when an iceberg may shoot to the surface and wreck their boat. Even larger craft are by no means safe, and tourists desiring a close approach should voyage with intrepid captains who sail safely through everything.

The wide, ceaseless sweep of a live glacier down the side of a great mountain and out into the sea holds a more compelling suggestion of power than any other action of nature. I have never felt the appeal of a mountain glacier—of a stream of ice and snow that, so far as the eye can discover, never reaches anywhere, although it keeps going forever. The feeling of forlorness with which, after years of anticipation, I finally beheld the renowned glacier of the Selkirks, will never be forgotten. It was the forlorness of a child who has been robbed of her Santa Claus, or who has found that her doll is stuffed with sawdust.

But to behold the splendid, perpendicular front of a live glacier rising out of a sea which breaks everlastingly upon it; to see it under the rose and lavender of sunset or the dull gold of noon; to see and hear tower, minaret, dome, go thundering down into the clear depths and pound them into foam—this alone is worth the price of a trip to Alaska.

We were told that the opaline coloring of the glacier was unusual, and that its prevailing color is an intense blue, more beautiful and constant than that of other glaciers; and that even the bergs floating out from it were of a more pronounced blue than other bergs.

But I do not believe it. I have seen the blue of the Columbia Glacier in Prince William Sound; and I have sailed for a whole afternoon among the intensely blue ice shallops that go drifting in an endless fleet from Glacier Bay out through Icy Straits to the ocean. If there be a more exquisite blue this side of heaven than I have seen in Icy Straits and in the palisades of the Columbia Glacier, I must see it to believe it.

There are three glaciers in Taku Inlet: two—Windham and Twin— which are at present "dead"; and Taku, the Beautiful, which is very much alive. The latter was named Foster, for the former Secretary of the Treasury; but the Indian name has clung to it, which is one more cause for Thanksgiving.

The Inlet is eighteen miles long and about seven hundred feet wide. Taku River flows into it from the northeast, spreading out in blue ribbons over the brown flats; at high tide it may be navigated, with caution, by small row-boats and canoes. It was explored in early days by the Hudson Bay Company, also by surveyors of the Western Union Telegraph Company.

Whidbey, entering the Inlet in 1794, sustained his reputation for absolute blindness to beauty. He found "a compact body of ice extending some distance nearly all around." He found "frozen mountains," "rock slides," "dwarf pine trees," and "undissolving frost and snow." He lamented the lack of a suitable landing-place for boats; and reported the aspect in general to be "as dreary and inhospitable as the imagination can possibly suggest."

Alas for the poor chilly Englishman! He, doubtless, expected silvery-gowned ice maidens to come sliding out from under the glacier in pearly boats, singing and kissing their hands, to bear him back into their deep blue grottos and dells of ice, and refresh him with Russian tea from old brass samovars; he expected these maidens to be girdled and crowned with carnations and poppies, and to pluck winy grapes—with dust clinging to their bloomy roundness—from living vines for him to eat; and most of all, he expected to find in some remote corner of the clear and sparkling cavern a big fireplace, "which would remind him pleasantly of England"; and a brilliant fire on a well-swept hearth, with the smoke and sparks going up through a melted hole in the glacier.

About fifteen miles up Taku River, Wright Glacier streams down from the southeast and fronts upon the low and marshy lands for a distance of nearly three miles.

The mountains surrounding Taku Inlet rise to a height of four thousand feet, jutting out abruptly, in places, over the water.

 **22**

On the Sheep Ranges

CHARLES SHELDON

When Charles Sheldon (1867–1929) arrived in the Yukon's Ogilvie Mountains in June 1904, he was already a self-made millionaire, having retired two years earlier at the age of 35 after making a fortune in a Mexican mining venture. Accompanying him on this now-historic trip was the artist Carl Rungius and Wilfred H. Osgood, a naturalist with the Biological Survey (the precursor of the U. S. Fish and Wildlife Service). A graduate of Yale University, an activist in the Boone and Crockett Club, and an acquaintance of President Theodore Roosevelt, Charles Sheldon brought with him to the far north one of the curious ironies of his time: many, if not all, of the leading conservationists—including Roosevelt—were trophy hunters determined, above all, to save their aristocratic sport from ruin.

This paradox is evident in this selection from The Wilderness of the Upper Yukon (Scribner's, 1911), Sheldon's first book. Sheldon commits what even in his time was a taboo among sportsmen—he kills a sow grizzly bear—and then leaves the spring cub to die from starvation. In a somewhat similar situation in Mississippi, Theodore Roosevelt refused to kill a yearling black bear. As a result of this famous incident, "Teddy Bears" were soon sold, as they still are today, from coast to coast. Oblivious to our modern ethics, Sheldon then waxes poetic about the experience: "What more could a lover of the wilderness and its wild life demand?"

In fairness it should be noted finally that in 1906 Sheldon visited Denali in Alaska (more sows and cubs killed), and was so moved by the experience that he labored tirelessly to create what became Mt. McKinley National Park on February 26, 1917. Questions of ethical hunting aside, conservationists owe this generation—Roosevelt, Grinnell, Sheldon, and others—an enormous debt. Our leading environmentalists may seem just as old fashioned to posterity.

From *The Wilderness of the Upper Yukon: A Hunter's Explorations for Wild Sheep in Sub-Arctic Mountains*. New York: Scribner's, 1911.

July 16

From the mountain top I had traced the course of the creek to a point about four miles above camp, where it was lost behind an obstructing ridge which projected at right angles to the main ranges. There it was close to timber-line and evidently the main divide was not far up the stream. We decided to advance four miles, make a camp, and remain for a few days to investigate the country. Though obliged to ford the creek several times, we traveled mostly on the west bank, on the way shooting some willow ptarmigan—beautiful birds even in their inconspicuous summer plumage. Red-squirrels were more abundant as we proceeded, although the spruces became smaller. Three miles from camp a large branch entered the creek, flowing from the east between high mountain ranges. A mile beyond this, where the main stream forked into two creeks of equal volume, was a small meadow, about three hundred feet wide, filled with excellent grass scattered among the clumps of willow and dwarf birch. It was early in the afternoon when we arrived, and some graylings were caught while lunch was being cooked.

At 3:30 we left camp, each taking a different direction to look for signs of game. I followed up the west fork, with the intention of reaching the divide if possible. The creek, fifteen to thirty feet wide, descended so abruptly that the source could not be far off. There were very few moose tracks so far up the creek, but several ptarmigan were flushed, some with young, and red-squirrels kept chattering as they skipped about. The tinkling notes of the water-ouzel often sounded from the creek, and once the exquisite harlequin duck was seen floating down among the rocks in the foaming torrent. We had seen harlequin ducks all the way along the creek, and I have since come to associate these beautiful birds with wild, dashing, northern streams. The walking was excellent and, two miles up, the stream forked again, one branch coming from a basin to the southwest, the other from the west. Just below this junction was a canon, two hundred feet long, filled with snow and ice. I walked through it and found myself at the limit of timber, mosquitoes still swarming about me. Farther up the west fork I saw the diggings and fairly fresh dung of a grizzly, and a mile and a half farther on the creek broke out from vast, bare, rolling hills on the south, fed by numerous streams formed from the melting snow above the canons and deep ravines. Here at last was the divide. From the summit could be seen the waters flowing into the Tatonduk River, or Sheep Creek as it is locally called, where it enters the

Yukon River, below Eagle City. Coal Creek has its sources in the numerous small streams flowing together, all formed from melting snow in the surrounding mountains.

The divide at this point was covered with green, rolling pastures, more than a mile wide and two miles long. On the south it was bordered by a high mountain chain, with a continuous jagged crest swelling up into high peaks, from which numerous spurs projected at right angles, enclosing deep and narrow basins, the bottoms of which consisted of rolling meadows of green grass. On the north was a range of mountains, more broken by peaks, crags, and canons, all sloping down to Tatonduk River waters, finally forming a long, smooth, rolling ridge. Heavy banks of snow lined every crest and peak; the canons and ravines were filled with it and the mountainsides appeared streaked with white. White limestone, dark, almost black, chert, and iron-stained rock, glowing red, all in sharp contrast, characterize these northern ranges. The summit pastures sloped gently toward the west, where another creek, formed between the ridges, flowed on to the Tatonduk River. A mile down, looking through an opening in the timber, I could see the creek, filled with snow and ice, glistening under the sunlight like a bright lake, while beyond it flowed through vast meadows toward the north and again curved west at the foot of the ranges, not far distant, which separated the waters of the Peel River from those of the Yukon, Dwarf birch and willow were scattered about the smooth, green sward, whose surface was soft and broken by tiny rivulets flowing to the creek below.

I seated myself and turned my field-glasses toward the south range. Suddenly within the field, two miles distant, appeared four sheep feeding on the saddle below the peak of a spur connecting with the range. More careful scrutiny proved them to be ewes. My first sight of the northern mountain-sheep! At last we were in the sheep ranges! As we had eaten no good meat except a few grouse and ptarmigan for eight days, and our bacon was being rapidly consumed, I immediately began a stalk, walking as rapidly as possible down the west slope of the divide on soft mossy ground, in some places miry and filled with willows. Now and then I paused to watch the sheep, which kept feeding quietly in the same place. At the northern end of the spur, then opposite me, the slope breaks, forming a cliff several hundred feet high, traversing the end of the mountain east and west. This cliff curves at the eastern extremity, cutting the smooth slope which, at the brink, rises steeply in a succession of benches to the top of the spur-mountain. The spur encloses a beautiful basin of rolling meadows in an amphitheatre of mountains.

I started to climb at the west edge of the cliffs, thereby keeping out of sight of the sheep. After climbing perhaps three hundred feet I looked up under the precipice, and at its base suddenly saw a grizzly bear walking on some snow toward the curving cliff, where it cuts the east slope. Quickly dropping, I almost slid to the foot, where I could conceal myself in the willows along the stream flowing from the basin. As the bear proceeded, I advanced parallel with it for about a hundred yards, until it climbed over a steep snow-bank to the top of the cliff and stood on the edge of the east slope. As it ascended this snow-bank I noticed a small cub playing about it. It was then 10 P.M. The bear stood for a moment on the highest bench at the edge of the cliff, about five hundred yards above me, and began to dig out a ground-squirrel.

Ground-squirrels, *Citellus plesius*, were everywhere. All the pastures and mountain slopes were filled with their holes and one was continually in sight of them, sitting straight up on their hind legs or running for their burrows. The most characteristic sound of the higher parts of the northern wilderness is their shrill chatter when they see a supposed enemy approaching, or when they disappear in their holes.

Through the glasses the bear could be seen digging, making the earth fly in all directions. At times she would sit and dig, again rise and strike the ground in apparent anger, twist around, watch for a moment, and then begin digging again. The squirrels always have several holes, connected by underground channels, and the bear kept digging out one after another, now and then making a jump to the next, evidently knowing that the squirrel was about to run out. Then she would again dig, until, finally, the squirrel was pocketed, and the bear made a great pounce and grabbed it with both forepaws. As her back was turned, the operation of devouring her prey could not be seen. While the bear was digging for the squirrel, the cub raced about, now sitting still a moment, then jumping up and running off playing, quite indifferent to the mother's task.

After spending twenty minutes digging and tearing out the hard earth until she caught the squirrel, the bear stepped to the edge of the cliff, took a long look below, started quartering down the slope, and disappeared. The wind was in my favor, so, after waiting five minutes, I started. The way was very steep, and because of the succession of benches it was impossible to see more than twenty or thirty feet above each one after it was reached. Holding my rifle cocked, expecting to meet the bear close as I came to the top of each bench, I climbed one after another, always very slowly to keep my breath for a steady shot, until I arrived on the last, when I saw the bear slowly walking along the upper surface of the basin close to the mountain-side, about three hundred yards off. She kept an irregular course, often pausing and looking for ground-squirrels. I followed rapidly, trying to gain, but always stopping when she stopped, ready to drop low if she faced in my direction. After gaining a hundred yards, I sat down, rested my elbows on my knees, and aiming at her left hind quarter as she paused, fired, and heard the bullet strike her. She jumped, turned, and stood with forelegs extended forward, apparently panting. The cub at once began to run about bawling. The bear dropped to a sitting posture for a moment and then rose. I fired a second shot at her foreshoulder and heard the bullet strike her. She gave a great jump and stood until a third shot was fired, when she fell, kicked once or twice, and was dead.

The cub was still running about crying, and I went slowly toward it, intending if possible to capture it for the New York Zoological Park. When within fifty feet the cub saw me. It ran around, looked at me with great curiosity, sniffing again and again, approached a few feet, then continued to run back and forth. Finally, as I kept coming closer, it stood on its hind feet, placed its forepaws on the dead mother and began spitting at me. I stooped low and crept within six feet, ready to place a noose, made from my belt and the straps from the kodak and field-glass, over its head, when suddenly it pushed forward its nose, sniffed at me several times in terror, turned and rushed up the mountain slope. I started to pursue, but it distanced me so rapidly that the chase was soon given up.

No one who reads this experience should miss the significance of the cub's final action. It was a tiny cub, born the preceding winter, and could have received no impressions of human beings from experience. It did not fear the *sight* of man, but the *scent* of man immediately inspired it with terror. Fear of the odor of man was clearly an *instinct*. What was the origin of this instinct? Surely, in that remote part of the country, the cub's ancestors could not have experienced a fear of the scent of man for generations numerous enough to have the trait registered in the nervous organization and fixed, so that it was transmitted by heredity to the young! This would require frequent repetitions of the experience, through too many generations, and it is not reasonable to believe this possible. In my opinion this instinct had its origin in a period so remote in the past that we have no facts at all to explain it, and we can only affirm its existence, as clearly exhibited in this case. The instinct may include the fear of any strange scent as hostile. All bears with which I have had experience before or after, had this same instinct, and I firmly believe that it was as potent in the grizzly bears encountered by Lewis and Clark as in those inhabiting remote regions at the present time. Casual observers have not always discriminated between sight and scent as they affect the action of animals.

It was then 11:30, and the mists had settled about the crest and extended half-way down the slopes. For a long time while I worked in the twilight, getting off the skin, and everything was hushed and still, the wailing cries of the cub sounded from the mountain top—a weird, wild noise in this mysterious solitude. At such an elevation it was very cold, and being lightly clad I soon became chilled and found difficulty in handling the bear alone, so the skin was not off until nearly two in the morning. The head was left in so that Rungius could sketch it. The bear was an old grizzly, fairly large, in excellent pelage; its claws were very long, and there was practically no fat on it. The first bullet shattered the hind quarter, penetrated through the vitals, and came out through a large hole in its side. The other two had struck within an inch of each other, both cutting the heart. Tired and cold, I shouldered the heavy skin and struggled back to camp, reaching it at 5:30 in the morning. Rungius and Osgood, neither of whom had seen any game during the day, came out from the tent to see the skin and hear my story.

The fire was started; tea, bacon, and bread refreshed me before the genial warmth. Now our hopes were brightened, and with the knowledge that we had found the game country all was enthusiasm, I soon rolled under my blanket, but for some time could not sleep. The experience of the night had deeply impressed me with the wild enchantment of the wilderness, the finding of the divide, the sublime mountains about it, the first sight of sheep, the unexpected meeting and killing of the bear, my experience with the cub; the charm of the location while skinning the bear high up on the green slope of the mountain in the midnight twilight; the absence of sound save the murmur of the creek below and the wailing of the cub pealing wildly through the mists above; the dim outline of the summits of the mountains to the west, their peaks tipped golden by the sun low behind them; the mystery of all that unknown country; the strange and beautiful lights and shadows playing on the mountains encircling me; what more could a lover of the wilderness and its wild life demand?

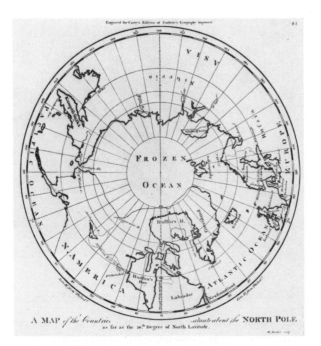

A British map (circa 1800) depicting the circumpolar north as far as the 50th degree of north latitude. Note how well the northern European and Asian arctic coasts are mapped as compared with those of North America. Reprinted with permission of Alaska and Polar Regions Collection, University of Alaska, Fairbanks.

Vitus Bering led the 1741–1742 Russian expedition of which the naturalist Georg Steller was a member. Reprinted with permission of the Alaska and Polar Regions Collection, University of Alaska, Fairbanks.

A Russian map (circa 1754) written in French indicating the route taken by Bering and Tchirikov in 1741–1742. Reprinted with permission of Alaska and Polar Regions Collection, University of Alaska, Fairbanks.

In this engraving from Captain Cook's *Voyages*, the crew can be seen firing their weapons at walruses, called here "Sea Horses." Reprinted with permission of Alaska and Polar Regions Collection, University of Alaska, Fairbanks.

"Many trees had been cut down since these regions had been first visited by Europeans; this was evident by the visible effects of the axe and saw . . ."— George Vancouver. This Russian drawing depicts the primeval forest of coastal Alaska in an undisturbed area. Reprinted with permission of the Alaska and Polar Regions Collection, University of Alaska, Fairbanks.

In this illustration from Litke's 1835 *Voyage Autour du Monde*, three Alaskan natives encountered on the voyage are depicted. Reprinted with permission of the Alaska and Polar Regions Collection, University of Alaska, Fairbanks.

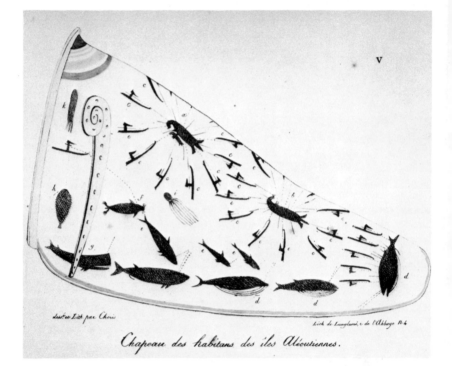

Chapeau des habitans des îles Aléoutiennes.

Venianimov spent considerable time as a missionary among the Aleuts. Pictured here is an Aleut hat on which have been drawn a walrus hunt, a seal hunt, a whale hunt, an octopus, a squid, and a flounder. The Aleuts, with their characteristic hats, can be seen in kayaks encircling their prey. From Louis Chorus' 1822 *Voyage Pittoresque Autour du Monde*. Reprinted with permission of the Alaska and Polar Regions Collection, University of Alaska, Fairbanks.

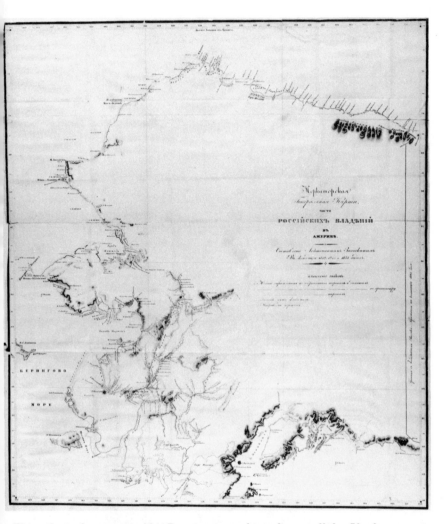

This relatively accurate 1844 Russian map shows how well the Alaskan coast was known at that time, but how little was known of the vast interior. Note that the Yukon River is mapped to a point about 100 miles upstream from Zagoskin's Nulato. Reprinted with permission of the Alaska and Polar Regions Collection, University of Alaska, Fairbanks.

Some of the native inhabitants of Alexander Murray's Fort Yukon. Note that the man fourth from the right on the bottom row is wearing a coat made of parka squirrel skins. Reprinted with permission of the Alaska and Polar Regions Collection, University of Alaska, Fairbanks.

John Muir and John Burroughs on the 1899 Harriman Expedition. Photographed by Edward S. Curtis in what is today Glacier Bay National Park. Reprinted with permission of the Alaska and Polar Regions Collection, University of Alaska, Fairbanks.

Lieutenant Henry T. Allen with Sargeant Robertson and Private Fickett while exploring in Alaska (circa 1885). Reprinted with permission of the Alaska and Polar Regions Collection, University of Alaska, Fairbanks.

Dogs were used to pull sleds and haul provisions long before the Klondikers arrived on the scene. Pictured here are Native Americans on the Copper River in Alaska. Reprinted with permission of the Alaska and Polar Regions Collection, University of Alaska, Fairbanks.

"They are the bedrock Alaskan article, the men to be first on the claims if an Eldorado is struck"—Robert Dunn. Reprinted with permission of the Alaska and Polar Regions Collection, University of Alaska, Fairbanks.

Grizzly bear sow and cub. Photograph by Adolph Murie. Reprinted with permission of the Alaska and Polar Regions Collection, University of Alaska, Fairbanks.

Barren grounds grizzly bear. Photograph by Adolph Murie. Reprinted with permission of the Alaska and Polar Regions Collection, University of Alaska, Fairbanks.

Mt. McKinley (20,320 feet), the highest mountain in North America. Although Alaskans refer to the mountain as Denali ("The Great One") the federal government has yet to officially change the name. Photograph by Adolph Murie. Reprinted with permission of the Alaska and Polar Regions Collection, University of Alaska, Fairbanks.

The same year that Reverend Stuck led the first expedition to the summit of Mt. McKinley, the first airplane arrived in the territory. The airplane would revolutionize life in the far north. Reprinted with permission of the Alaska and Polar Regions Collection, University of Alaska, Fairbanks.

"Oceangoing vessels navigate to Bethel, river steamers churn the waters to McGrath, and graduated sizes of canoes and kayaks sail on the narrow, shallow streams that are little more than babbling brooks"—May Wynne Lamb. Reprinted with permission of the Alaska and Polar Regions Collection, University of Alaska, Fairbanks.

In remote arctic mountains such as these, Robert Marshall led the first expeditions. Photograph by Charles W. Murray, Jr.

A mature black-phased Alaskan wolf from the Savage River pack in Mount McKinley National Park (now Denali National Park). Photograph by Adolph Murie. Reprinted with permission of the Alaska and Polar Regions Collection, University of Alaska, Fairbanks.

Barren-ground caribou on high mountain ridge. Photograph by Adolph Murie. Reprinted with permission of the Alaska and Polar Regions Collection, University of Alaska, Fairbanks.

Lituya Bay, 1965. Cenotaph Island (left) and Spur (right) stripped to 1740 feet by the giant wave of 1958. Photograph by Dave Bohn. From *Glacier Bay: The Land and the Silence*, by Dave Bohn. Sierra Club Books, San Francisco, 1967. Reprinted with permission of Dave Bohn.

Dall sheep ram feeding on tundra vegetation. Photograph by Adolph Murie. Reprinted with permission of the Alaska and Polar Regions Collection, University of Alaska, Fairbanks.

Photograph of Thomas Merton by John Lyons. Reprinted with permission of New Directions.

"I went out hunting and trapping, I went out twenty days and came back. I had $2200 worth of beaver skins and that is more money that I ever made in five years of trappings"—Johnny Taku Jack. Reprinted with permission of the Alaska and Polar Regions Collection, University of Alaska, Fairbanks.

The moose is a major protein source for the Koyukon Athabaskans. Photograph by Adolph Murie. Reprinted with permission of the Alaska and Polar Regions Collection, University of Alaska, Fairbanks.

River rafters on the Kongakut River in the Arctic National Wildlife Refuge. Reprinted with the permission of the United States Fish and Wildlife Service.

Oil and gas development in the remote coastal regions of arctic Alaska have sometimes led to changes that have been devastating for native cultures. Reprinted with the permission of the United States Fish and Wildlife Service.

Dwellings of the King Island Eskimoes. Note the use of stretched walrus hides to cover the roofs. A stretched polar bear hide can be seen in the top center, with the skins of bearded seals to the right. Reprinted with permission of the Alaska and Polar Regions Collection, University of Alaska, Fairbanks.

Ragged Ear and one of her two 1989 cubs feeding in a soapberry patch at the bottom of Igloo Canyon in Denali National Park. Note the radio collar and the blond-color phase, which is typical for the grizzlies in the park. Photograph by John A. Murray.

 **23**

The Barren Grounds
Grizzly Bear

VILHJALMUR STEFANSSON

Vilhjalmur Stefansson (1879–1962) and Rudolph M. Anderson led one of the earliest expeditions into the high Arctic, studying the anthropology and biology of the northern Mackenzie and southern Franklin districts of the Canadian Northwest Territories from 1908 through 1912. Stefansson and Anderson returned and explored the western Canadian Arctic, including Herschel Island, from 1913 through 1918. Stefansson also actively explored the northern and western coasts of Alaska. His career was marked by controversy. In his book Arctic Dreams (Scribner's, 1986), Barry Lopez compares Stefansson with Robert Peary, who claimed to have reached the North Pole on April 6, 1909, a feat later disputed: "Both were avid, sometimes unscrupulous promoters of their own enterprises and accomplishments."[1] Lopez states that all of Stefansson's grandiose claims to develop the Arctic "showed more than anything how illusionary Stefansson's understanding of the Arctic was."[2] Stefansson was famous in his day as an arctic explorer and ethnographer, and is perhaps most important historically as a figure who made a few scientific contributions and inspired others to explore the Arctic.

In this selection, first published in My Life with the Eskimo (Harper and Brothers, 1912), Stefansson provides one of the first scientific reports on the barren grounds grizzly bear, a species genetically identical to that found in the Rocky Mountains and once present in California and the Southwest. What is particularly significant about this account is that Stefansson places the species further to the east—Great Bear Lake and the Horton River of the Northwest Territories—than was previously thought.

1. Barry Lopez. Arctic Dreams. New York: Scribner's, 1986, 346.
2. 347.

From My Life with the Eskimo. New York: Harper, 1912.

Brown Bears, or Grizzlies, are found sparingly throughout the Arctic mainland from western Alaska to Coronation Gulf. There are undoubtedly two or three races or species in this region, but, owing to lack of specimens from important localities and lack of time for critical examination of the material at hand, I am obliged to nominally refer to the Arctic Brown Bears under the above heading. In northern Alaska they do not appear to be very common on the north side of the Endicott Mountains, and seldom, if ever, come out on the coastal plains. The inland Eskimo occasionally kill specimens and often use the skin for a tent door. I saw the skins of two which were killed on the Hula-hula River, in October, 1908, by a Colville River Eskimo named Auktel'lik. Auktel'lik told me he had killed forty-four Aklak [Eskimo word for *ursus arctos horribilis*] in his time, and that only two of the lot came towards him and tried to attack him. From what I could learn he had not hunted very far west of the Colville [River] or at all east of the Mackenzie [River]. Most Eskimo, however, speak with much greater respect of the pugnacity of *Aklak* [brown or grizzly bear] than of *Nannuk* (the Polar Bear) and are much more cautious about attacking him. On July 3d, 1912, Mr. Frederick Lambart, Engineer on the Alaska-Yukon Boundary Survey, shot a Brown Bear on the Arctic slope of the mountains on the 141st meridian, about forty-five miles from the Arctic Ocean at Demarcation Point. From three photos of the dead Bear, it appeared to be of the long-nosed type, with a pronounced hump on the shoulders. Mr. Lambart informs me that this bear had been examined by Dr. C. Hart Merriam [a biologist actively involved in bear taxonomy early in the twentieth century] and declared to be a new species hitherto undescribed [no longer considered true]. In the Mackenzie delta tracks of Brown Bears are occasionally seen, but the bears are seldom killed, owing to the impracticability of hunting them through the dense underbrush on the islands in summer.

I have been warned many times by natives against shooting at a Barren Ground Bear unless from above—as a wounded bear has greater difficulty in charging uphill. So far as our experience goes, however, the Barren Ground Bear is an inoffensive and wary brute, preferring to put as much ground as possible between himself and human society. I saw but one unwounded bear come towards me, but as he did not have my scent his advance was perhaps more from mere curiosity than from hostility. As the bear was on the uninhabited coast between Cape Lyon and

Dolphin and Union Straits, and he had probably never seen human beings before, this inference seems plausible. Wounded bears are another story, of course, and it is generally admitted that the Barren Ground Bears are tougher or more tenacious of life than the Polar Bears.

We found the center of greatest abundance of the Barren Ground Bears in the country around Langton Bay and on Horton River, not more than thirty or forty miles south from Langton Bay. One was killed at Cape Lyon, and another on Dease River east of Great Bear Lake [Great Bear Lake is in the Northwest Territories of Canada, an unusually eastern arctic location for this species]. In this region our party killed about twenty specimens, most of which were obtained on our dog-packing expeditions in early fall. The Bears here showed two very distinct types, which for convenience we designate as the long-snouted types. The skulls are readily separated on this basis. It is rather hard to distinguish them by color, as late summer skins are usually much bleached out [by the sun in a treeless habitat]. In general the long-snouted Bears were inclined to a reddish brown cast of color (sometimes almost bay color), while the others were often very dark—dusky brown, with tips of hairs on dorsal surface light grayish brown on fulvous, sometimes with tips a faint golden yellowish tint. The Barren Ground Bears go into hibernation about the first week of October and come out early in April while the weather is still very cold.

While ascending the Horton River we saw at intervals the nearly fresh tracks of three Barren Ground Bears on December 29th, 1910 and January 1st, 1911, going along the river and over the shortest portages, at least forty miles in approximately a straight line. Neither the Eskimo nor the Slavey Indian who were with us had ever before seen evidences of Brown Bears out of their holes [winter denning sites] in midwinter. They seem to be nearly as fat on their first emergence from their long sleep as in the fall, but speedily lose weight, and early summer specimens are invariably poor. This is natural from the nature of their food, which is to a large extent vegetable. Although the Bear's native heath [tundra] is often conspicuously furrowed in many places by the unearthed burrows of Arctic spermophiles (*Citellus parryi* or *C. P. kennicotti* [the author refers to arctic ground squirrels]) I believe that the Bear's search is more for the little mammal's store of roots than for the little animal itself. The Bear's stomach is much more apt to contain *masu* roots (*Polygonum* sp.) than flesh. A bear must needs be very active to catch enough spermophiles above ground in spring and early summer, and if carcasses are not to be found, the Bears evidently suffer most from hunger at this season, when they can neither dig roots for themselves in the frozen ground nor dig out the spermophiles and their caches. One specimen was killed by an Eskimo of our party on Dease River, east of Great Bear Lake, after the Bear had gorged himself on a cache of Caribou meat, having more than fifty pounds of fresh meat in his stomach. A few Bears were met with in the Coppermine country, but throughout the Coronation Gulf region they are apparently rare. The Eskimo say that the Aklak is not found on Victoria Island. The fact that the Barren Ground Bears seem to always have at least two cubs at a birth, that old bears are often seen followed by two young cubs and one yearling cub, and that we never saw more than one yearling cub accompanying its mother, is evidence that there must be considerable mortality among the cubs in the first year, probably during the second spring. The new-born cubs, of course, are nursing in the spring, while the older cubs presumably have to depend upon their own foraging. Otherwise these Bears have practically no enemies besides man. As there is little market for their skins, neither Eskimo nor Indians make any special effort to hunt them, the specimens obtained being in general upon summer Caribou hunts.

24

Koyukon Riddles

Collected and
translated by
JULIUS JETTÉ, S.J.

In the long tradition of *New World* Jesuit missionaries, Father Julius Jetté (no dates available) lived almost thirty years with the Koyukon Indians of northern Alaska, carefully studying their culture and recording everything that he learned. The contemporary cultural anthropologist Richard Nelson (see "The Subsistence Cycle") has also lived with the Koyukon and has stated that "the depth, insight, and magnitude of [Jetté's] work are unequaled in all of Alaskan anthropology."[1] That is an impressive claim, but is more than born out here in Jetté's translation of several Koyukon riddles. Jetté writes:

> A riddle is a creation of ingenuity. It resembles one of those little nick-nacks, which a small boy will often whittle out of a stray bit of wood, with no other tool than a common pocket-knife. In itself the trifle is worthless, void of artistic qualities, and still, despite its uncouthness, one looks at it with a feeling akin to admiration, for it bespeaks coordination and planning in the mind, and deftness in the hand . . . [these] reflect, as it were, the mind-characteristics of their authors.[2]

One is reminded that among the works of greatest antiquity in the English language are the Anglo-Saxon riddles that pre-date even the reign of King Alfred (871–899 A.D.). Like the Old English riddles, these riddles of the Koyukon tell of a world austere and governed by unbending laws. They are full of irony, sardonic laughter, and a keen sense of nature.

1. Richard Nelson. *Make Prayers to the Raven: A Koyukon View of the Northern Forest.* Chicago: University of Chicago Press, 1983, 8.
2. Julius Jetté. Riddles of the Ten'a Indians. *Anthropos.* 8: 181.

From "Riddles of the Ten'a Indians." *Anthropos* (1913), 8: 181–201, 630–51.

RIDDLE: Wait, I see something: It has taken the color of cloudberries.
ANSWER: The bill of the white-fronted goose.

RIDDLE: Wait, I see something: It scatters like little wood crumbs from the trees.
ANSWER: The ruffed grouse, feeding in its high roosting places.

RIDDLE: Wait, I see something: Tiny bits of charcoal scattered in the snow.
ANSWER: The bills of ptarmigan.

RIDDLE: Wait, I see something: They are like bushes bending in the wind.
ANSWER: The "ears" of the great horned owl.

RIDDLE: Wait, I see something: We are wide open in the bushes.
ANSWER: The snowshoe hare's eyes.

RIDDLE: Wait, I see something: I drag my shovel along the trail.
ANSWER: A beaver, with its broad, bare tail.

RIDDLE: Wait, I see something: It looks like a bit of charred wood waving around in the air.
ANSWER: The short-tailed weasel's tail in winter.

RIDDLE: Wait, I see something: Far away yonder a fireflash comes down.
ANSWER: A red fox, glimpsed as it dashes brightly through the brush.

RIDDLE: Wait, I see something: I am looking everywhere for a lost arrow.
ANSWER: The search for a bear's den.

RIDDLE: Wait, I see something: The stars are rotting on my sides.
ANSWER: Deenaalee, or Mount McKinley.

25

The Ascent of Denali (Mount McKinley)

HUDSON STUCK

It was Hudson Stuck (1863–1920), the archdeacon of the Episcopal Church in Alaska, who led the first successful assault on the south peak of Mount McKinley (20,320′) on June 17, 1913. With Stuck on that day were Harry Karstens (Charles Sheldon's old hunting partner and future superintendent of Mount McKinley National Park), Walter Harper (the half-Athabascan son of Arthur Harper who was in 1873 the first white man to describe the mountain from the interior), and Robert Tatum.

Being a religious man by profession, Hudson Stuck, like Thomas Merton (see "The Alaskan Journal"), brought with him to Alaska a unique spiritual perspective. Most remarkable in this regard is the author's lively discussion of faith and science in this passage describing the glorious moment when man finally conquered the highest mountain in North America. Stuck descended from Denali (the federal government still insists on calling it Mount McKinley) as Moses came down from Mount Sinai, with a renewed commitment to serve humanity. Such is the power of great mountains.

From *The Ascent of Denali* (*Mount McKinley*). New York: Scribner's, 1914.

The climbing grew steeper and steeper; the slope that had looked easy from below now seemed to shoot straight up. For the most part the climbing-irons gave us sufficient footing, but here and there we came to softer snow, where they would not take sufficient hold and we had to cut steps. The calks in these climbing-irons were about an inch and a quarter long; we wished they had been two inches. The creepers are a great advantage in the matter of speed, but they need long points. They are not so safe as step-cutting, and there is the ever-present danger that unless one is exceedingly careful one will step upon the rope with them and their sharp calks sever some of the strands. They were, however, of great assistance and saved a deal of laborious step-cutting.

At last the crest of the ridge was reached and we stood well above the two peaks that mark the ends of the horseshoe [the top of the mountain resembles a horseshoe].

Also it was evident that we were well above the great North Peak across the Grand Basin [In 1910 the North Peak was climbed by the Brown expedition]. Its crest had been like an index on the snow beside us as we climbed, and we stopped for a few moments when it seemed that we were level with it. We judged it to be about five hundred feet lower than the South Peak.

But still there stretched ahead of us, and perhaps one hundred feet above us, another small ridge with a north and south pair of little hay-cock summits. This is the real top of Denali. From below, this ultimate ridge merges indistinguishably with the crest of the horseshoe ridge, but it is not a part of it but a culminating ridge from beyond it. With keen excitement we pushed on. Walter, who had been in the lead all day, was the first to scramble up; a native Alaskan, he is the first human being to set foot upon the top of Alaska's great mountain, and he had well earned the lifelong distinction. Karstens and Tatum were hard upon his heels, but the last man on the rope, in his enthusiasm and excitement some-what overpassing his narrow wind margin, had almost to be hauled up the last few feet, and fell unconscious for a moment upon the floor of the little snow basin that occupies the top of the mountain. . . . So soon as wind was recovered we shook hands all round and a brief prayer of thanksgiving to Almighty God was said, that He had granted us our heart's desire and brought us safely to the top of His great mountain.

This prime duty done, we fell at once to our scientific tasks. The instrument tent was set up, the mercurial barometer, taken out of its leather case and then out of its wooden case, was swung upon its tripod and a rough zero established, and it was left awhile to adjust itself to conditions before a reading was attempted. It was a great gratification to get it to the top uninjured. The boiling-point apparatus was put together and its candles lighted under the ice which fills its little cistern. . . . Meanwhile, Tatum had been reading a round of angles with the prismatic compass. He could not handle it with sufficient exactness with his mitts on, and he froze his fingers doing it bare-handed.

The scientific work accomplished, then and not till then did we indulge ourselves in the wonderful prospect that stretched around us. It was a perfectly clear day, the sun shining brightly in the sky, and naught bounded our view save the natural limitations of vision. Immediately before us, in the direction in which we had climbed, lay—nothing: a void, a sheer gulf many thousands of feet deep, and one shrank back instinctively from the little parapet of the snow basin when one had glanced at the awful profundity. Across the gulf, about three thousand feet beneath us and fifteen or twenty miles away, sprang most splendidly into view the great mass of Denali's Wife, or Mount Foraker, as some white men mis-name her, filling majestically all the middle distance. It was our first glimpse of her during the whole ascent. Denali's Wife does not appear at all save from the actual summit of Denali, for she is completely hidden by his South Peak until the moment when his South Peak is surmounted. And never was nobler sight displayed to man than that great, isolated mountain spread out completely, with all its spurs and ridges, its cliffs and its glaciers, lofty and mighty and yet far beneath us. On that spot one understood why the view of Denali from Lake Minchumina is the grand view, for the west face drops abruptly down with nothing but that vast void from the top to night the bottom of the mountain. Beyond stretched, blue and vague to the southwest, the wide valley of the Kuskokwim, with an end of all mountains. To the north we looked right over the North Peak to the foot-hills below, patched with lakes and lingered snow, glittering with streams. We had hoped to see the junction of the Yukon and Tanana Rivers, one hundred and fifty miles away to the northwest, as we had often seen the summit of Denali from that point in the winter, but the haze that almost always qualifies a fine summer day inhibited that stretch of vision. Perhaps the forest-fires we found raging on the Tanana River were already beginning to foul the northern sky.

It was, however, to the south and the east that the most marvellous prospect opened before us. What infinite tangle of mountain ranges filled the whole scene, until gray sky, gray mountain, and gray sea merged in the ultimate distance! The near-by peaks and ridges stood out with dazzling distinction, the glaciation, the drainage, the relation of each part to the others all revealed. The snow-covered tops of the remoter peaks, dwindling and fading, rose to our view as though floating in thin air when their bases were hidden by the haze, and the beautiful crescent curve of the whole Alaska range exhibited itself from Denali to the sea. To the right hand the glittering, tiny threads of streams draining the mountain range into the Chulitna and Sushintna Rivers, and so to Cook's Inlet and the Pacific Ocean, spread themselves out; to the left the affluents of the Kantishna and the Nenana drained the range into the Yukon and Bering Sea.

Yet the chief impression was not of our connection with the earth so far below, its rivers and its seas, but rather of detachment from it. We seemed alone upon a dead world, as dead as the mountains on the moon. Only once before can the writer remember a similar feeling of being neither in the world or of the world, and that was at the bottom of the Grand Canyon of the Colorado, in Arizona, its savage granite walls as dead as this savage peak of ice.

Above us the sky took a blue so deep that none of us had ever gazed upon a midday sky like it before. It was a deep, rich, lustrous, transparent blue, as dark as a Prussian blue, but intensely blue; a hue so strange, so increasingly impressive, that to one at least it "seemed like special news of God," as a new poet sings. We first noticed the darkening tint of the upper sky in the Grand Basin, and it deepened as we rose. Tyndall observed and discussed this phenomenon in the Alps, but it seems scarcely to have been mentioned since.

It is difficult to describe at all the scene which the top of the mountain presented, and impossible to describe it adequately. One was not occupied with the thought of description but wholly possessed with the breadth and glory of it, with its sheer, amazing immensity and scope. Only once, perhaps, in any lifetime is such vision granted. . . . Only some peaks in the Andes and some peaks in the Himalayas rise above [Denali] in all the world. . . .

It was 1:30 P.M. when we reached the summit and two minutes past three when we left; yet so quickly had the time flown that we could not believe we had been an hour and a half on top. . . . All the way down, my thoughts were occupied with the glorious scene my eyes had gazed upon and should gaze upon never again. In all human probability I would never climb that mountain again; yet if I climbed it a score more times I would never be likely to repeat such vision. . . . Only those who have for long years cherished a great and almost inordinate desire, and have had that desire gratified to the limit of their expectation, can enter into the deep thankfulness and content that filled the heart upon the descent of this mountain. There was no pride of conquest, no trace of that exultation of victory some enjoy upon the first ascent of a lofty peak, no gloating over good fortune that had hoisted us a few hundred feet higher than others who had struggled and been discomfited. Rather was the feeling that a privileged communion with the high places of the earth had been granted; that not only had we been permitted to lift up eager eyes to these summits, secret and solitary since the world began, but to enter boldly upon them, to take place, as it were, domestically in their hitherto sealed chambers, to inhabit them, and to cast our eyes down from them, seeing all things as they spread out from the windows of heaven itself. . . .

Oh, wisdom of man and the apparatus of the sciences, the little columns of mercury that sling up and down, the vacuum boxes that expand and contract, the hammer that chips the highest rocks, the compass that takes the bearings of glacier and ridge—all the equipage of hyposometry and geology and geodesy—how pitifully feeble and childish it seems to cope with the majesty of the mountains! Take them all together, haul them up the steep, and as they lie there, read, recorded, and done for, which shall be more adequate to the whole scene—their records?—or that simple, ancient hymn, "We praise Thee, O God!—Heaven and earth are full of the majesty of Thy Glory!" What an astonishing thing that, standing where we stood and seeing what we saw, there are men who should be able to deduce this law or that from their observation of its working and yet be unable to see the Lawgiver!—who should be able to push back effect to immediate cause and yet be blind to the Supreme Cause of All Causes; who can say, "This is the glacier's doing and it is marvellous in our eyes," and not see Him "Who in His Strength setteth fast the mountains and is girded with power," Whose servants the glaciers, the snow, and the ice are, "wind and storm fulfilling His Word"; who exult in the exercise of their own intelligences and the playthings those intelligiences have constructed and yet deny the Omniscience that endowed them with some minute fragment of Itself! It was not always so; it was not so with the really great men who have advanced our knowledge of nature. But of late years hordes of small men have given themselves up to the study of the physical sciences without any study preliminary. . . . Here is no gibe at the physical sciences. To sneer at them were just as foolish as to sneer at religion. What we could do on this expedition in a "scientific" way we did laboriously and zealously. . . . But when all this business is done as closely and carefully as possible, and every observation taken that there are instruments devised to record, surely the soul is dead that feels no more and sees no further than the instruments do, that stirs with no other emotion than the mercury in the tube or the dial at its point of suspension, that is incapable of awe, of reverence, of worshipful uplift, and does not feel that "the Lord even the most might God hath spoken and called the world from the rising of the sun even to the going down of the same," in the wonders displayed before his eyes.

 **26**

The Kuskokwim River

MAY WYNNE LAMB

In 1916, May Wynne (1899–1975), a young woman from rural Kansas, arrived in Akiak, a small Eskimo village on the Kuskokwim River of southeastern Alaska, to teach at a government school established for the residents. She remained in Akiak for three years, eventually marrying Frank Lamb, a physician assigned to build a hospital there. A year after their marriage, Dr. Lamb died while making his rounds in the bush. May subsequently left for the Lower 48 and never returned to Alaska.

In this chapter from her book Life in Alaska: The Reminiscences of a Kansas Woman, 1916–1919 (University of Nebraska), published posthumously in 1988, the author provides a description of the second most important river in Alaska. In a region that to this day does not have any roads, the Kuskokwim remains for almost a thousand miles the major artery of travel. May Wynne Lamb writes quietly but convincingly of this great river, evoking the "bloodcurdling tales" of "its treachery and devouring terror" as well as the "glamorous, lively parade" of its drifting ice.

From Life in Alaska: The Reminiscences of a Kansas Woman, 1916–1919, by May Wynne Lamb, edited by Dorothy Wynne Zimmerman; reprinted by permission of University of Nebraska Press. Copyright © 1988 University of Nebraska Press.

Tourists who visit Alaska seldom travel far enough west to see the beauties and magnificence of the Kuskokwim River. It is the second largest river in Alaska, with its headwaters in the many unexplored regions of the majestic Alaskan range. All the small, rushing, leaping streams unite in power to provide a water basin of 50,000 square miles, and it affords 800 miles of navigation for various kinds of watercraft. Oceangoing vessels navigate to Bethel, river steamers churn the waters to McGrath, and graduated sizes of canoes and kayaks sail on the narrow, shallow streams that are little more than babbling brooks.

The waters of the South, East, and North Forks together with the Takotna River unite and combine to form the Kuskokwim proper. Here it gains in momentum and power, mile by mile, as it is fed by the melting snow and ice, flowing through the many unseen canyons of the great ocean. The Swift, the Stony, the Hoholitna, Crooked Creek, and Tuluk-sak, with untold and unnamed sloughs, flow from all points of the compass to help swell its magnitude. The mouth of the river, where it enters the Bering Sea, is a great source of worry to most navigators. The river channel is forever changing. The mud flats spread out in low water as far as the eye can see. Sailors travel on half-tides. The low tides are too shallow and the high tides might leave them stranded on mudflats as the water reaches low ebb.

This awe-inspiring river has little recorded history since it is so isolated and inaccessible. It is practically unknown, compared with the much-written-about river Jordan, so inextricably interwoven with human life. Its history and its people are just coming to the front; in fact, many outside of Alaska have never heard of the word "Kuskokwim," meaning "cough river," "Kus" (cough) "kwim" (river).

This fast-moving stream sparkles on its way, animated and endowed with a fighting spirit; it twists and turns, whirls and leaps, burrows and squirms, both sides seeking madly to reach a goal. It has never been dammed or spanned; it stops for no umpire. It just keeps moving along as we do in life, intent on winning.

The Kuskokwim River not only gives pleasure and beauty, but bloodcurdling tales are told of its treachery and devouring terror. Dog teams and drivers have plunged headlong through the ice to a watery, unknown grave; skaters at a gay and merry party have rushed heedlessly into unexpected air holes and been hopelessly lost under the ice; men in heavy trucks have crashed into the cold, deep water, tragically pinioned with no human means of escape; boats have been carried swiftly downward with all lost in the river's might and power.

The freeze-up was interesting, but it was quite different from what my geography led me to believe. The old river never waited until we were ready; year in and year out it had a task to perform. We might be caught far from home or with the boat held in its icy fangs. When nature set the time, it began blanketing itself with a lusty layer of ice, sometimes thinner and sometimes thicker, as the universe demanded. It made its own hibernal covering in much the same fashion as we would piece together a crazy quilt. The myriads of blocks of various shapes and sizes of one glistening color were so firmly integrated that only through the mighty power of old Sol could they be torn asunder.

A swift stream with whirlpools and powerful currents does not usually freeze over in just one night like a calm and tranquil lake; to begin with, the mighty Kuskokwim starts its refrigeration along the edges and then each day and night reaches out into the stream. When the action of the strong current breaks the ice loose from its moorings, it then floats downward toward the sea, joining to other broken parts. This process continues until the entire mass is consolidated and the river is firmly tucked in from bank to bank with its winter wrap. The days covered in this operation depend on the state of the weather and how quickly it acts to accomplish this enormous task. The ice now freezes thicker and deeper until it is safe for travelers—a seasonal highway that lasts for at least six months.

There is no temporizing with the weather either in the fall or spring; when the snow and ice in the many tributaries begin to melt, the water in the main river rises. This inundation lifts the ice, breaking the shore clasps loose from their anchor and leaving the whole mass free to follow the current. In its destructive and devouring momentum the ice is jammed and crushed into smaller pieces, producing a terrific thunder-like noise as it fights its way ruthlessly onward to the sea. In its mighty and mad force it works like an excavator, digging up the spruce and willow trees, shaving and gouging into the banks along the way, ever changing the bed of the river.

As the ice drifted by in a glamorous, lively parade, our imaginations pictured all kinds of sights on this fast-moving body. We fancied seeing men and their dog teams, cabins, animal life, and property of all kinds caught in the dangerous, monstrous, turbulent flow of ice and water; but our field glasses soon allayed our fears and put our minds at rest. It was only debris collected along the way.

The ice jammed our station, causing extreme high water for one day, and as a result we had a jolly good time sailing around the village in boats while it lasted. The government house and the church were the only spots high enough to escape the rip-roaring deluge. A boat was anchored at each door for emergency. During this time, we were packed with refugees for the night almost as tight as in our camp on the portage. Huge cakes of ice floated through the main street, and when the water suddenly dropped, these mammoth icebergs were left at our front doors to melt—a refrigeration that lasted for several days.

The Kuskokwim, a mellifluous name, flows through a very rich country, rich in various kinds of minerals, in many kinds of fish, in animal life, in grass and flowers, rich in beauty, a wonderful playland to those who love nature and the great God-given out-of-doors.

 **27**

Eskimo Poems

Collected and
translated by
KNUD RASMUSSEN

The Danish ethnographer Knud Rasmussen (1879–1935) led the Fifth Thule Expedition across northern Canada from Baffin Island to Alaska during the years 1921–1924. This expedition constituted the first traverse of the Northwest Passage by dog sled. Along the way, Rasmussen made detailed ethnological and archaeological studies of the Inuit, a research project that eventually produced a monumental ten-volume work totalling over 5,000 pages. Rasmussen was interested in all cultural aspects of the Eskimo as they are found in the circumpolar north. Toward this end, he gathered and translated Eskimo folk tales, oral narratives, religious myths, songs, and poems. These poems are found scattered through the many volumes of his study, a few volumes of which were published posthumously. While some of the poems included here come from areas to the east of Alaska and the Yukon, others do not, and all are part of what is now emerging as a single northern Eskimo culture. Each speaks eloquently to the beauty of nature in the north, and to a life lived in harmony with the land and the seasons. In places evoking the finest Greek lyric poetry, in others sounding almost like the verse of the Chinese poet Wang Wei or the lyrics of English Romantic William Wordsworth, these poems can legitimately claim a place in world literature. These are very literal translations. Rasmussen places the original Eskimo side by side with his translations in each case. Their extremely concentrated, laconic quality communicates the underlying austerity of life in polar regions.

From *The Report of the Fifth Thule Expedition 1921–1924*, the Danish Expedition to Arctic North America, 12 vols. Copenhagen, Gyldendalske Boghandel, 1929. Eskimo poetry selections are from Volumes seven and nine.

Alas, I spy and search about,
Impatient, full of eagerness,
after caribou among the hills.
Am I grown dull and old
since I now hunt in vain?
I, that once could shoot
With my bow and my arrow
Standing erect, without aiming,
so that a bull with broad-spreading tines
Tumbled down dead from the hillside
With its muzzle deep in the clay
Song by *Avane*. Caribou Eskimo.

The great sea
Has sent me adrift,
It moves me as the weed in a great river,
Earth and the great weather
Move me,
Have carried me away
And move my inward parts with joy.
By *Uvavnuk*, mother of the shaman
Niviatsian. Iglulik Eskimo.

I will walk with leg muscles
which are strong
as the sinews of the shins of the little caribou calf.
I will walk with leg muscles
which are strong
as the sinews of the shins of the little hare.
I will take care not to go towards the dark.
I will go towards the day.
Words to be spoken when setting out on a
long journey. Iglulik Eskimo.

And I think over again
My small adventures
When from a shore wind I drifted out
In my kayak
And thought I was in danger.
My fears,
Those small ones
That I thought so big,
For all the vital things
I had to get and to reach.

And yet, there is only
One great thing,
The only thing:
To live to see in huts and on journeys
The great day that dawns
And the light that fills the world.

> Song from the Kitlinguharmiut.
> Copper Eskimo.

Glorious it is to see
The caribou flocking down from the forests
and beginning
Their wandering to the north.
Timidly they watch
For the pitfalls of man.
Glorious it is to see
The great herds from the forests
Spreading out over plains of white.
Glorious to see.
> Yayai—ya—yiya.

Glorious it is to see
Early summer's short-haired caribou
Beginning to wander.
Glorious to see them trot
To and fro
Across the promontories,
Seeking a crossing place.
> Yai—ya—yiya.

Glorious it is
To see the great musk oxen
Gathering in herds.
The little dogs they watch for
When they gather in herds.
Glorious to see.
    Yai—ya—yiya.

Glorious it is
To see young women
Gathering in little groups
And paying visits in the houses—
Then all at once the men
Do so want to be manly,
While the girls simply
Think of some little lie.
    Yayai—ya—yiya.

Glorious it is
To see long-haired winter caribou
Returning to the forests.
Fearfully they watch
For the little people,
While the herd follows the ebb-mark of the sea
With a storm of clattering hooves.
Glorious it is
When wandering time is come.
    Yayai—ya—yiya.
               By *Netsit*. The Musk-Ox people.

I sighted a bear
On the drifting ice,
It seemed like a harmless dog
That came running towards me gladly,
So eager was it to eat me up on the spot,
That it swung round angrily
When I swiftly sprang aside out of its way.
And now we played catch-as-catch can
From morning to late in the day.
But by then it was so wearied
It could do no more,
And I thrust my lance into its side.
    Polar Bear hunting song of Iglulik Eskimo.

I could not sleep,
For the sea lay so smooth
near at hand.
So I rowed out,
and a walrus came up
close beside my kayak.
It was too near to throw,
And I thrust the harpoon into its side,
and the hunting float bounded over the water.
But it kept coming up again
And set its flippers angrily
like elbows on the surface of the water,
trying to tear the hunting float to pieces.
In vain it spent its utmost strength,
for the skin of an unborn lemming
was sewn inside as a guardian amulet,
and when it drew back, blowing viciously
to gather strength again,
I rowed up and stabbed it
With my lance.
And this I sing
because the men who dwell
south and north of us here
fill their breathing with self-praise.

    Walrus hunting song of Iglulik Eskimo.

 **28**

The North Fork
of the Koyukuk

ROBERT MARSHALL

There is no figure more important to the history of conservation in the twentieth century than Robert Marshall (1901–1939). Born to a wealthy New York family (his attorney father helped found Adirondack State Park), Marshall was educated at Syracuse, Harvard, and Johns Hopkins, where he received a Ph.D. in plant pathology. "As a boy," Marshall once wrote, "I spent many hours in the heart of New York City, dreaming of Lewis and Clark and their glorious exploration into an unbroken wilderness. Occasionally, my reveries ended in a terrible depression, and I would imagine that I had been born a century too late for genuine excitement."[1] After hardening himself with 30- and 40-mile day hikes in New York, Marshall went on to explore the Rocky Mountains and in 1929 made the first of three extended forays to Alaska. During the 1930s, as a federal forestry official, he opposed popular New Deal public works projects that threatened wilderness. In 1937 Marshall was named Chief of the Recreation and Lands Division of the Forest Service and in that capacity helped to increase the number of primitive and wilderness areas; today one of the largest wilderness areas in the Lower 48 is named for him. "The Bob," as it is known, straddles the Continental Divide in northern Montana.

In this selection, taken from Alaska Wilderness (University of California Press, 1956), Marshall describes his pioneering exploration of the North Fork of the Koyukuk River in the Brooks Range. Here, in what has since been set aside as Gates of the Arctic National Park (Marshall's name for one of the valleys), a boyhood dream came true as Marshall camped "more than a thousand miles from the nearest automobile." Here he found at last a land such as Lewis and Clark knew, populated with grizzlies and wolves, and, as we soon discover, full of perils and challenges.

1. Robert Marshall. Alaska Wilderness. Berkeley: University of California, 1956, 2.

Robert Marshall, Alaska Wilderness: Exploring the Central Brooks Range. 2nd edition, The University of California Press. Copyright 1956 © 1970 by the Regents of the University of California.

On the morning of July 25, we left Wiseman for twenty-five days of exploration. Al led the spirited and strong Brownie, I took the docile and weak Bronco—horses we had rented from fat Jack Hood, farmer and teamster of Wiseman. Brownie carried 175 pounds, Bronco 150. In an intermittent rain we followed the dirt road for seven miles to a smaller gold-mining settlement on Nolan Creek. Here, Ed Marsan, one of the miners, who first came to Alaska in the gold rush of 1898, insisted we go no further that day. We could not decline his and his wife's hospitality.

After lunch I climbed Smith Creek Dome just back of Nolan, which the Nolanites scale every June 22 to see the midnight sun. It afforded a fine view of wave after wave of mountains stretching northward nearly to the Arctic Divide. All peaks were barren, most of them gray or greenish, except those to the east and northeast in the Hammond and Dietrich River countries which were a reddish brown. To the south the mountains were slightly lower but just as barren. Looking northward again, I suddenly realized that probably not a single one of the hundreds of mountains before me had ever been climbed.

Two other settlers who were digging for gold on Nolan Creek, Charlie Irish and Jesse Allen (who lived most of the year in Wiseman), drew maps, showed us pictures, and explained as much about our planned route as anyone could who had never been over it in the summer. Apparently, only five white men had ever been up the North Fork as far as the point where Clear River—an eastern branch of the North Fork—empties into it: our host Ed Marsan who had reached the Clear River in 1907; Charlie Irish and Jesse Allen who had hunted there the previous winter with another miner and woodsman. Kenneth Harvey; and Ernie Johnson of Bettles, the most famous trapper of the North Fork, who had trapped there several winters and even built himself several winter huts in the region, including one at the North Fork-Ernie Creek junction. The latter creek was named after him after I came to know him on a later trip. There was no record of anybody having explored Clear River, except for a short stretch above the mouth, fifteen miles at the most. The Tinayguk River, however—a western branch of the North Fork—had been visited many times by people traveling to the Wild Lake mining camps.

From Nolan we headed west for Pasco Pass, about five miles away, aided at first by wood roads, but later gave up looking for them. We crossed much burned territory, found an old cabin in the pass, and descended the steep hillside to a flat between two ponds. There we had our first taste of arctic sedge tussocks. These curses are tufts mostly of cottongrass, which gradually build up out of the swamp, the younger plants growing out of the dead remains of the earlier ones. As they grow larger, they also grow wider so that they are much bigger on top than below, becoming more or less mushroom-shaped. They get to be eighteen inches high, some even higher. They are very topheavy, and when you step on them they are almost certain to bend over and pitch you off into the swamp. When you try to walk in the swamp, you have to step over these high humps, and sometimes they grow so close together your foot catches in between. Three-quarters of a mile of this seemed like five, and at one place we were afraid we could not get the horses through. We were to find later that this was easy compared with some places on the North Fork.

Near the west end of the western pond we struck an old sled road which led south to Glacier River (a North Fork eastern tributary) and across toward the Charlie Yale cabin. Yale, an old hermit prospector, for ten years had lived alone in this cabin, eight miles over the hill from his nearest neighbor on Nolan Creek. For ten winters, every night his lonely light shone out on the snow with never a soul around to see it. I have camped more than a hundred miles from the nearest person, but this never seemed to me to be half so lonely as this cabin, where a human being sacrificed ten years of social intercourse for the sake of a fortune he never attained.

On the way to the cabin, Al pulled a stunt I had never seen before. In a small brook he spied a grayling, grabbed the shovel, and by a quick thrust caught the fish in its middle, pinned it against the bottom and cut it in two. It tasted nice for lunch.

We rested the horses for four hours at the abandoned old cabin, now filthy, but a haven from the mosquitoes. When we left the cabin, we left the last trail behind. We continued in our—temporarily—southern direction, descending Glacier River five miles, crossing it twice. On one occasion, Al demonstrated his skill as a fisherman in a more conventional way. "Just a couple of minutes," he said, "and I'll catch those two grayling in that pool for our dinner." And within two minutes Al had cut a pole, tied his line to it, and landed both fish.

That evening we camped at the ruins of another old cabin. Our mosquito-proof tent was a great blessing. This was the first night I had ever slept entirely comfortably in the mosquito season. The swarms were thick, but our tent was designed perfectly, with its attached canvas floor and funnel-shaped door, which could be sealed by pulling two strings. After we had killed forty or fifty mosquitoes which had entered while we were getting in, not one disturbed us all night.

We descended Glacier River for a further mile to Conglomerate Creek, coming in from the north, where Al fished a couple of hours and caught thirty-five grayling, while I made ecological observations. These studies which I made frequently during the course of our trips, included, in addition to the investigation of tree growth, the study of smaller plants, and noting of slope, soil, moisture, and elevation factors. Among other things, I measured the temperature of the soil on the surface and at a depth of six inches, and the depth at which the ground was frozen. I also recorded daily maximum and minimum air temperatures.

Our fishing and observations concluded and the horses rested, we left Glacier Valley, swung west, crossed Jack Delay Pass and reached the North Fork of the Koyukuk, which we followed north, traveling alternately on the hillsides above the river and on the gravel bars. We made camp on the side of a hogback between the mouth of Richmond Creek and the North Fork, and after pasturing the horses, pitched our tent in a cluster of fire-killed spruce.

The small cooking fire which we built on the moss started racing away through the dry lichen peat moss, and dead blueberry bushes. He had to trench all around the fire to make it safe. I dug down from six inches to a foot without hitting mineral soil, but it was so wet down there that the fire could not spread. Ordinarily in this country, despite its long winters, bogginess, and rain, there is a great fire hazard.

A limestone bluff rose 400 feet sheer from the river about a mile ahead. We had to keep to the hillside above it all morning. We dropped down to Bonanza Creek for lunch and let the horses feed for three and a half hours. Al fished; I took pictures and enjoyed the magnificent, rough mountain scenery of the North Fork on a perfect afternoon.

We started again at six in the evening and struck five miles of exceptionally tough travel. We had to pick our way over and through sedge tussocks almost all the time. The last mile, despite the hard work, was very cold; it felt as the Arctic should feel.

When we reached the river bars at eight-thirty and the sun dipped behind the high western mountains, every hardship and discomfort was forgotten in the presence of rugged mountains sprayed by the soft light of evening, and the turbulent river rolling wildly from the unexplored north.

We made camp among the gravel bars of several sloughs, about 600 feet from the river. Here was the best horse feed we had found; some grass, but mostly *Equisetum*. The sloughs were all cut up with moose tracks.

It became very cold in the night, dropping below freezing. At nine in the morning small puddles of water were still covered with ice.

The river was filled with broad bars of coarse stone on one side or the other, or in the center. In places the stones, which were as large as six inches in diameter, gave way to gravel, sand or oozy mud. Above the bars—or above the river itself when the bars were submerged by high water—were cut banks from three to eight feet high with only occasional gradients traversible by horses. The principal trees growing in the flats above the banks were cottonwood, but there was also willow, alder, and some white spruce. Back of these flats were successively higher terraces, flat or gently rolling, interspersed with occasional low ridges. They were covered almost completely with sedge tussocks. Their only tree growth was white spruce, dwarf birch, and rarely white birch. The footing on the terraces was abominable, but there was no brush to fight. Just above the river the footing was good, but the brush fierce. The river bars were good in both respects, but never continued for long. No matter which way we went, we were in trouble.

We alternated all morning from bar to brush, making about three miles an hour on the former and half a mile per hour in the latter. At one place, we had to cut a path for an eighth of a mile through a jungle of fallen cottonwood and live alder. It took us an hour and a half to make this eighth of a mile.

In the early afternoon, we reached the mouth of the Tinayguk River. Tinayguk means moose in Eskimo. We stopped for lunch at a place where we were afraid to hobble the horses for fear they would break their legs, so we tied them to trees. The mosquitoes were a pest, but by crawling inside our tent we were able to eat quite comfortably though somewhat cramped. Just as we were ready to start we saw a big black bear. Al took two shots at 1,200 feet, but missed.

As we continued along the North Fork, we hit three miles of the worst sedge tussocks we had yet encountered. It was mount up and fall off and stumble and sink into mud above your shoe tops and drag the horses and, in general, wear yourself out. Finally we spotted a mile of easy bars and descended to the river. We camped early at a lovely island at the junction of the North Fork and Clear River. It was separated from the peninsula formed by the rivers by a shallow slough. On this island we found the only passable horse feed of the day. Back of it, across the main channel of the river, rose a 3,500 foot mountain, with ravines and ridges which were covered by dark green spruce below and a thousand feet of gray rock to cap the summit.

After a rainy day in our island camp, we spent one of those days on which most everything goes wrong and yet the net result is as good as if everything had happened perfectly.

It started all right. We got breakfast, broke our two nights' camp, cached 25 pounds of food in the branches of a cottonwood, packed and were away before nine. It rained a little in the morning, but by eleven cleared into a fine day.

For three miles things went nicely as we walked along Clear River; but then we came to the foot of a canyon, where the river boiled between precipices which came down steeply to the water's edge. It seemed impossible to get the horses through, so we decided to try the left-hand hillside. As we progressed we had to rise continually because the walls of the canyon kept rising. After three miles we obtained a superb view of the upper end of the canyon where the river raged between giant cliffs for ten miles. Although there are probably a couple of hundred canyons as fine as this scattered throughout the North American continent, there was an indescribable joy at viewing this bit of perfection and a great thrill at the thought that we were surely the first white men who had ever gazed upon it.

The steepness which added so much to the grandeur of the canyon made a descent into it with the horses impossible. As we continued, our hillside route grew rougher. We scouted for ways down, but without avail. After another mile we had to rest the horses, so we ate lunch. During this pause, Al found a snail in the dry bed of a recently receded glacier—a surprising place. I bored several spruce trees and found the exceedingly slow growth one would expect.

A mile after resuming our journey, our hillside route became so rough that we didn't dare take the horses a step further. We decided to try, instead, for the summit of the hill on the side of which we were traveling. At this point we were probably 1,200 feet above the water and about 1,300 feet below the peak. We reached the summit, but only after nearly losing the horses several times in the soft underfooting. There had been large landslides on the sides of this mountain which accounted for our naming it Moving Mountain.

The view from the top gave us an excellent idea of the jagged country toward which we were heading. The main Brooks Range divide was entirely covered with snow. Close at hand, only about ten miles air line to the north, was a precipitous pair of mountains, one on each side of the North Fork. I bestowed the name of Gates of the Arctic on them, christening the east portal Boreal Mountain and the west portal Frigid Crags. To the east and southeast also stretched range after range of unscaled mountains, less wild than those to the north. Directly below us to the northeast was a low pass connecting the North Fork with Clear River. Across it were several cliffy peaks, including a strange mountain of which we had been told in Nolan, whose top is covered by a design in the shape of a five-pointed red-colored star, which I was to explore on a later occasion. We could see three of the star's points.

In the pass were about half a dozen ponds, which emptied into the North Fork, except one which flowed into Clear river. We decided to descend to the single Clear river pond and camp there for the night. In the morning we would cross over to the North Fork, giving up for the present our plans of further exploration of the Clear River, because of our difficulties with the horses.

We descended rapidly to within half a mile of the pond. Here a few spruce trees seemed to furnish the most eligible site for a camp. The rest of the country for miles around was treeless, the feed poor, the water some distance away, and the mosquitoes intolerable, but we stopped because the horses were tired after this strenuous day.

The ground was so rough that we thought we could take a chance and leave the horses without hobbles. We thoroughly enjoyed the evening in this barren land as we cooked supper. As usual we ate inside the tent, because to have lifted our mosquito nets long enough to consume our meal outside would have been agony.

After supper, stretched out in that luxurious ease which can only follow a hard day, Al regaled me with stories of moose hunts. He had just killed his third or fourth when we noticed that the horse bell had stopped ringing. We crawled from the tent—it was still full daylight. The horses were nowhere to be seen. Following tracks, Al ran up the mountain at breakneck speed in the direction from which we had come. Twenty minutes later he was back leading the two renegade horses, after having chased them nearly a mile. This time we hobbled them.

While the sun was setting far to the north, Al fished unsuccessfully in the little pond below and I collected a few snails, until we chanced to look up the mountain and saw the horses disappearing again. A wild dash by both of us followed. After a mile of heartbreaking sprinting over sedge tussocks, we got above the horses, caught them, and led them back to camp. The mosquitoes had been so bad, and brush to scratch on so lacking, that the horses had simply been driven crazy and had run away, hobbles and all. We realized we could not stop here. So at ten-thirty we broke camp and started for the North Fork, eight miles away.

That journey was an unforgettable experience. It never got really dark, though at midnight it was distinctly dusky. We were both just tired enough to be in a placid mood of resignation to punishment. But the punishment did not come; the going was relatively good. Only at a few creek crossings did we have trouble, and on one soft side hill where Bronco, whom Al was leading, went down in the muck. I thought for a moment he was lost. But Al talked to the excited animal just as one would speak to a baby, and, while calming it down, took off the pack. Meanwhile, under Al's directions, I led Brownie safely across the ooze. Then, together, we pulled Bronco out and brought him to dry land. We repacked him—the sixth time that day.

The remainder of the night passed peacefully. The red glow of the sunset moved from the west to the north and then around to the east. We passed numerous gray ponds. Once at about one o'clock in the morning we came to a pond bigger than the rest. At the water's edge a large bull moose stood outlined in the dawnlight against a hillside covered with a pale yellow mat of reindeer moss. The pink eastern sky mingled with the black of scattered spruce trees in the reflection in the water.

At two o'clock we reached the North Fork, just as the sun was tipping the high peaks to the west. Over Boreal floated a single pink feather. We soon found a fine place for the horses to feed, with plenty of brush on which to scratch. They were quickly unpacked and turned loose, and very shortly thereafter the tent was up. Finally we were enjoying our long-deferred slumber.

We slept off our night's debauch until ten, and spent the remainder of the morning doing minor jobs in a leisurely manner. At one o'clock in the afternoon we started up the North Fork again, following bars virtually all of ten miles. We waded the river a dozen times, the water being from a foot and a half to three feet deep and always quite swift.

As we advanced, the mountains became more and more precipitous until finally they culminated in the Gates of the Arctic. Here on the west side of the valley a whole series of bristling crags, probably at least a score, towered sheer for perhaps 2,000 feet from an exceedingly steep 2,000-foot pedestal. From a similar base on the east rose the 4,000-foot precipice of Boreal. This mountain rose straight up for almost 6,000 feet. Between these two stupendous walls, the valley was probably two miles wide, consisting mostly of dry gravel bars.

Fortunately this gorge was not in the continental United States, where its wild sublimity would almost certainly have been commercially exploited. We camped in the very center of the Gates, seventy-four miles from the closest human being and more than a thousand miles from the nearest automobile.

 **29**

The Wolves of Mount McKinley

ADOLPH MURIE

Adolph Murie (1899–1974), the son of Norwegian immigrants and a graduate of Concordia College in Moorhead, Minnesota, arrived in Alaska in September 1922 to assist his older stepbrother Olaus Murie in a study of caribou. Adolph Murie, or "Ade" as he was known to friends and family, fell in love with the far north, and, after completing doctoral work at the University of Michigan, returned often to Alaska. A figure of considerable importance in the history of modern science, Murie is regarded as the "father" of wolf ecology, largely on the basis of his pioneering work The Wolves of Mount McKinley (U. S. Government, 1944). At a time when many wildlife researchers and managers regarded predators as intrinsically destructive of prey populations, Murie came to the startling conclusion that "Wolf predation probably has a salutary effect on the [Dall] sheep as a species. At the present time [in Mount McKinley National Park] it appears that the sheep and wolves may be in equilibrium."

While Murie's immense erudition and knowledge of canis lupus are evident in this selection from The Wolves of Mount McKinley, so are his skills as a narrator, for he is able to put the specialized language of the monograph aside as he blends hard science and human observation together into his own unique form of natural history. His skills as a nature writer were later recognized in 1963 when he was awarded the John Burroughs Medal for nature writing for his book A Naturalist in Alaska (Devin-Adair, 1961). Part of the reason that Murie could write with such fluency and authority about the wild fauna of Alaska is that he was such a meticulous observer—he once spent thirty-three hours (non-stop) watching the activities of a wolf den on the East Fork of the Toklat River in Alaska.

Reprinted by permission of University of Washington Press from The Wolves of Mount McKinley, by Adolph Murie, University of Washington paperback, 1985.

In front of our cabin at East Fork River, on May 15, 1940, wolf tracks were seen in the fresh snow covering the gravel bars. The tracks led in both directions, but since there was no game upstream at the time to attract the wolves, it appeared that some other interest, which I hoped was a den, accounted for their movement that way. I followed the tracks up the bar for a mile and a half directly to the den on a point of the high bank bordering the river bed. In contrast to the Toklat den, which was located in the woods in a flat patch of timber, this one was 2 miles beyond the last scraggly timber, on an open point about 100 feet above the river where the wolves had an excellent view of the surrounding country. Apparently a variety of situations are chosen for dens for I was told of two others which were located in timber, and of a third which was in a treeless area at the head of a dry stream.

Foxes had dug the original den on the point, and wolves had later moved in and had enlarged a few of the burrows. It seems customary in this region for wolves to preempt fox dens. Former Ranger Swisher, who had found at least four wolf dens, said that all of them had originally been dug by foxes. There are many unoccupied fox dens available so it is not strange that they are generally used by the wolves. The soil at the sites is sandy or loamy, at least free of rocks, so that digging is easy. Only a little enlarging of one of the many burrows is required to make a den habitable for a wolf. Although the adult wolves can only use the enlarged burrow, the whole system of burrows is available to the pups for a few weeks. This advantage is incidental and probably has no bearing on the choice of fox dens as homes.

When I approached this den a black male wolf was resting 70 yards away. He ran off about a quarter of a mile or less and howled and barked at intervals. As I stood 4 yards from the entrance, the female furtively pushed her head out of the burrow, then withdrew it, but in a moment came out with a rush, galloped most of the way down the slope, and stopped to bark at me. Then she galloped toward the male hidden in a ravine, and both parents howled and barked until I left.

From the den I heard the soft whimpering of the pups. It seemed I had already intruded too far, enough to cause the wolves to move. As I could not make matters much worse, I wriggled into the burrow which was 16 inches high and 25 inches wide. Six feet from the entrance of the burrow there was a right angle turn. At the turn there was a hollow, rounded and worn, which obviously was a bed much used by an adult.

Due to the melting snow it was full of water in which there was a liberal sprinkling of porcupine droppings. A porcupine had used the place the preceding winter. Its feeding signs had been noted on the many nearby willows. From the turn the burrow slanted slightly upward for 6 feet to the chamber in which the pups were huddled and squirming. With a hooked willow I managed to pull three of the six pups to me. Not wishing to subject all of them to even a slight wetting, and feeling guilty about disturbing the den so much, I withdrew with the three I had. Their eyes were closed and they appeared to be about a week old. They were all females, and dark, almost black. One appeared slightly lighter than the other two and I placed her in my packsack to keep for closer acquaintance. The other two were returned to their chamber and I departed.

After my intrusion it seemed certain that the family would move, so the following morning I walked toward the den to take up their trail before the snow melted. But from a distance I saw the black male curled up on the point 15 yards from the entrance, so it was apparent that they had not moved away after all. In fact, they remained at the den until the young were old enough to move off with the adults at the normal time.

On a ridge across the river from the den, about a half mile or less away, there were excellent locations for watching the wolves without disturbing them. There was also a view of the landscape for several miles in all directions.

Between May 15, when the den was discovered, and July 7, when the wolves moved a mile away, I spent about 195 hours observing them. The longest continuous vigil was 33 hours, and twice I observed them all night. Frequently I watched a few hours in the evening to see the wolves leave for the night hunt. Late in the summer and in the early fall after the family had left the den, I had the opportunity on a few occasions to watch the family for several hours at a time.

So far as I am aware it has been taken for granted that a wolf family consists of a pair of adults and pups. Perhaps that is the rule, although we may not have enough information about wolves to really know. Usually when a den is discovered the young are destroyed and all opportunity for making further observations is thereby lost.

The first week after finding the East Fork den I remained away from its vicinity to let the wolves regain whatever composure they had lost when I intruded in their home. On May 25, a few days after beginning an almost daily watch of the den, I was astonished at seeing two strange gray wolves move from where they had been lying a few yards from the den entrance. These two gray wolves proved to be males. They rested at the den most of the day. At 4 p.m., in company with the black father wolf, they departed for the night hunt. Because I had not watched the den closely the first week after finding it I do not know when the two gray males first made their appearance there, but judging from later events it seems likely that they were there occasionally from the first.

Five days later, a second black wolf—a female—was seen, making a total of five adults at the den—three males and two females. These five wolves lounged at the den day after day until the family moved away. There may have been another male in the group for I learned that a male had been inadvertently shot about 2 miles from the den a few days before I found the den.

Late in July another male was seen with the band, and a little later a fourth extra male joined them. These seven wolves, or various combinations of them, were frequently seen together in August and September. Five of the seven were males. The four extra males appeared to be bachelors.

The relationship of the two extra males and the extra female to the pair is not known. They may have been pups born to the gray female in years past or they may have been her brothers and sister, or no blood relation at all. I knew the gray female in 1939. She was then traveling with two gray and two black wolves which I did not know well enough to be certain they were the same as those at the den in 1940. But since the color combination of the wolves traveling together was the same in 1940 as in 1939, it is quite certain that the same wolves were involved. So apparently all the adult wolves at the den in 1940 were at least 2 years old. In 1941 it was known that the extra male with the female was at least 2 years old for he was an easily identified gray male which was at the den in 1940. The fact that none of the 1940 pups was at the 1941 den supports the conclusion that the extra wolves at the 1940 den were not the previous year's pups.

The presence of the five adults in the East Fork family during denning time in 1940 and three in 1941, and three adults in the Savage River family, suggests that it may not be uncommon to find more than two adults at a den. The presence of extra adults is an unusual family make-up which is probably an outcome of the close association of the wolves in the band. It should be an advantage for the parents to have help in hunting and feeding the pups.

Wolves vary much in color, size, contour, and action. No doubt there is also much variation in temperament. Many are so distinctively colored or patterned that they can be identified from afar. I found the gray ones more easily identified since among them there is more individual variation in color pattern than in the black wolves.

The mother of the pups was dark gray, almost "bluish," over the back, and had light under parts, a blackish face, and a silvery mane. She was thick-bodied, short-legged, short-muzzled, and smaller than the others. She was easily recognized from afar.

The father was black with a yellowish vertical streak behind each shoulder. From a distance he appeared coal black except for the yellow shoulder marks, but a nearer view revealed a scattering of silver and rusty hairs, especially over the shoulders and along the sides. There was an extra fullness of the neck under the chin. He seemed more solemn than the others, but perhaps that was partly imagined by me, knowing as

I did that many of the family cares rested on his shoulders. On the hunts that I observed he usually took the lead in running down caribou calves.

The other black wolf was a slender-built, long-legged female. Her muzzle seemed exceptionally long, reminding me of the Little Red Riding Hood illustrations. Her neck was not as thick as that of the black male. This female had no young in 1940, but had her own family in 1941.

What appeared to be the largest wolf was a tall, rangy male with a long silvery mane and a dark mantle over the back and part way down over the sides. He seemed to be the lord and master of the group although he was not mated to any of the females. The other wolves approached this one with some diffidence, usually cowering before him. He deigned to wag his tail only after the others had done so. He was also the dandy in appearance. When trotting off for a hunt his tail waved jauntily and there was a spring and sprightly spirit in his step. The excess energy at times gave him a rocking-horse gallop quite different from that of any of the others.

The other gray male at the den I called "Grandpa" in my notes. He was a rangy wolf of a nondescript color. There were no distinctive markings, but he moved as though her were old and a little stiff. Sometimes he had sore feet which made him limp. From all appearances he was an old animal, although in this I may be mistaken.

One of the grays that joined the group in late July was a large male with a light face except for a black robber's mask over the eyes. His chest was conspicuously white. He moved with much spring and energy. The black mask was distinctive and recognizable from a distance.

The other wolf, which joined the group in August, was a huge gray animal with a light yellowish face. In 1941 he was mated to the small black female which had no young the preceding year.

All these wolves could be readily distinguished within the group but some of the less distinctively marked ones might have been confused among a group of strange wolves. The black-faced gray female, the robber-masked male, and the black-mantled male were so characteristically marked that they could be identified in a large company.

PART III

A1959–1989
ALASKAN
STATEHOOD
AND THE
AGE OF
ENVIRONMENTALISM

We are not just protecting the walrus and polar bear and caribou, we are protecting a world, pretty much the same world that some of our reindeer-hunting ancestors inhabited 50,000 years ago, a world that evolved as the Pleistocene ice sheet plowed across the continents, driving the older world of warm grassland and broadleaf forest southward. It is a vulnerable but strong and sustaining world. . . .

> David Rains Wallace
> from "At the End of the Earth," an essay in
> *The Untamed Garden, and Other Personal Essays*

If Alaska is the last frontier it may be because it represents the last full-scale attempt in North America to build a society worthy of human life, worthy of the claims made for America at the beginning.

> John Haines
> from "The Writer as Alaskan:
> Beginnings and Reflections,"
> an essay in *Living Off the Country,*
> *Essays on Poetry and Place*

 January 3, 1959, Alaska is admitted to the Union. 1960, the nine million-acre Arctic National Wildlife Range is established. 1962, an important offshore oil discovery is made in Cook Inlet. March 27, 1964, the Good Friday Earthquake, registering 8.6 on the Richter Scale, levels parts of Anchorage and generates killer tidal waves that devastate Kodiak, Valdez, and Seward. 1967, Kenneth Brower, Steve Pierce, and John Milton cross the Brooks Range on foot. 1968, Thomas Merton visits Alaska. 1968, Atlantic Richfield estimates oil in Prudhoe Bay on the north slope at 9.6 billion barrels. 1969, The S.S. *Manhattan* successfully navigates the Northwest Passage. 1971, the Atomic Energy Commission detonates an atomic bomb at Amchitka in the Aleutian Islands. December 18, 1971, the Alaska Native Claims Settlement Act allows Alaska natives to select over 40 million acres of federal lands for ownership. 1972, Chugach State Park is established near Anchorage. 1974, pipeline construction begins and on August 1, 1977, the first oil is shipped from Valdez. December 2, 1980, the Alaska National Interest Lands Conservation Act triples the wilderness system and doubles the lands administered by the National Park Service. July, 1983, Edward Abbey rafts down a wild river in the Arctic National Wildlife Refuge. 1987, as emigration from the Yukon continues, nearly 19,000 of the province's 27,000 residents live in Whitehorse. 1988, forest fires devastate an area the size of Connecticut in central Alaska. 1988, three whales trapped in the pack ice near Barrow capture world attention as the Russians dispatch an ice-breaker to assist in their rescue. January 1989, new cold records are set for North America as temperatures in Alaska and the Yukon plunge to −80° F. February 1989, as solar flare activity reaches a 100-year peak, dazzling northern light displays are seen in Alaska and the Yukon. March 24, 1989, the *Exxon Valdez* grounds south of Valdez and spills 11 million gallons of crude oil into Prince William Sound.

 **30**

Other Days

JOHN HAINES

John Haines (1924–   ), a resident of Alaska's interior for over thirty years, is the author of six books of poetry and five works of prose. His awards include two Guggenheim Fellowships in poetry, a grant award from the National Endowment for the Arts, and a Governor's Award for his contributions to the humanities in Alaska. He currently is a visiting professor at Ohio University in Athens, Ohio. He returns each summer to his homestead near Delta Junction, Alaska.

In this selection, a preface to his long essay on wilderness living Of Traps and Snares (Graywolf Press, 1977), John Haines describes his homestead on the Tanana River. During this period (late 1950s), the struggling writer made his living partly from fur-trapping, and the book describes the rigors of self-sufficiency in the wilderness in a manner similar to Richard Proenneke's One Man's Wilderness (Alaska Northwest Publishing, 1973). "Little by little," the author writes, "I am learning the ways of the north. In the darkness and cold that is coming, we will not go hungry." Haines, like Thoreau in his cabin at Walden Pond, has seen life reduced to its essentials. In this passage, time slows almost to a stop as the author relates what existence is like when it is governed not by the mechanical clock, but by the naturally relaxed ebb and flow of the arctic seasons.

It is evening, early in November. I am sitting on the closed porch of the cabin at Richardson, making snares. Working with a few strands of cable and a pair of pliers, I make a sliding noose seven to eight inches in diameter; it will be for lynx, or coyote if I am lucky. The wire is tough and springy, and I find it hard to make the knots hold.

I have spent part of this day cutting wood. Out in the yard by the sawhorse there is a pile of freshly sawn birch, and slabs of it already split to be stacked against the outside wall of the cabin. The woodflesh, the sawdust and chips, are a pale yellow on the evening snow.

The cabin is warm, a fire smolders and sparks in the big black wood-range in the room behind me. Something is cooking there on the stovetop; the big kettle hums in the silence. Out the window, in the southwest, a cloudy light fades slowly over the mountains. The river channel at the foot of the hill is frozen, but there downriver I see a dark streak in the snow: open water.

The land changes slowly in a thousand years. The river itself has shifted from one side of the valley to another, worn its bed deeper in the sediment and rock. Islands have formed, grown grass and willows, and then been washed away, driftpiles buried in sand. The spruce forest on these slopes gave way to fire, to birch and aspen, and in the spaces among these now the spruce come slowly back. The birch will die, stand punky, and fall, and moss thicken once more on the downed and rotting trunks.

Of all I can see from this hillside, the only recent things are the narrow roadway below the house, and my own cluster of cabins and sheds. Everything else is as it has been for thousands of years. It was colder then, or warmer. Brown coalbeds were forming the swamps to the south. Animals and birds very like those here now roamed the windy meadows, made their way south, and flew north again in a far spring-time. Enormous herds left tracks in the snow, browsing the willows and lichens. And others no longer here, huger, with hairy sides and heavy tusks. They were hunted, pursued by shadows on the snow. They have passed through, they have been eaten and killed.

Days and years run together. It is later and colder, past the middle of December, the shortest days. The sun has gone down behind Mt. Deborah, a cold, pyramidal slab in the southwest. I am fitting together a new harness for the pup I am training. I have cut the leather from strips of tanned moose, made from the back of the animal, the thickest part of the hide. By the light of this window I sew the collar seams with an awl and heavy flax thread. I have already punched holes for the bellyband and the collar buckles.

A large piece of hide taken from a hindquarter of moose is soaking in a tub behind the stove. The hair has slipped, and I have scraped the hide clean. It soaks in a solution of soap and snow water. Stirred and wrung out once or twice a day, it will be ready in a week or two to be washed clean, then pulled and stretched until it is soft and dry. Later I will hang it in the smokehouse and smoke it with dry alder until it is a light or deeper brown. I will cut new moccasin soles from it.

I remember things. Names, friends of years past, a wife far off. Last week I saw a magazine article on contemporary painters in New York City, photographs of people I once knew. I wrote one of them a letter, telling of myself here in the north. There will be no answer, and all that seems very far and ages distant.

In that same magazine—or it was another sent to me, or borrowed from the roadhouse—I have read something of the politics of this nation and the world. Names again: Truman, MacArthur, Eisenhower, a place named Korea. But these too are distant and unreal. My life is here, in this country I have made, in the things I have built. In the world of Richardson and Tenderfoot, of Banner Creek, and the Tanana at the foot of the hill. I do not want more than this.

Winter comes dark and close; there is snow, and wind on the hills. It is a lean year, and there are few rabbits in the country now. Two years ago they were thick in the willows and alders; when snow went off in the spring, the gnawed bark showed pale near the height of the snowfall. Lynx followed the rabbits everywhere, and it was no trick at all to catch a dozen or so of the big cats in a few weeks' time. Now the snow in the woods shows little sign of anything, only dust and leaves, the occasional track of a fox or squirrel. I may catch a few marten on the ridges over behind Redmond Creek, a lynx in Banner flats or a fox here along the river. I have a small cabin at the mouth of Tenderfoot, six miles upriver. I built a new dogsled this fall, and I am eager to use it. I have dried fish stacked in the shed, potatoes and cabbage in the cellar, and wood in the yard. A moose, shot late and none too fat, hangs from the tall rack behind the cabin, frozen like a rock. Little by little I am learning the ways of the north. In the darkness and cold that is coming, we will not go hungry.

I put down my work; the light is poor, and I listen. A car drives slowly by and is gone over the hill. There are not many now so late in the year.

Seasons, years. The sun will rise over the hill next spring, the cold will come again, and more or less snow will fall. If I live here long enough, I may see a new migration of people from Asia. Here below me is the corridor, the way into the continent, a way still open until stopped once more by ice.

I am alone in my thirty-third year, strange to myself and the few people I know. In this immensity of silence and solitude, my childhood seems distant as the age of mastodons and sloths; yet it is alive in me and in this life I have chosen to live. I am here and nowhere else.

It is dark in the cabin now, the fire in the stove is going out. I am done with these snares. I hang those I have finished on a nail by the doorway to the porch; I put away my tools and the lengths of unused wire. It is time to feed the dogs, and begin supper for myself. Tomorrow I must be up early, and out on the trail before light.

A breath of wind pulls smoke down across the south window. Out on the river, there is fog on that open water.

 **31**

The Old Crow

MARGARET MURIE

Margaret Murie (1902–   ) has been, and continues to be, one of the most influential conservationists of the century. Born in Seattle, she moved to Fairbanks, Alaska—then a frontier town—at the age of nine when her father was appointed Assistant U. S. Attorney for the region. She later became the first woman graduate at the University of Alaska and married Olaus Murie (1889–1962) two months after graduation. Olaus, like his stepbrother Adolph (see "The Wolves of Mount McKinley"), was a biologist, and, to confuse matters further, Adolph later married Margaret's sister Louise. Olaus served as director (1946–1949) and president (1950–1957) of the Wilderness Society during its formative years and was instrumental in shaping it into the powerful alliance it is today. "Mardy," as she is known to her friends, is the author of several nature books, including Two in the Far North (Knopf, 1962) and Wapiti Wilderness (Knopf, 1965). Much of her writing chronicles her life and travels through North American wilderness areas with her husband.

There is a plaque over the mantel of Margaret Murie's log home near Jackson, Wyoming, with an inscription taken from an old gravestone in Cumberland, England: "The wonder of the world, the beauty and the power, the shapes of things, their colours, lights and shades; these I saw. Look ye also while life lasts." That same spirit of delight in nature infuses this chapter from Two in the Far North, which relates a six-week excursion she, Olaus, their infant son, and an assistant made to the remote Old Crow River region of the Northern Yukon. There are trials and tribulations here—the mosquitoes are "unbelievable, vociferous, indescribable"—but there are also wonders—they find a 125-pound fossilized mammoth tusk. No one is better at narrating an arctic wilderness adventure than Mardy.

When a whole season's planning and effort is focused on one little piece of world, on one river, when it takes a whole precious month to reach it, that spot on the map takes on a great deal of importance. We had no other considerations to deflect our thoughts. Every bit of information, every conversation had been about Old Crow.

We came to a tall clay bluff, a brown tide staining the waters of the Porcupine. Then we turned left, over the lip of a sand bar. We were in it at last. A small stream compared with the Porcupine, it would be a big river in the middle west; it twisted and flowed rapidly here at its mouth, walled by ramparts of clay and rugged wooded slopes. We camped on a wide gravel beach, the last one we would see for six weeks.

Here we met the much-touted Old Crow mosquitoes! Since we had been warned a thousand times about them, they didn't seem so awful, ("Do you know what you're getting into, with that baby?" "Even the natives stay out of that country in summer." "There's mosquitoes all over Alaska, but they're nothing compared to the Old Crow." "They couldn't be thicker unless they were smaller!")

So here, after a month of pure pleasure, began the real part of the trip. A mosquito routine was established. As soon as Jess reached for the lever to slow the motor for a landing, I reached for the little roll of mosquito netting and draped it over the baby, box and all. By talking and singing and making all kinds of funny sounds, I kept him under the net till the men got our tent set up. Then Olaus came, picked up the box, made a dash, lifted the netting door, shoved the box in quickly, and then let the netting down. I came along behind him with all the small articles. Crouching, I shoved all these objects in one at a time, closing the netting each time. Then I took off my stiff-brimmed, netting-draped hat, left it outside, wiggled in quickly myself, turned, and pulled the netting down securely behind me.

Inside there was a curious stillness, for only a few bugs had got in. From the Boston bag came a thick tin lid and the can of Buhach. A tablespoon of the yellow Pyrethrum powder went onto the lid and a match was set to it. It burned like incense with a delectable odor, and in a few moments the tent was entirely free of bugs. Buhach! How we loved it! It was the one thing that made life possible, that insured sanity.

Now I could undress the baby and let him crawl about while I fixed his supper, a jar of stewed fruit, ready since morning in the bag, a bottle of milk mixed with water from the Thermos. Then I gave him a talc rubdown, got him into his flannel nightie, fed him, and put him to bed, in a mosquitoeless haven.

Then I had to reverse the process. From a vaccumlike peace I crawled out into the buzzing inferno, grabbed my hat, draped the head net down, pulled the leather gloves out of my pocket, and buttoned down my shirt sleeves. By now the men would have smudges going around the central cooking fire, the grub boxes would have been brought up, and I could proceed to the night meal and my day's work. We could eat with the nets up if we sat in the smoke. As soon as we had eaten, the nets came down and the gloves went on again. Everything was all right as long as I had my hands in wash water, except that, of course, dozens of bugs dropped into the water and drowned, but the moment I pulled my hands out of the water they would be black with mosquitoes. Yet, with our routine established, and satisfied that it was the best we could make it, we were able to concentrate on other things. Conversation at meals was animated, we heard a lot about Jess's adventurous life in the real frontier Alaska; we talked about the camping we had done together in the past; we shared the plots of books we had read; we learned about birds and animals from Olaus's quiet stories of his many collecting trips; we conjectured a lot on where we'd find the breeding grounds, or why we hadn't found them; and each night we relived the day's adventures. And let the mosquitoes hum.

But I won't try to say that, when, around midnight, chores done, we crawled in through the netting into that little oasis of stillness, we didn't sigh with relief and gratitude—every time.

From the diary:
"June 25: Finally came to the canyon, about five in the evening. I was thinking of Bill Mason's words: 'If you get through the canyon all right, there's nothing to the rest; it's different country from there on; just sluggish water.'"

If we got through! I sat on the seat near the men, Martin in my arms, with one of the big life-preserver vests pinned on to him with any safety pins.

As we started up into the fast water a gale of wind swept down the canyon, against us. We were halfway through but had a real drop to go over. Between groups of big rounded boulders, the whole river was boiling down through a very narrow channel.

We dropped in to shore in an eddy just behind this jumble of rocks, and on a beach made of boulders as big as tables, we stood to survey our situation. The wind was increasing; clouds were piling up; it was suddenly cold. The men built a fire behind a vertical rock; we heated some beans and the baby's mush and had supper close to the fire. The wind and cold had driven away the mosquitoes. Against the rocky wall the men found a little shelving space where, by laying alder branches, they could put up one tent. As the tent went up the heavy rain came. We all crawled in, and with the clamor and the roar of rain and river in our ears, slept.

One morning from Fairbanks!

The morning came bright and clear, and we breakfasted on mush and coffee. Now we were about to try it. The rope "bridle" attached to the bow was tested, and all the stout line was coiled neatly on shore, Olaus and I holding the end. Behind us on the shore, harnessed firmly into his box with all his toys, the baby sat, watching the maneuvers.

Jess and his boat slid out into the stream. Then the current caught him and he slid down some more, to get straightened out. Soon he yelled: "Hold her!"

The coil of rope was going out fast now, and Jess and Olaus were both yelling: "Snub her, snub her!" I had the very end and the rest was going—a panicky moment till I got a turn around a small boulder while Olaus took a new purchase and we both put our shoulders under and pulled. We drew in line, and pulled again, scrambling over and round the rocks. By now we were in the next little cove; we must be getting somewhere. Then we heard Jess shout: "We got 'er; we got 'er. Keep takin' in line; I'm comin' in now."

Now I could hurry back over the rocks to that packing case sitting all alone in the next cove downstream. The baby was not crying, but he gave a big chuckle when he saw me coming down over the rocks to him.

We were all back in the boat again and chugging away. I mixed a bottle for the baby and put him down for his morning nap. Then I heard Jess say: "Oh-oh, guess we aren't through yet. But I don't think this one will be bad. Just hop ashore here and give me a little pull."

So we hopped ashore blithely. "Guess we needn't take the baby ashore."

We had the line; Olaus had the loop at the end over his shoulders, but we hadn't quite braced ourselves when Jess, boat, and baby hit the current and went downstream like a streak. We were being suddenly dragged over the rocks, scrambling for footing, fighting to keep that rope. Olaus went down full length, I crashed to my knees behind him, and we were still being pulled. Now Olaus was frantically working with the loop, trying to get it off over his head, and he was already in the edge of the current before he succeeded. I kept running with the rope, but of course that was futile. I ended up in a jumble of sharp rocks at the water's edge.

We picked ourselves up and looked out over the river. No red boat, nothing but boiling, churning water. We both raced downstream, tumbling over the rocks. I heard Olaus say, under his breath: "Hope the rope didn't get in his wheel."

But the picture in my mind was that other boiling place below. Could Jess get out of the current before he was carried down into that, boat, baby, and all? We pulled ourselves up over a little point of rocks. There below us was the eddy, and in it the boat, idling serenely, and Jess, standing up, coiling in line. I sank down limply onto the rocks. Jess looked up and grinned at us. "Hey! Took your baby for quite a ride, didn't I? I was thinking, out there when we went round the bend, 'My gosh, Mardy'll be wondering where her baby's gone.' I knew you couldn't see us from where you were. We'll make it O.K. next try. I know how the current is now."

And we did, with tremendous pulling. But Martin, still asleep, was carried ashore first! Gratitude swelled in our hearts as we traveled on into the "different" country.

Just above the canyon, in still, slack water, was an old trappers' cabin and clearing. Here we put up camp for the rest of that day. We were about to leave the hills and enter the great flat tundra of the Arctic, and Olaus wanted to hike into the Shafer Mountains, a long bald hill stretching for about seven miles along the east side of the Old Crow Basin. Higher and farther away in the southwest toward the village were the high blue hills called the Old Crow Mountains. Northward, just flatness.

There were no breezy sand bars here. In the clearing Jess built excellent smudges from rotten stumps—we were not quite out of the timber country yet—and without nets to impede us we accomplished a lot of camp work while Olaus was gone. Here was a chance to air all the bedding in the hot sun. Jess was always busy—cleaning and oiling the guns; making me another pan or utensil out of a gas can or making another canvas stool; patching his clothes—all to a running comment. Many a tale I heard; much practical skill I should have absorbed.

From the diary:

"June 27: The Old Crow is really the descendant of an enormous Pleistocene lake which occupied this whole region north of the canyon and the hills, so it winds and curves back upon itself in an amazing way. And often in the sandy clay banks we see lens and layers of ice—the Ice Age still with us.

"Sometimes at night we are sure we are only a mile or two, overland, from our last camp. The country is alternating high yellow sand banks or mud banks or bluffs, and on the opposite shore low willow-grown mud shores or cut banks topped with small spruces on the mossy tundra, wild roses and red and pink Indian paintbrush blooming everywhere, the vivid light green of goose grass near the water—the deep, quiet, brown water.

"A great empty quiet land; its only voice the steady whine of the mosquitoes—until we round a bend and see, high up in a crevice or shelf of a mud bluff, a duck-hawk nest, and out over our heads come the parents, 'Ka, ka, ka'—but no syllables can truly convey the rasping, raucous, upsetting quality of that fairly intolerable cry. It was the only sound which, even above the roar of the engine, always woke the baby. He would rise up in his box and start imitating that cry, jumping up and down. With us it wasn't a matter of just passing a duck-hawk nest. We had to stop, and tie up under it, while Olaus, and sometimes Jess too, climbed up, banded the young, and took pictures while the two parents swooped and swung and made the whole wilderness ache with their protest.

Two duck-hawk nests, three flocks of geese, several ducks, a bald eagle, and many small birds, singing. While we travel the breeze of our motion keeps mosquitoes away. Sometimes there are storms at night, so we have to get the work done and get under cover, but the days are bright and hot. Every time some geese go over Olaus calls to them, and Martin has amazed us by imitating this sound perfectly—a good little goose-caller!"

A fairly typical entry—typical of our first days on the Old Crow, the serene days before the thing happened [the author refers to the breakdown of their boat engine on June 28 near Black Fox Creek, Yukon Territory].

 **32**

Glacier Bay Journal

DAVE BOHN

Dave Bohn (no birthdate available) is a distinguished wilderness photographer and author whose works include Glacier Bay (Sierra Club, 1967), Backcountry Journal (Capra Press, 1974), and Rambles Through an Alaskan Wild (Capra Press, 1979). In this selection from Glacier Bay, Bohn describes a wilderness trip to Glacier Bay National Park in 1965 where, like so many others before and since, he had to struggle to keep himself, his camera equipment, and his sense of humor dry in the midst of a torrential deluge. The same rainfall that produces the lovely rain forests of southeastern Alaska has ruined many a hiking and photo expedition, but not so here as Dave Bohn regroups after the May storm and continues his explorations of Glacier Bay.

1 May 1965, Lituya Bay

I am sitting here in the small—much too small—tent, in the rain. In the pouring rain. It is 10:00 a.m. At least I had a hot breakfast over a fire before the skies opened. I notice water around the tent beginning to rise a bit. Possibly the drainage here is not quite as good as I thought.

It is now 8:00 p.m. It is still raining, but rain is not the word. I thought I had seen it rain last year at Goose Cove. Negative. It only sprinkled. This is a monsoon. I saw almost the monsoon on the Fairweather Glacier in 1962. I am now in a gray two-man tent. No difference. I am beginning to think I will learn a wilderness lesson in the next few hours. . . . Lesson: When traveling alone in rain country, do not try to save too much weight by carrying a small tent.

At any rate, I am here, and the month of May is always the best month for the coast. Statistically. The monsoon is definetly outside the door. It will probably stop by late tonight. Yet, it does not look that way at all. It looks as if this is the long monsoon. I can feel it. I notice the water around the tent has risen about a half inch since this morning.

Midnight

I notice there is now a great deal of water under the tent as well as around it. The floor is billowing as if there were air underneath. I wish it were air. And a moment ago the left guyline pulled out and deposited the whole side of the tent on the sleeping bag and in my face. The wind out there is really very high. Which means I may lose the entire tent in a few minutes, unless I can get the line anchored again. Which means I must get dressed, including oilskins and very wet boots. In a gray two-man tent with one side collapsed. Without touching the other side, in dark screeching wind and rain. I think it will be a hard lesson.

1:00 a.m.: I am standing outside the tent deciding. I pulled too hard on the tie string of my rubber jacket and it ripped open fourteen inches. Considerable water will enter a slit that long. I don't know what I am deciding. There is nothing to decide. The tent is going to be washed away unless I move it. Immediately. In the dark screeching wind and rain.

4:00 a.m.: It is beginning to get light. The monsoon is still with me and the water is still rising around the tent. The foam rubber mattress is soaked, the down sleeping bag damp through, all clothes damp. I think I have lost. The tent must be moved again, and on the next move all will get wetter, including the cameras. It is no longer the monsoon. It is the deluge, and below me across the waters of Lituya Bay, through the dim light, horizontal rain, and fog, I can see the mast lights of what must be the entire halibut fleet. I am no longer alone. They have come in from the sea—across the bar and into the Bay. But out there beyond La Chaussee Spit, what must the open sea be like early this morning? It must be insane. The wind here is increasing.

10:00 a.m.: I have moved the tent a second time. I am in the forest, under the swaying trees and the occasional falling limbs. The sleeping bag is now soaked through. Which is why it just took me ten minutes to wriggle into it. One does not slide easily into soaked rip-stop nylon.

In wilderness, when you get behind you often cannot catch up. I am behind. The deluge is still with me and the wind is yet higher. In fact, I can see through the glasses that some of the boats have thrown shore lines. In Lituya Bay? Where according to Lapérouse not a ripple marred the face of the waters? Yes. Shore lines in Lituya Bay. I think I am too far behind. If the cameras go the way of the rest of the gear, I am finished. I think I shall stand on shore in the screeching wind and rain, hail the fleet, and re-group aboard a halibut troller. You win, deluge.

30 May, Strawberry Island

All of Bartlett Cove saw us off this morning in our sixteen-foot boat. Three of us with gear and food for three weeks. The logistics are solved. The extra four feet makes the difference.

I have just looked through the ground glass at Carl Swanson's bird house. Swanson fox-farmed here in the 1930's. The building to which the bird house is attached is leaning considerably. The roof is falling in and all will collapse in a year or two, I presume. In fact, both roofs are falling in. But I am glad Swanson bothered to build a bird house out here on isolated Strawberry Island. Through the ground glass it looked beautiful, and from a distance so did the main house.

31 May, en route Reid Inlet

From Berg Bay this morning, where John Muir camped eighty-six years ago, we moved off for Reid Inlet. It has been raining steadily and we are all somewhat cold. Sitting for hours in an open boat in the weather is no way to keep warm. But one learns about the land. Glacier Bay is under mist and the peaks are not revealed to us. Nevertheless the land forms are with us hour after hour. The magnificent land forms pushing down into the water on all sides of us and disappearing into the clouds. Land forms scraped and rounded by the glaciers. Birds constantly flying out of the mist. Mammoth flocks of ducks rising from the water in confusion. Two thousand ducks taking to the air at once. Cormorant you are the fifth cormorant I have watched since Berg Bay, and each one of you has circled the boat exactly two times. Cormorant, why do you circle this boat two times? Pigeon guillemot, I am watching you also with the glasses. I see how you kick your feet like hell as you leave the water. Fatty with red feet. Hundreds of fatties with red feet.

Hour after hour. The trees are thinning out, but not the mist. Moving north through the fog and the rain and the cold. Beyond the mist two more headlands, then Reid Inlet. The wind is rising now and our freeboard is not ample. And then appearing from behind the last obstacle—if one knows where to look—the red cabin finished in 1940 by Joe and Muz Ibach. The cabin on the small piece of land which, on the back of a fuzzy photograph Joe Ibach called 'HOME AT GLACIER BAY.' Hello red cabin. All of us are relieved you are still here. Including Cicely who has never met you before. Who cares that we are cold and stiff, that we have been sitting in the cold rain for five hours, that we are hungry and the food boxes wet? Who cares. It was as if the red cabin would not be here, somehow, but it is here still standing and we are back at Reid Inlet.

2 June, Reid Inlet

The light! Look at the light on the glacier. The boat. Drag the boat off the beach and go, instantly. The race to the terminus of the Reid Glacier and up on the rocks at the east side. In stillness in front of the now silent glacier. Light on the ice cliff. Luminous. Great silence.

6 June, at Margerie Glacier

I am sitting here at the tent watching an iceberg trying to dislodge the bowline. The boat is two hundred feet offshore. If the iceberg wins we might be in poor shape, even though we brought extra food.

The same food that fell overboard as we arrived earlier. The box was set on the bow for a moment, just after landing, and then the glacier calved. It was big, and as I turned to look the swell from the preceding explosion hit the boat and all our food went over the side. Surrounded by floating grapefruits I shouted and cursed at the Grand Pacific, but it kept right on calving. It paid no attention to me. This country doesn't pay attention to anybody. Vice versa, or else.

We are camped alongside the Margerie Glacier, which is two hundred feet away. The Grand Pacific is very noisy and so is the Margerie. From the promontory between the two I can see for miles and miles to the south, almost all of the fjord under ice when John Muir was in Glacier Bay. And up here, ground cover is sparse. This is the end of the line by water. No farther north unless one travels up over the Grand Pacific on snowshoes. Canada over there, not very far from the terminus.

7 June, behind Russell Island

Returning from the Grand Pacific Glacier. Lunch in the hot sun. Rare hot sun. Tide incoming. No worries about the boat, avalanches, icebergs, wind. Rare moments when one does not have to pay attention. Just be here, nothing more. With the wild landscape, not sublime landscape even under hot sun. Still brooding always brooding landscape. With the glasses looking across for miles to the peaks, to Russell Island, to the spruce colonizing on the mainland east of Russell Island, the ravens and eagles on the beach . . . eagles on the beach? Why eagles on the beach? Beyond, a half-mile from us, coming toward us directly . . . BROWN BEAR.

Enormous. The great carnivore. Here he is, close, the incredible power as he moves . . . I have seen you, brown bear, before you know of us. And then I watch you as your head goes up and swings side to side. Now you know of us and the reaction is superb. To the right instantly and at twenty-five miles an hour away for the hills. I am glad you so decided, brown bear.

9 June, Reid Inlet

The Ibachs of Reid Inlet. This is what is different about the little red wilderness cabin. Muz and Joe built a small monument here, though of course they would never have seen in that way—a small monument to an immense piece of land.

When I discovered that fuzzy old photograph of the red cabin near completion in 1940, the one on which Joe printed 'Home At Glacier Bay,' I objected to the unsharpness, a predictable reaction from a photographer. I also noticed the horizon was tilted. But I am looking at that photograph now, and now I know better. It should be fuzzy and the horizon should be tilted. It is a fine photograph and what counts is what is written on the other side.

11 June, upper Muir Inlet

Last year we came north through the ice of Muir Inlet in a seventy-foot boat, but now we are in a sixteen-foot boat in the heaviest ice I have yet seen anywhere in Glacier Bay. Mountains of floating ice all around us, fog and rain, miles and miles of ice. I have the same feeling I did last year, only much more so. I keep thinking about the land coming out from under—land that has been covered, at least this far north in the Monument, for perhaps two thousand years. But surrounded by mountains of almost-silent floating ice in the fog and rain, I cannot quite account for the strange intensity of thought. I think the intensity and the recognition go back. I think it has something to do with a man wrapped in animal hide and fur, crouched at the edge of a glacier twenty thousand years ago.

14 June, in camp, Wachusett Inlet

This is a strange, wonderful, desolate inlet. Heavy alder at the entrance which thins out quickly and then gravel. Hundreds of acres of gravel deposits, brown and gray, and two dying glaciers—the Burroughs and the Plateau. Almost the entire inlet under ice in 1930, an inlet now ten miles long. And if the ice is reducing in thickness by forty feet a year, the exquisite forms I photographed just two hours ago at the terminus of the Plateau Glacier will be gone next year and there will be more land out from under. Change, phenomenal change year after year, century after century.

 **33**

Sheenjek

KENNETH BROWER

In 1967 Kenneth Brower (1944–   ), *the son of conser-*
vationist David Brower, John Milton, and Steve Pearson
made an historic 300-mile back-packing trip over the
Brooks Range from south to north. John Milton wrote of this adventure in
his book Nameless Valleys, Shining Mountains *(Meredith, 1970) and*
Kenneth Brower told of the same trip in his format-series book Earth and
the Great Weather, The Brooks Range *(Friends of the Earth, 1973). This*
selection is from Brower's version of the trip. He writes here of their first
days in the region, spent reconnoitering around Last Lake, in the
Sheenjek Valley, before beginning their epic journey to the Arctic
Ocean: "There were tracks everywhere on the river-bars—wolf, bear,
Dall sheep, caribou—and we left our tracks too."

"Sheenjek" from *Earth and the Great Weather: The Brooks Range* by Kenneth Brower.
Reprinted by permission of Kenneth Brower.

As the plane set down on Last Lake it frightened two moose from the edge of the water. From the plane window the scale of the country was so hard to understand, and the black spruces of that latitude were so stunted, that the moose looked larger than life. We were being set down among the giant beasts of the kind of lost continent that Arthur Conan Doyle imagined. The moose watched us unalarmed until the pontoons hit the water, then ran heavily off. We taxied to the tussock-grass shore of the lake, unloaded our things and paid the pilot, counting the bills into his hand. He was a Korea veteran who had played bush pilot well, I thought, reading a magazine most of the flight, looking up only occasionally. He had identified the moose as caribou, either to have fun with us or because he didn't know. He took off with an impressive roar, for a Cessna pilot, and dipped his wings as he turned back over the lake and headed homeward. The plane was dramatic somehow; slow moving, for a long while remaining a point among the foothills, a human point above the great face of the land. Then it disappeared and we were alone in the middle of the country.

From the plane on our approach we had seen a cache a short distance from the lake. The small platform of dead white branches had stood out clearly against the living signs of man, but now the cache became as curious to us as a stranger would have been. Steve Pearson, John Milton, the cache and I were the only man-made things for many leagues around. We walked over to meet the cache.

Steve Pearson was twenty-seven, of medium height, with sturdy walking legs. He had grown up in New York. As a boy in that crowded city he had begun to think there was nothing in the world he liked. Then, on a train trip to the Middle West, he looked out the window and saw the great plains. He suddenly had discovered space, and could not believe his good fortune. When he grew up he became a wanderer. In the Army he was stationed in Korea and California, then traveled everywhere, preferring warm countries like Italy and Australia. He had hated Korea's cold. Most recently he had served as a press photographer in Vietnam, but he came to hate the war and left. Steve never felt comfortable staying anyplace long. He was more than anything else an emigrant.

John Milton was twenty-eight. He had grown up in New Jersey, where as a boy he had read, and been much influenced by, Lewis and Clark. As a student at the University of Michigan, and later as an ecologist for the Conservation Foundation, he had traveled all over Latin America. He had gone to school in Mexico City, researched his master's thesis in Costa Rica, been pursued by Indians in the Oriente of Peru. His work had taken him to the Azores, the West Indies, the Canadian Arctic, and Europe. He and I had spent three months together in the Galapagos Islands off Ecuador's coast.

The heavy branches of the cache platform were all cut to a uniform length and nailed in place halfway up two spruces that grew closely together. The ground under the trees was littered with things that the ravens or wolverines had pulled from the cache. There was a teapot, some pans, a page from an Indian bible, an assortment of weathered funny papers, a letter to someone named Ambrose William, and a Selective Service card in Ambrose William's name. Above us, a pair of faded jeans was just visible over the edge of the cache platform. The jeans were full of something. We climbed a little uneasily, expecting I don't know what—a burial platform? But on top there was more of the same. There was the remainder of the Athabascan language bible, an Athabascan book of prayers, a child's English reader, several good unrusted traps, some Calpec in a blue bottle, some aspirin, some Turpin Hydrate Elixir, and some medicinal powders, the remains of a parka, and a pair of ragged blue jeans, stuffed with old shirts. There was a model 1895 Winchester with a lever action too rusted to open. The rifle apparently had fed from a clip, but this item was so rusted that it was impossible to tell. There was a knife with a wooden handle. There were several USGS maps of the Gulf of Alaska and other areas far to the south, and a map drawn in pencil on blue-lined paper, with no place names on it, no clue at all to what land the map represented, just an X beside one of the hand-drawn lakes.

That was all there was. It may seem a lot, taking up as much room as it does in the paragraph, but it did not take up much room in the Sheenjek Valley. It was the only mark of man we would see for many weeks, the only human sign in all that arctic country.

In the next days we camped at Last Lake and wandered around. I fished for grayling in the lake and in the small stream that ran from it, and John and Steve explored the hills to the east. I waited to feel at home in the country, but the feeling did not come. I wondered what was wrong. I was not understanding the rhythm and resonance of the place, or its whatever; its mood, spirit, idiosyncrasy. Fishing, I watched the grayling—they tasted like trout but had great dorsal fins that they spread under the water—and I wondered what was missing from the country.

The Arctic had no smell. The summer snow did have a faint odor, and the smoke from our willow fires had a fragrance, and the black soil had a cold earth-smell when you dug a hand in it, but the wind brought no messages. The wind came raw and untinged, like the breath of an ice age. There was nothing like the resinous smell of the Sierra Nevada or the wet green growing smell of the Washington Cascades. Could a country be simply too big, too severe, to have a smell. I realized how important smell was to me. I remembered that the lynx of this country had a poor olfactory sense—maybe smell was not part of the scheme here? I wondered if I was just catching a cold.

Another thing about the Arctic was that you could not lie around it. There were no warm rocks to lie shirtless on. The Arctic was cool even in summer, and there was surface wetness everywhere because permafrost prevented drainage. I wanted, perhaps because I am nearsighted, to bring everything to my nose, but I couldn't. There was no rolling around in this country. A certain contact with the land was missing; that might be the trouble.

John took to the Sheenjek country more easily. Every night he was busy writing in one of the journals, bound in red plastic, in which he keeps records of all his travels. He noted bog violets near the lake, small flowers that, in order to make up for the lake of nitrogen in boggy soils, trap insects in their basal rosettes. He noted the red squirrels around the lake, and wondered why they were so silent. Was it, he asked his journal, a consequence of the scarcity of cover in this northern environment? He noted an "overwhelming sense of great distances, mysterious valleys, and an indefinable light air . . ." [Milton would later title his book on this expedition *Nameless Valleys, Shining Mountains*]. He noted the pair of arctic loons (*gavia arctica pacifica*) that swam, calling now and again, far out on the lake. "How well," he wrote, "their lonely cry suits this solitary land." I myself was not sure yet about the solitary land, or how well the loons' cry suited it. The cry fitted the country well enough, I suppose. Steve kept no journal and I did not know how he felt about it. . . .

The day after Thayer [Averill Thayer was at that time a public lands manager for the Arctic Wildlife range, now the Arctic National Wildlife Refuge] left, we broke camp and departed. John was not yet strong enough [John Milton is suffering from a bad cold] to carry a full load, and Steve and I began with more than ninety pounds each. It seemed an incredible weight. It was a task just getting our packs to our shoulders, but we set out, walking through intermittent rain and wind, and as we moved through the country it began talking to us. The sky was gray and turbulent above and the land was green, yellow, and orange under our feet. The green was dominant, a soft wet green luminous under the somber sky. Equisetum grew in fragile sprays, like a green mist over the ground. The yellow was mostly in the willows that bordered the streams and it showed up here and there in the tussock grass. The rarest color was the orange of a lichen that grew on certain rocks. It was a solitary orange. There was seldom more than one lichen-covered rock in sight at any one time. The rocks occurred as points of intensity—quintessence of orange, painfully orange—amidst green fields of tussock grass.

There was a duller orange in the moss at the edges of streams. Every fourth stream or so, for reasons we could not guess, was bordered entirely by green. The moss grew in gentle hummocks by the streamside. The hummocks were full of water and delicate, easily disrupted by our feet. The entire country was full of water. Streams ran everywhere and the tussocks held water like sponges. The tussock hillsides were bright under the dark northern sky, as if in the absence of the sun their duty was to illuminate the world. It was not with an inward light that they glowed, precisely, but with a real light nonetheless, a refracted light better than the original source.

Walking under the weather I relearned all my mountain lessons. I looked up into the rain—no reason to be afraid of it—and the rain beat my face. I made myself comfortable in the cold, and at ease in the storm. These are ways of living I have to remember each time I go to the mountains. I was now relearning in my own right all the things my father [David Brower] had learned, and relearned, in his time in the mountains. Mountains were the most important thing in my father's youth, and as a young man he has taken me into them, and to a considerable extent he and the mountains were, and are now, inextricable. The farther I walked, the more of my father's good lessons were substantiated. We stopped and rested. My green poncho, reaching to my knees in front, was pulled back over my pack to keep the pack dry, and it made the kind of tent that a table and blanket make for children. Sitting in the slanting rain and arctic wind, I ducked my head inside the tent. I was alone in there with my hands. I watched my hands, which resemble my father's. They were folded in my lap, pale in the undersea light beneath the poncho. I thought about the gifts of my father. The light inside was steady and green, though outside the poncho snapped in the wind.

Moving again. Under the weight of the packs it was most comfortable to watch the ground at our feet, but from time to time we looked up from the tussocks and arctic flowers to the peaks on either side of the valley. Mist and cloud were playing about the mountains, wreathing the cols, spilling out of high cirques and down the slopes. Above the mists was the ridgeline of peaks, a black lace of rock against white snow (or, if you wished, a white lace of snow against black rock) and above the ridgeline, sometimes obscuring it, was the gray sky, full of the promise of snow, or of rain at least—so heavy with promise that the gray verged on blue. The sky set off the lacework of rock, making the snow whiter and the rock blacker, making the ridgeline sharp, high, cold, and uninhabitable. For me high ridges, like the stars, have always been symbols of the severity of the universe. The ridges don't care about us. As I walked under the Sheenjek peaks I felt a renewed conviction about the impartiality of God. I wondered if the holy men who sat in Asian mountains usually came to the same conclusion. Or did holy men only go to the mountains in cartoons?

Storm after storm was blowing out of the north. In this weather the ridge looked like all the other alpine ridges in the world, but was very beautiful.

We came to a beaver pond. It was the northernmost beaver pond in the Sheenjek Valley, we guessed, for a few miles ahead the spruces gave out. Nothing but willow and dwarf birch grew between that final stunted treeline and the shore of the Arctic Ocean, and beyond that shore, to the Pole, there was nothing but ice. It may have been the northernmost beaver pond in the entire Brooks Range, and perhaps the entire planet, unless somewhere there were Siberian beaver more adventurous. The two northernmost beaver who lived in the pond were not adventurers, in truth, but drudges who paid with hard work for their distinction. Their great pond was the work of generations and dynasties of beavers—a complex of four dams and four ponds that completely enclosed, as if by a moat, what once had been a steep hill and was now an island. We pitched camp across from the island. The larger beaver, the male of the pair, we assumed [sexual dimorphism is a characteristic of most mammals], swam up and regarded us with what John described in his journal as "suspicious old maid's eyes." It was not an unfair description, I think. In his journal John mapped the pond, and it made for an impressive blueprint, but like the human engineering feats that call attention to themselves—the longest spans and highest towers—the northernmost pond was unbeautiful. There were snags of drowned trees visible under the water, and the country around looked altered and drab. When we woke by the pond the next morning the beavers were nowhere in sight. A solitary duck landed on the water, ate a plant or two from the bottom of the pond, and flew south.

We continued north. The Sheenjek Valley widened and the river made a great turn across the valley floor. We could look miles across to a low place in the far valley wall and see beyond to the drainage of the Kongagak, a river that flowed north into the Arctic Ocean. Ahead the Sheenjek became an impressive river. It flowed in many channels over the wide gravel floor of the valley. The water was the same gray as the gravel, reflecting as it did the gray sky, and walking close to the river we could see the channels only as differences in texture, as streams of motion among the river bars. The river slipped along at different speed, in eddies and countercurrents, but always against us. We were walking against the stream, toward the source.

In the next days we walked along the river whenever we could. Above the flat gravel floor of the valley, the long slopes were cobbled with tussock grass, and the tussock hummocks made for bad walking. We could not relax when traveling on them because we were always making decisions; whether to step on this one, which looked likely to tip us off, or to step in the interstice between one hummock and the next, and have to pull a boot free. The gravel shore of the river was better going, though then it was necessary to cross and recross the channels, and to fight through occasional clumps of river willows. At first I unslung my rifle as we entered the willows, in case we surprised a bear in the closeness of the trees, but after a day or two I thought no more about it.

When the rain stopped the mosquitoes came. Sometimes they arrived in such numbers that we stopped and put on our headnets. The headnets were uncomfortable, but they had a virtue. When the rain returned and we took the netting off, the world came back in all its color. It was like pushing back the hood of your parka and hearing the sound of the air again. It was like what happens when you turn a corner in the mountains, cutting yourself off from the others in your party, and find yourself suddenly alone on the land.

Walking through the rain, our route took us away from the river, out of sound but seldom out of sight. It rained for days, and rain beat our tents through the night, quickening all the streams in the Sheenjek country. Rivulets ran everywhere. Some larger streams had cut down to bedrock, but most streams were new and wandered over the land as they chose. The grass beneath the surfaces of these itinerant streams were flattened somewhat, but looked perfectly healthy down there. The new streams were inviting. They elicited from me a kind of dog's response, strangely reversed. Instead of peeing at every post I drank at every stream. The streams tasted as good and cold as the high ridges they flowed down from. When the streams were fast we linked arms and forded, six legs working against the current. I felt us moving toward the heart of the country.

Once we came to a stream too fast to wade, and we searched up and downstream until we found a spruce log spanning it. Crossing, I dropped my hat, and it was carried quickly out of sight. It was a green tyrolean hat that my parents had bought in Salzburg for my little brother. It was headed for the Sheenjek, and then, if nothing snagged it, for the Yukon, and then for the Bering Sea. I wondered if the Austrian hatmaker would be pleased. It seemed a noble end for the hat, lost in the unexplored wastes of northern America.

Back to the river. There the valley floor was flat, and the larger streams joining the river had lost the speed they gained on the gradient of the hillside, so that our crossings were easier. The smaller streams running down to the Sheenjek had disappeared completely under the gravel before they joined the river. We made good time. There were tracks everywhere on the river bars—wolf, bear, Dall sheep, caribou—and we left our tracks too. It was clear from the tracks that a great volume of life passed through this valley. We saw little of it—a porcupine and two ptarmigan in the morning, an eagle in the afternoon. We were not seeing the country as it really was. If we could somehow pass through this valley invisible and odorless, we agreed, it would be a different valley.

**34**

One Man's Wilderness

RICHARD PROENNEKE

Dick Proenneke (1917–   ) has led the sort of life many dream of. Born in Iowa, he served in the U. S. Navy during World War II, worked as a sheep herder in Oregon for a few years, and then eventually came to Alaska for the first time in 1950. In 1967, after having lived and worked around Kodiak Island and King Salmon on the Alaska Peninsula, Proenneke stayed at a friend's cabin on Lake Clark. The area impressed him and the next summer he returned to construct his own cabin in this remote wilderness, a story related in One Man's Wilderness (Alaska Northwest Publishing Company, 1973). Today Dick Proenneke is a living legend around what has since become Lake Clark National Park. Here he describes a ritual that is repeated all across the north country every autumn—the hunt for winter meat—and does so in a manner that is strikingly different from Charles Sheldon's description of the grizzly hunt found elsewhere in this book.

"Camp Meat" from Richard Proenneke, One Man's Wilderness: An Alaskan Odyssey. Sam Keith, editor. Reprinted by permission of Alaska Northwest Publishing Company.

September 20th

If I was going to stay the winter, I would need more meat. Today was the last day of the sheep season and I liked sheep meat better than caribou. The sight of four good rams in a bunch convinced me.

I put the butchering outfit, camera gear and musket [bolt-action 30.06 rifle] into the canoe and paddled across the calm lake in the shadow of Crag Mountain. The big rock face of the mountain would hide my approach from the sheep. The camera gear I decided to leave in the canoe. This was serious business today. Up through the spruce and into the high country that I loved, careful not to expose my movements to the sheep. They must know now what a stalking figure on two legs means. I stopped to examine a lone spruce deformed by the wind, a few tufts of branches left near its top. There were fresh tooth marks in the bark and long brown hair hanging from every sliver. The claw marks were higher than I could reach. This was the bears' social register, and the one who had signed it recently was big.

I climbed to a rocky outcrop and eased my head just barely above the rim. There were the rams out of range, lying down and soaking up the sun on a ridge line. I watched until they rose, stretched, took long looks down the mountain and then trailed off out of sight. I climbed fast. I didn't want them to be out of range next time.

As I peered over the rim where they had been bedded, I saw them again. Closer now, but still out of range—my kind of range, at least. They were on another ridge and climbing slowly. In between was a rocky point and a little saddle. I left my packboard and jacket behind and climbed, keeping the rocks between the sheep and myself. I was breathing hard from the fast scramble and wondered whether I would be able to hit anything when I reached the rocks.

I peeked over the top of a granite boulder. About two hundred yards away, the rams were moving behind a grassy knoll. They would appear on the other side of it. The first legal-curl ram to step into the clear would be my target.

I wriggled to some dry grass and waited there on my belly, the safety off the Ought-Six, my heart thumping against the earth.

Suddenly there he was, a big ram stepping out. A full curl at least. I held the tip of the front sight blade just below the top of his shoulder . . . took a deep breath . . . and as I slowly let it out, squeezed the trigger. The shot crashed loud in the high stillness.

I heard the whunk of the bullet hitting. The ram did a flip, and down he came sliding and rolling in the new snow. I could see a red spot growing larger on his front shoulder. Down past me he rolled and kept right on going. Maybe he would make it to the timber. I watched him until he stopped. Then I went back for my packboard and pulled on my jacket. My hands were trembling. Up above me three rams posed against the sky for a thrilling moment and dropped out of sight.

My sheep was stone dead. If the bullet hadn't done the job, the fall had. He was a big one, with a little better than full curl and both tips intact. Plenty of meat and a beautiful snowy pelt. I had opened and closed the season in one day, with one shot.

I took him by one heavy horn and dragged him on down the mountain to a level place beneath some spruce trees. As I dressed the big ram out, the camp robbers came gliding in. They perched on the limbs, watching me with inquisitive tilts of their heads as I peeled off the hide. Some ravens croaked from the crags. They had seen the whole show and were talking it over.

At first glance I figured three loads. I took the neck, front quarters, and ribs the first trip. A record trip down to the beach, non-stop. Steady going is the way to do it. Each time you stop to rest, it is harder to go again. One careful step at a time and eventually you're there.

Back up through the timber again to find the camp robbers picking away at the kill. The hind quarters didn't seem too heavy. Maybe I could clean up what was left in one super-load. I had sawed off the skull cap, with horns attached. I put the head, feet and some other scraps in the hide, which I rolled into a compact bundle. The heart, liver, tenderloin, and brains I put into a flour sack and tucked it between the hindquarters roped on the board. I tied the horns atop the hide bundle. All that was left were the entrails and a few small scraps that the birds and other prowlers of the slopes could share.

A much slower trip down the mountain this time. I was glad to get down on the level and see the gleam of the canoe through the brush. It had been a rugged load, but I had saved myself a trip.

Paddling across the still lake, I felt like an Indian hunter returning to a hungry tribe. I glanced up at the high place where I had made the kill. It seemed clouds away.

I put the heart, liver and brains to soak in a pan. The bloody flour sacks, the pelt and the horns I put into the lake to soak. I hung the meat in the woodshed for the night, cleaned up all my gear and put it away.

The pelt must have weighed a hundred pounds when I dragged it from the water. Nearly all the blood had soaked out of the white hide, but after I fleshed it I put it back into the lake to finish the job.

Sheep liver and onions for supper. The liver fried two minutes to the side. Pink in the middle, full of flavor and I ate enough of it. Maybe some of that old boy's ability to romp the high places will rub off on me.

A satisfying day. The search for meat is over. I hate to see the big ram end like this, but I suppose he could have died a lot harder than he did.

**35**

The Alaskan Journal

THOMAS MERTON

In 1968 Thomas Merton (1915–1968) was permitted to travel beyond the walls of Gethsemani Abbey, located in the rolling green hills of northern Kentucky, for the first time in many years. A member of the Cistercian Order, Merton had quietly built an international reputation as a lyric poet, philosophical essayist, and commentator on contemporary affairs (including nuclear weapons, human rights, and the Viet Nam War). He remained in Alaska for two weeks before continuing on to a Buddhist convention in Bangkok, Thailand, where he died in a bizarre accident involving an electrical fan and a running shower. Merton's fascination with the mountains of Alaska—the peaks are "graceful, mysterious," "sacred and majestic," and "enormous, noble, stirring"—reflects a broader concern with uplifting the spiritual condition of humankind. His view of Alaska—a place "better than Kentucky" for him "to be a hermit"—is strikingly different from most others encountered in this book. The contemplative rigors of Trappist life gave this soft-spoken monk a unique perspective on civilization and wild nature, and his has been a voice sorely missed. Had Merton lived, it is possible that we would have returned, as he indicates here, to write and minister in the seclusion of a small village.

September 29: Anchorage/17th Sunday after Pentecost

. . . All this flying around Alaska has been paid for by the Bishop. We had a good talk last evening & he agreed that if I came to Alaska it would be simply to live as a hermit with no kind of parish responsibility.

September 30

Light snow in Anchorage on the last day of September.

Flew to Dillingham in a Piper Aztec (two engines), a fast plane that goes high. Bristol Bay area—like Siberia! Miles of tundra. Big winding rivers. At times, lakes are crowded together & shine like bits of broken glass. Or are untidy & complex like the pieces of a jigsaw puzzle.

Two volcanoes: *Iliamna*—graceful, mysterious, feminine, akin to the great Mexican volcanoes. A volcano to which one speaks with reverence, lovely in the distance, standing above the sea of clouds. Lovely near at hand with smaller attendant peaks. *Redoubt* (which surely has another name, a secret & true name) handsome & noble in the distance, but ugly, sinister as you get near it. A brute of a dirty busted mountain that has exploded too often. A bear of a mountain. A dog mountain with steam curling up out of the snow crater. As the plane drew near there was turbulence & we felt the plane might at any moment be suddenly pulled out of its course and hurled against the mountain. As if it would not pull itself away. But finally it did. *Redoubt*. A volcano to which one says nothing. Pictures from the plane. . . .

Dillingham—grey sky, smelling of snow. Cold wind. Freezing.
Gruening in the airport & shook his hand. Famous people are never as tall as you expect.

Night in the comfortable bishop's house. Torrent in the channel outside. Sound of water racing smooth & even at fifty miles an hour into the bay. I oversleep. Get up just in time to put a few clothes on—but not to shower—before Fr. Manske arrives (7:30) with the car to take me out along the shore. The clouds lift a little & beyond the green islands are vague, snowcovered peaks. A beautiful channel full of islands.

September 29: St. Michael

Quiet Sunday morning in the (empty) bishop's house. Anchorage. Rain. Wet carpet of fallen birch leaves. Wind. Gulls. Long road going off past a gravelpit toward Providence Hospital where I preached a day of recollection today. More & more leaves fall. Everyone's at Palmer, celebrating St. Michael & the Parish. . . .

There were three or four copies of *Ave Maria* on the table but I did not get to look at them to see if my statement on draft record burning was there [Editor of *Thomas Merton in Alaska* notes that the article referenced here was titled "Non-violence does not—cannot—mean passivity," and that it appeared in *Ave Maria* 108: no. 8, pp. 9–10]. Nor have I had any repercussions. A letter from Phil Berrigan (Allentown Prison, Pa.) was forwarded from Gethsemani [Gethsemani Abbey, Kentucky, where Merton lived]. He does not mind prison life. But demonstrations & draft card burnings are not understood: they help Wallace [George Wallace, Governor of Alabama, was seeking the presidency in 1968]. Is it possible he [Wallace] may be President? Yes, possible.

September 24: Valdez (Valdeez)

At the far end of a long blue arm of water, full of islands. The bush pilot flies low over the post office thinking it to be the Catholic Church—to alert the priest we are arriving.

The old town of Valdez, wrecked by earthquake, tidal wave. Still some buildings leaning into shallow salt water. Others, with window smashed by a local drunkard. I think I have lost the roll of film I took in Valdez & the mountains (from the plane).

Most impressive mountains I have seen in Alaska: Drum & Wrangell & the third great massive one whose name I forget, rising out of the vast birchy plain of Copper Valley. They are sacred & majestic mountains, ominous, enormous, noble, stirring. You want to attend to them. I could not keep my eyes off them. Beauty & terror of the Chugach. Dangerous valleys. Points. Saws. Snowy nails.

September 26: Anchorage

. . . I walk briefly through the streets of Anchorage, viewing the huge lift of land after the 1964 earthquake, looking out at the barges drilling for oil in Cook Inlet. The mountains to the west are hidden in fog & snow clouds. Behind the city, the tops are powdered with clean snow.

. . . Behind Palmer: Pioneer Peak, badly named, tall & black & white in the snow—mist, rugged armatures, indestructible, great. It vanishes into snow clouds as we retreat up the valley into birch flats. McKinley hidden. . . .

September 27: Yakutat

Bay with small islands. Driving rain on the docks. A few fishing boats. Beat-up motorboats, very poor. An old battered green rowboat called The Jolly Green Giant.

It is a village of Indians, with an FAA station nearby. Battered houses. A small Indian girl opens the door of the general store. Looks back at us as we pass. Cannery buildings falling down. Old tracks are buried in mud & grass. A dilapidated building was once a "roundhouse" though it is a large rectangle. After all, all there is is a long straight gravel road pointing in the mist between tall hemlocks out into the nowhere where more of the same will be extended to a lumber operation. The woods are full of moose & black bear, & brown bear, & even a special bear found only at Yakutat—the glacier bear (or blue bear).

Frank Ryman had in his lodge the skin of a wolf—as big as a small bear.

Yakutat has plenty of wolves & coyotes, besides bears. . . .

September 27: Juneau

Alone in the empty bishop's house at Junea (he has retired—the see is vacant) after concelebration, dinner & conference at the Cathedral. Driving rain, & a long spectacular thin waterfall down the side of the mountain becomes, in a concrete channel outside the house, the fastest torrent I have ever seen. It must be running fifty miles an hour into the choppy bay.

This morning—we flew in bad weather to Yakutat, came down out of thick clouds on to a shore full of surf & hemlock & muskeg. Desolate airstrip.

Frank Ryman drove us into the village to show me the village. Broken down houses, mostly inhabited by Tlingit Indians, an old fish cannery, & a small dock with a few fishing boats on a lovely broad bay with islands. Everything seemed covered with hemlock. Driving rain, mountains invisible. Frank Ryman has a quarter acre of land he offered me—& it is enough to put a trailer on. But it is right at the edge of the village. If I lived there I would become very involved in the life of the village and would probably become a sort of pastor.

We left Yakutat after dinner (at Ryman's "lodge" out at the airstrip), flew in rain to Juneau which turns out to be a fascinating place clinging to the feet of several mountains at the edge of a sort of fjord. I never saw such torrential rain as met us when we got out of the plane!

Earlier in the week; visit Cordova on Monday. The road that goes around to the back of Eyak Lake is one of the most beautiful places in Alaska—silent, peaceful, among high mountains, wild geese & ducks on the flats. Perhaps in many ways the best place I have seen so far. The bay there, too, is magnificent.

Tuesday we flew with a bush pilot—over the mountains & glaciers to Valdez. Then up through the pass in the Chugach to Copper Valley & Copper Center school, with the Wrangell Mountains beyond it. And down again through the Matanuska Valley to Anchorage.

Generous hospitality of Archbishop Ryan in Anchorage. I have been staying at his house since Tuesday night. A comfortable bed in the basement where he also has his bar. He is from New York & has a New York humor & urbanity.

Whatever else I may say—it is clear I like Alaska much better than Kentucky & it seems to me that if I am to be a hermit in the U. S., Alaska is probably the place for it. The SE is good—rain & all. I have still to go out to Western Alaska—& missed Kodiak where there is, I hear, an old Russian hermit. (Last week I saw the Russian church in the Indian village of Eklutna, up the road from the convent.)

Last Sunday I climbed a mountain behind the convent, guided by a boy who knew the trail. Very tired after it!

Wednesday & Thursday—wrote letters in the Chancery Office at Anchorage, two of them to Fr. Flavian, trying to describe Alaska.

September 28: Juneau

Green walls of mountains in the rain. Lights of the Federal Building in rainy dusk. Narrow streets ending up against a mountain. A towering waterfall snaking down out of the clouds. Green.

Bluegreen Juneau. The old cathedral. The deserted hospital. The deserted hotel. The deserted dock. The deserted school. We met Senator. Brown tundra. Low hemlocks. In the distance, interesting mountains. We flew to them, between them. Brown vacant slopes. A distance somewhat like New Mexico (flat, dark blue line). Another distance with snow covered mountains vanishing into low clouds. Lake Aleknagik speaks to me. A chain of lakes far from everything. Is this it?

 **36**

On Building a Raft

DAVID J. COOPER

In the summer of 1976 David J. Cooper (1950–   ), a doctoral candidate in plant ecology at the University of Colorado, Boulder, undertook a solitary trek of nearly 300 miles through the Brooks Range, some of the most rugged and remote mountains in Alaska. Beginning at the Eskimo village of Anaktuvuk Pass, Cooper hiked 120 miles with a 100-pound backpack to the Arrigetch Peaks, where he built a log raft from spruce trees (he had never rafted before in his life) and floated 160 miles down the Alatna River to the Athabascan village of Allaket. Certainly one of the great solo wilderness feats of all time, Cooper's perilous journey ranks with some of the folk epics of the American West. Because of his detailed scientific knowledge, Cooper's narrative provides an intimate look at the varied, and often edible, native plants of the Arctic, which include Eskimo potatoes, blueberries, fireweed, and others. The scholar Thomas Lyon has written of Cooper's remarkable narrative that "he reports his gradual assimilation to the requirements of the wild in a fittingly unpretentious, unwriterly style. He claims no great breakthrough, but simply in his learning to live with the rain there is a passage indeed."[1] In this selection, Cooper describes what it is like to build a raft from standing trees in the middle of nowhere and then float on it down a wild river where one has never been before. Four years after Cooper made his epic trip, the area through which he traveled was set aside forever as Gates of the Arctic National Park. His book Brooks Range Passage (The Mountaineers, 1982) is already considered a classic of Arctic literature.

1. Thomas Lyon. A Literary History of the American West. Fort Worth: Texas Christian University Press, 1987, 1250.

July 24

I have never built a raft and have never floated a river, though I have spent time with rivers, watching them and fishing. In Bettles, Ray Bane (one of the National Park Service men) had told me that the Kobuk natives of years ago used to hike into these mountains in the spring and spend the summer hunting, fishing, and gathering. In the late summer or fall, they would build large rafts and float down the rivers back to their village. The rivers are long, broad, and meandering. Over the years, the natives developed a design for rafts that suited their purposes. An odd number of logs is used, with the longest one in the center. All other logs progressing in jumps are a bit shorter, with the small end of each log at the front of the raft, the big end at the back. It produces a pointed rear end with an expanded width. A cross log is used to lash the raft together at the front and middle, with no crosspieces at the rear. The cross logs are tied to the top of the raft so they will not drag in shallow water. A small rack is built at the rear of the raft for stacking the gathered products of summer (my pack in this case), and a person stands near the front with a long pole to direct the movement of the raft by pushing off objects or the river bottom. The lightness of the front and heaviness of the rear would seemingly cause a friction differential, resulting in the front end going faster than the rear, and thus keeping the front forward in the flow. A square raft would go in any direction, control would be limited, and a rudder necessary.

I unfold my bow saw and take to the forest. Standing dead (but not rotten) trees are the best for my purposes because they are the driest logs and will float the longest. I locate a spruce stand that is closer to the river than other patches of forest and start looking over suitable trees. What a surprise! Almost all the standing dead trees are larger than the up to eight-inch diameter I need. It is incredible that they can grow so large this close to the tree line.

I find a suitable tree about thirty feet tall and saw through it until I almost come through the other end. Then I push on the tree several times to develop a rocking motion; it cracks and topples to the ground. I saw off the branches and the top of the tree and fasten a rope onto it. I start pulling it along the gravel toward the riverside. It is about a hundred yards from the forest to the river and the rope bites a groove in my hand even though I wear leather gloves. It is a long, slow, hard drag, the log being about fifteen feet long and weighing more than I wish to carry.

There are several little gullies lined with gravel where I must drag the log down and then up the other side. I lean forward and chug, gritting my teeth where the log catches on a large stone. When I reach a patch of sand near the river, I am able to hold the front part of the log a bit above the sand and skid the log along almost effortlessly.

Up to the riverside I drag it, each step an effort as I concentrate on maneuvering around the rocks and other obstacles that slow progress. I sit by the river for a rest and then head back to the forest to hunt for another log. I am clothed only in leather boots and gloves since days are warm and summery with enough breeze to keep mosquitoes away. Flies are more persistent, however. These huge, biting creatures never land on the front of the chest or the thighs, but always on the back of my legs, buttocks, or neck—always someplace that is difficult to swat. I jump as I walk, dancing to the music I sing and whistle, and I realize that my song has changed. Instead of singing a sad song or questioning why I am here and alone, I sing happy music, lyrics of togetherness and love. I am happy to be here building. Perhaps it is an age-old trait of man to be content when his hands and mind are busy constructing things for himself. Here I build something new, as yet unplanned, and a vessel for my future travel.

I search for another log and find one a bit larger than the first. I take it down, trim it, tie it up, and slowly drag it to the river in the fashion of the first one. I stop for a blueberry break, but find no berries in the woods, so I settle for my lunch biscuits, with honey and peanuts. I try my luck at fishing again, but the swift river shows me no strikes and no fish. I try slow pools, eddies, every place imaginable. I cannot understand why I am unable to find fish in the river.

Log dragging takes all day—solo raft building is slow work. I make it enjoyable, taking my time to choose only the logs I want, taking down only the trees that I need—no crooked, bent, rotten, or still living individuals; only the tall, straight, dead, but not rotten trees. There is an equilibrium with regard to the size of the raft. It must be large enough to float me and my gear down the river, but cannot be too large and heavy to be dragged from sandbars and shallow areas, or even to be pushed off banks and landed each evening or anytime I need to get off the raft.

I ponder a number of questions. How much buoyancy does one log have? How much weight will it float? How much water will the logs absorb sitting in the river in the days to come? Will the logs become saturated with water after being submerged by my weight? How much will the raft weigh when all the pieces are lashed together? Will I be able to budge it from sandbars if it gets caught? These questions trouble me, but as with any other questions, I answer them as best I can and trust my judgment.

I believe that farther downstream from here, the Alatna is a much slower, meandering river, with many sandbars and slow places of shallow water where a raft could get stuck, but only time will tell what I will see. These are leisurely days of construction. The warmth and sandy expanses cause me to lie in the sun. To relax is an emotional experience. Now that I am here at the Alatna, I can relax.

July 25

When I see the dew sparkling in the morning's first light, I understand why people give up money to capture a piece of this. Something so pure must be treasured.

The sun climbs over the ridge to the northeast, and with the first rays I can feel the valley warming with the streaming energy of light and heat. Sitting by the river, I eat my ration of granola with powdered milk and raisins. I watch the river's water flow away, constantly replaced by more from the infinite number of valleys, tributaries, gullies, seeps, springs, and snowbanks of this drainage system. I try to think of all the places this water could have come from and I am boggled by the number of named and nameless places and the forms the water has taken before flowering here to compose this moving body. This river's sources and resources are vast and unending, and it is comforting to know that it will not suddenly run out if one spring dries up or when one snowfield gives its last flake. This ribbon of river is the product of diversity. Water has flowed over many types of stones, leaching and carrying many types of minerals and many sediments with intricate histories, all moved again to be deposited elsewhere and begin another history.

I cut two more logs for the raft, drag them over, and put them on the sides. Then I do a final trim to make things as smooth as possible where knobs are left from cut branches. I also cut the lengths of logs to make a symmetrical V-shaped rear end (the front is cut straight across). I make crosspieces from the topped-off sections of the trees, then line it all up and decide how to tie the whole works together. I first put a bowline at the end of the rope and pass the rest through it to make a slip knot. This I place around one end log where the front crosspiece goes, and I cinch it as tightly as possible. I use ground line, which is used in commercial longline fishing for saltwater fish, principally halibut. It is nylon, with a lot of stretch, and has about a thousand-pound test strength, which I hope is strong enough. I wear my goatskin gloves to protect my hands while pulling and knotting. I put my feet on the log, grab the line, and push with my legs and pull my arms, shoulders, and back as hard and continually as I can.

I continue this for all the logs across the raft, pulling, pushing, wrapping tightly, securing the logs together. I end the line with a series of half hitches to make sure the end will not come loose. Then I lie on the sand to rest my exhausted body. I feel the sun upon my face and watch the clouds drift by. I can feel the river moving near my feet, and I know the great stride I have just taken to move with the river's flow. I had forgotten how incredible human hands are at building. I get up and lash the logs together in the middle of the raft, just as I had in the front. The most important part is to get it all as tight as possible, because the strength of the river could pull apart any flimsily tied raft. This tying and lashing, when finished, gives the whole works a solid feeling as if it were one unit of wood instead of many.

Next I find two long poles, perhaps twice my height and sturdy enough to push the raft in the current without breaking, yet small enough so I can wrap my hands around them and light enough for easy mobility. I also cut four sections of a downed tree and build the small rack on the back of the raft, lashing the rack pieces together and to the raft. It is finished. I pick up the scraps of sawdust and branches and throw them into the river.

Now I stand back and look at the result of my two days' labor, two days of pleasure, actually, it is a nine-log raft, symmetrically designed with poles and a rack, and tightly lashed—a thing of beauty, created by me to be used by me as a part of my life. I believe it just might float.

The Alatna River valley is a completely different environment from the other valleys I have seen so far. Every morning here is as cool and calm and clear as anyone can imagine. And when I look away toward the south to the great interior of Alaska or north toward the skies over the Arctic plain, I see a mist of cool air that has settled during the brief evening. As the morning heat, which proliferates in these lowlands, cause the air to rise and circulate, some moves into these mountains. Raised by orographic processes, the air heated by the day and the heat of condensation form cumulus clouds. The clouds build into whopper thunderheads that boom and blow until the landscape runs with mois-ture, the rivers with mud.

The wind picks up in violent gusts. Sand blows along the riverbank and stings my bare legs. I cover my eyes and run toward the trees as a violent downpour begins. I reach camp and huddle under my poncho for the few minutes of downpour, the few crashes of thunder, the few minutes of chill. Then it's over. My bare feet leave prints in the wet sand, the poplars drip until their leaves are dry, and the fresh smell of balsam again fills the air.

As the sun makes its way northward, dipping toward the horizon on its ceaseless circular path, all becomes cool once more. Calm returns and draws the valley into a tiny, closely related unit again. I go back to the raft and see if it needs any further work. It doesn't, and I see it waiting in anticipation of our journey. Now my thoughts run wild with ambition to travel, to try my handmade vehicle.

July 26

The day of the trial has come. I pack all my gear and haul it down to the riverside. I munch on breakfast as I lash my pack onto the raft. When all is secured and my belongings packed and ready, I sit on the shore and think. I have some fears about this part of my travels. This is my first rafting experience and I am alone, with no one around to show me how and make sure I start off right. Rivers can never be trusted. They are strong, ceaseless, and capricious. What is visible on the surface does not always indicate what is underneath, what most of the water is doing, and why. I know this can be a great way to travel, but never having floated a river, I am not sure how to make it safe.

I look up the winding valley toward the north and spots of clouds that pattern the sky, and I believe I will learn how to handle this raft very quickly. I plan to travel only a mile or so downriver to where Arrigetch Creek joins the Alatna and then hike up to Arrigetch for a few days of looking at granite pinnacles. I think back to the many days since Anaktuvuk Pass, and I christen my raft *Blueberry*. I wish I had a bottle of blueberry wine to drink (but I would never break a bottle in this valley, not even upon the bow).

I stand up and prepare to be off when I notice a slight complication to my departure. I built the raft on the sand alongside the river, not on logs that I could use to roll it into the water. How could I have been so stupid! I run around to the back and see if I can push it, but it does not budge. The raft is about fourteen feet long and perhaps five feet wide at the widest spot; the weight, I cannot guess. I have constructed a wooden blob that may be immobile. I do not want to untie the lashings, so I move around one side and try to lift it and actually get it a few inches from the ground. Swinging my body toward the river, I shove the raft in that direction, and it moves a few inches. Then I go to the other side and duplicate that motion; again a few inches. It is stressful work, but I keep up the pulling and shoving, with many sweating rests in between, for an hour or so until the front end starts to float. I take a twenty-foot section of ground line and tie it to the longest log at the rear of the raft. I use this as my reins to hold the raft as the current starts to take it downstream. I hold it near shore, then coil the line as I walk toward the raft and try to climb on. I put my foot on one side but it starts to sink, so I go around back where the stern is still on sand and step over my pack. I move forward enough so that the rear rises. I pick up a pole, push against the sand to direct us out into the river, pushing, pushing, gritting my teeth. We are free from sand and floating. Away from the bank we move!

Standing is too hard, as any motion of mine upsets the balance of the floating craft, so I kneel on the logs and use the pole to try to keep the raft pointed forward, but it is difficult. The water is deep, and in places the current is too swift. I plunge the pole into the water, feed it deeper, and then shove to right myself or change the direction of the front end. It doesn't seem to work. I must be doing something wrong, or maybe poling is used only in still water or to push off of large stones. The river seemed so fast from the bank, with water passing by rapidly. But now upon the same waters, it seems much slower. The river is broad and features are big. There is time to see obstructions and react. It is not fast water where I need to manipulate the raft constantly. I start to look around and feel comfortable about being on the river.

I float for an unknown time, a distance of perhaps a mile, until I come to where Arrigetch Creek pours into the Alatna. Poling toward the bank, I look for a place to tie the raft for the several days while I am up the creek. I see a small raised island at the riverside. There are a few spruce trees and a seemingly sheltered cove away from the current. Expansive sand and gravel bars surround it, and it looks as if it would be easy to relocate when I come back from Arrigetch. I steer toward it and grab the reins of *Blueberry*. I put my pole down and for lack of a better way of doing it, jump into the water. It is about crotch deep here and wants to pull me and the raft away, but I manage to land both of us. I tied the rear end line onto a spruce and put another line on the front for safekeeping and also tie it to a tree.

I sort through my gear and take out a few odds and ends that will be unnecessary for the next few days: the saw, bow, and arrows, among other things. I take all my food, though, afraid to leave anything that could provide a meal for a hungry animal.

I hoist my pack for the first time in three days, and it still feels a part of me. Off I walk across the expanse of open, naked gravel into the forest. Bear tracks dot the mud everywhere, and patches of dug-up earth in the forest tell me more bear stories. The forest is open, mossy. Light streams through to the ground, and there are wet areas in lowlands and depressions between small hills.

Blueberries are abundant, and I take time and great pleasure in feasting on these foods that also feel a part of me even though it has been three days since I last tasted them. I even sample the black juicy crowberries, happy to see them, though they are not nearly so sweet as blueberries.

I get to a small, open knoll and look out across the Alatna valley and up to Arrigetch. I dwell for a moment on my most recent experiences. Rafting is different from what I had expected. It is hard to steer and stay in the main current or middle of the river and away from banks, shores, and over-hanging trees. I have gone about one mile; one hundred more and I will be a raftsman. Until then, I will just try to keep afloat and intact.

Looking up toward Arrigetch, my eyes are treated to spectacular views. I raise the question of whether or not the mountains are real. I must go touch at least one to satisfy my curiosity. I plan to hike alongside Arrigetch Creek, but soon it shows its rocks, taking on cliffs and grand rapid proportions, forcing me back into the forest. Alder and willow brush is thick, and walking upon the hillsides, I follow the faint netlike patterns of moose paths that are obscured by growth. They zigzag, branching into many routes, but the moose have plowed decent paths, and I follow any route I can. I learn to follow marks, such as broken branches on alders, to note the direction of travel of these biotic bull-dozers.

These are long miles with many hills and gullies. Clouds come early this day. They are not the kind of clouds that spit rain, bend the trees with wind, and then go away, but clouds that fill the sky with darkening gray and rain. It is calm and quiet, and starts to drizzle, then rain harder. I crawl under my poncho and wait a while—one hour, two, who knows how long? I nap, awaken, eat, wait. The rain stops, then I walk. The alders get thicker and thicker as if the rain has put endless growth-inducing elements into these soils, and thickets have developed. It turns into a physical challenge to push and bend my way through these dwarf jungles.

The alder leaves are like tiny, precariously perched buckets, each one filled with the rains of this afternoon. Any movement of a branch or leaf causes them to spill. I push branches, and entire shrubs drop their water, and always I am underneath. It is too hard to walk in my loose-fitting poncho so I walk in wool, which soon is damp, then as soaked as it can be.

Mosquitoes come out in hoards and my repellent is soaked and runs all over my face, burning my eyes and lips. Water is everywhere, yet to stop in a brief opening in the forest is immediate pleasure. Berries provide sweetness and alders are green, soaked with shining silver bark. Lichens, swollen with their drinking, abound on the ground and bark. I delight in cooling off during these brief minutes and feeding my stomach and eyes. It is such a needed switch from the bruising work of crashing through alder thickets.

I head toward the creek because I think that walking on its opposite side will be much easier walking than in these alders. But the creek has cut steep cliffs and I dare not attempt to climb them. So I break through brush for the afternoon, always looking for a place to cross the crashing stream. I finally find an outcrop of flat rocks at the riverside and decide to make camp.

I find deadwood and carve it into shavings, some of which are dry. Soon a fire warms my pot of grains and my body. I try to dry my shirt over the fire, and it takes on the incredible stink of wet wool with wet smoke woven into it. I spend several hours holding my clothes by the flames, but it really is just an excuse to warm my body by fire, something I have not yet done on this trip.

This is my first really wet experience. I am soaked from the bottom of my boots to the top of my hat. But my determination to climb into this valley is not dampened, and soon I will be ready to set off again.

I do not set up my tentlike shelter this evening, thinking the rain has ended, as the sky is clearing in patches. I stretch my dry sleeping bag upon a patch of sand alongside the creek, take off my wet clothing, and crawl in. The creek here is a ribbon of rapids and falls. Water rushes over rocks, roaring into the small, deep pool below. This is followed by many loud, rolling rapids. I bathe in the sounds of the creek, living with it these many hours. It is the only noise I hear—no song of a warbler, no jet airplane, no words from a soft-spoken companion. I speak not, and hardly notice the difference between singing and humming, because either mode rings similarly in my mind.

 **37**

Here I Am Yet!

JOHNNY TAKU JACK

In this selection a Tlingit Indian recalls a lifetime of working in the outdoors in the southern Yukon and northern British Columbia. Born near Atlin, British Columbia, in April 1903, Johnny Taku Jack worked as "railway section foreman, steamboat officer, big game hunter's cook, carpenter, and maintenance supervisor." Trapping supplemented seasonal summer employment. Trapping is still a mainstay of the northern village economy, but was threatened in 1989 when European Common Market Nations, an important market for raw furs, signed a resolution banning the import of furs taken by leg-hold traps. This measure favors furs imported from the Soviet Union, where fur-farming is practiced on the scale of a small industry. The life that Johnny Taku Jack describes in this oral history, which originally appeared in Robert G. McCandless's Yukon's Wildlife: A Social History *(University of Alberta Press, 1985), may soon become a thing of the past.*

Ever since I was a kid at Atlin I started off with snares, trying to catch rabbit and even minks, weasels. It takes practice. You may set when you ask an older man how to do it. You have to regulate the size just right and you never miss. We use deadfall. In the old days they used to use sinews, thread, to make a big mesh net which they used for beaver. They used a rattle on a pole at one end where the net is tied. The rattle was made of caribou hooves. At five o'clock, about that time, the beaver are coming out. They set the net away from the house so that you won't catch the young beavers. Have to hurry and catch the beavers before he cuts the net and gets out.

When we kill the beaver we are not supposed to feed the meat to the dogs because the beaver is just like people. Amongst the fur, the wild animals, the spirit of the dead beaver goes back to the spirits of the live ones and tells them they are feeding out meat to the dogs. For that reason they get bad luck and can't catch any more beaver. The beaver meat is the kind we don't eat all the time, just once a year when the trapping season is over. That's the only meat that's not poor. Bear is good then too. . . .

In the early days beaver was really cheap. The beaver and otter skins went up when the Japanese invade Attu Island; we hear that was because they use the short fur to line the fliers' clothing. That's when the beaver went sky high, marten went up as well. One hundred and fifteen dollars for a marten skin, pale or brown just the same, they all came in one price. Beaver went up to $79 just for one pelt.

I went out hunting and trapping, I went out twenty days and came back. I had $2200 worth of beaver skins and that is more money than I ever made in five years of trapping. Twenty-four hours after I sold my furs the Hudson's Bay Company got a telegram saying no more beaver than $25 a pelt. Some trappers came in with seventy beaver, they don't get half as much as what I made.

The word got around fast. When I was coming back I saw Fred Callison. I was taking a rest because I was tired. He said, "If I was you Johnny I'd keep going. Do you know what the beaver is now? I sold there and got $79 dollars." I said, "O.K. I'm going tonight." So I left and sold them. Just in twenty-four hours, the time I would have stayed in Callison's ranch that price went way down.

In the old days if they had four or five beaver streams in their line they never used to clean them up all at one time. They used to take one stream per year and next year go on to the next. In four or five years he would come back to the first stream and have four or five litters. But nowadays these young fellows it's money, money, money. They'll take everything and they clean out their trapline.

In my time when I was a young fellow, the best price I ever got was nine dollars for a blanket beaver. That's in 1924, 1928, and we go hundreds of miles for that. But nowadays they don't because . . . it's the government; I do blame the government for that. They go and give money out to teenagers because they say "We're hungry, we've got no money, nothing!" They give them lots of money. They give them money right out. They like liquor and stay in the beer parlor. . . . It doesn't matter how much money is in the fur nowadays, they say it's not enough. At the same time the young Indian fellows they don't know how to trap. The reason why is because their father and mother don't show them how to trap.

Trapping is just like anything else, you have to practice at it which way you can make money, and you have to figure things; how many traps you're going to set. If you set a bunch of traps, you lose that many days to take care of the other traps you have set. For my part, the way I used to trap myself, fifty traps was good enough for the winter, that's including from number 0 trap to number 4 and I never used more than that. Fifty traps can keep you very busy.

Every three days I run the traps. Anything beyond three days he might cut his paw off or something else will come along and tear up the hide and you lose it. By using fifty or sixty traps you've got lots of work to do on that I've heard it said that some people had two hundred traps set out and at the end, during the winter, sometimes he lose ten skins—the animals get away or the fur is damaged.

When we go trapping, we are always happy to get what we trap before we lose it. That's how a lot of us Indians find out if we use fifty-sixty traps, even only forty traps, we do as much trapping as we did with two hundred traps because we don't lose any. But for beaver trapping, I do believe the more you put out the more you're going to get.

Sometimes when I was in the Taku River we set out beaver traps over forty miles. My partner and I were in a boat. We put sinkers on the traps. When they jump over they fall down into deeper water and are drowned. It's guaranteed you'll catch every beaver you get; even if you get him by the claw, it's drowned. The more traps you put out the more you get because you don't lose it. It's not like a dry land fur animal.

They say the government doesn't allow to sink beaver, that it's cruel. Well I do believe it's cruel to trap beaver on dry land and it suffers for two or three days. And another thing, if you shoot a beaver while he's in the trap they say you can get pinched for that because they don't allow using a rifle on the beavers. So if it's a live beaver we have to use a club on it and I think that's cruel; but that's the law, we have to follow it.

The only thing that don't fight the trap at all—and I have pity on them too—is the lynx. You could catch them even by one toe, one little claw with the trap hanging on it, it would sit there. We kind of hate to kill that animal when we catch one because he's not fighting, he'd just sit there and growl at you . . .

 **38**

Lake Dwarves and Giant Rat

ANNA NELSON HARRY

Like so many vanished peoples of this world, the Eyaks, historically residing along the Gulf of Alaska coast between Yakutat and Cordova, are no more. Anna Nelson Harry (1906–1982), the author of this story, was one of the last Eyak, a tribe that apparently never exceeded five hundred in number. Scholar Michael Kraus has written of these two stories that "One can not help comparing this pair of stories with another pair of stories, justly among the most famous, in Gulliver's Travels, published in 1726, by Irishman Jonathan Swift, specifically of course Gulliver's Voyage to Lilliput and Voyage to Brobdingnag."[1] Kraus sees Anna Nelson Harry's position as "precisely that of Swift," a "biting satire" told from the "view-point of a smaller nation" who "has seen her own Eyak people struggling to survive beside larger nations, Tlingit and Aleut (Chugach Eskimo), and has seen those in turn now threatened by a still more giant one."[2] But the stories have a greater universality, as Kraus observes, and their ultimate meaning is a simple one: "We must not take ourselves too seriously. To laugh is to survive."[3]

1. Michael Kraus, editor. In Honor of Eyak: The Art of Anna Nelson Harry. Fairbanks: University of Alaska, 1982, 37.
2. 38.
3. 38.

Lake-Dwarves

A man was out hunting on foot. He came upon some lake-dwarves. He stood there and watched. Before him, boating around, were two little canoes filled with these lake-dwarves.

Just then a mouse came out. To their eyes it was a brown bear, that mouse. The dwarves got into a scurry over the mouse. Many dwarves shot at it with their bows and arrows, until at last they killed it. Then, lo, they saw a second mouse, and they were going to kill this one too.

The man was watching that. 'Wha-? What is that?' he pondered.

After the dwarves had killed the second mouse, they landed their canoes and proceeded to tow the two mice to shore. These wee people began butchering the mice the way brown bears are butchered. They took off the skin. Then they cut up the carcass. It was quite a struggle to load that mousemeat into their boats. It took two dwarves to carry the hind-quarter, the mouse-thigh. They worked very hard until all the meat from the two mice was loaded into their boats—the ribs, the spine. They took the mouse-spine too. That lesser little mouse, for them, was a black bear.

While they were bustling about over their work, preoccupied with the mice, the man reached down and plucked up one of the wee people. He took him and tucked him under his belt.

The dwarf pleaded with the man. 'Please, these things I hunt with, I'll give them to you if you release me. They are yours if you let me go. You will become a great hunter if you free me.' The little fellow was begging the man quite pitifully. 'I will show you my weapon.' He handed it to the man. It was the size of the man's thumb, like a strawberry leaf. Then the dwarf said, 'Put this inside your rifle whenever you are going to shoot anything.' The man set him free.

The other lake-dwarves were at their boats and ready to leave, waiting for their comrade who was missing, who had disappeared from their midst. The hunter had freed him and he was running back to his people. When he arrived they asked him, 'Where are your weapons?'

'I gave them away. That's how I managed to get back here. A huge man, big as a tree he was, grabbed me. I got him to release me by giving him all my things.'

'Maybe it was a tree-man,' they said to him.

'No, no, He was a person. He was the size of a tree, though. A huge person. He was enormous. He had clothes on and he stuck me under his belt. I offered him everything to pay him off. I finally gave him my lucky hunting leaf and for that he let me go.'

'Quick! Hurry up! He'll come upon us again!'

The dwarves put out their boats, paddled across the lake, and got home.

My, how their women came running down to meet them! Their little husbands had killed a brown bear and a black bear and had come boating home to them. The little people brought the meat ashore. Although it was already evening, the women hung the meat in the curing-house, right away, just as it was. The next day they would cut it into strips. Some went to bed, but it was expected that at any time the man would come.

They had boated clear across the lake. There was no way for the man to walk across, because it was such a deep lake.

He too went home. After all, he was out hunting for black bear when he came across these lake-dwarves.

Giant Rat

A man and woman and their child were boating along, looking for berries, when they came upon the cliff where the monster reputedly had its hole.

'I wish we might see it,' said the woman.

The man said, 'Shhh! Don't ask for trouble!' And just as he spoke the rat emerged behind them, capsizing their canoe. The woman was lost. The man grabbed the child and jumped onto the back of the big rat.

It took them into its hole, where they jumped off. The man held the child. She was afraid of the monster. Nevertheless, they lived a long time with this giant monster rat.

When it got dark the rat would go out hunting. It would bring home seals and ducks for the man and his child. Then it would lie down on top of them to cook them. When the food was cooked, the rat gave it to the man and his child and they ate it. They were living this way for some time. The man would try climbing the spruce-roots which hung from above, while the rat was gone. He got out. But he knew the rat would look for them as soon as it came back, so he hurried back in. When the rat returned, they were sitting there. It lay in under itself what it had killed and gave it to the man and his child to eat.

When it was pitch-dark the rat would leave, returning as it began to get light out. One day just before it got light the man put the girl on his back and climbed out of the rat-hole. He was going along, and had not yet gotten very far, when the rat returned. It immediately missed them and started banging its tail around, knocking everything down.

The man and his daughter returned to their people safely. He told them, 'Go get some young ravens. Snare them. Snare lots of them.' They did as he asked.

When the moon was full, they went there. (The rat would stay in and never go out when the moon was full.)

They sharpened their knives and axes, packed the young ravens on their backs, and headed for the rat-hole. 'Now dump the ravens down into the rat-hole to see if they'll be quiet.' (If the birds remained quiet, that would mean the hole was empty.) Immediately they clamored. The rat jerked his tail partway down but the people chopped it off, thus killing the monster.

The rat moved forward as it died, but only about halfway out. They were going to tow it down to shore but it was too big. They had to leave it there, until a big tide came and carried it down to the shore.

The monster rat was more massive than a very big whale, and had enormously long upper teeth. Its hair was longer than a black bear's fur.

The corpse of the giant rat floated out and as it washed around, they towed it ashore. They butchered it to get the skin. When they cut it open, they found all sorts of things in its stomach. People who had been disappearing mysteriously, they now found, had been killed and eaten by this big rat. They found people's skulls in its stomach. The people butchered it for its skin. The hair was already going in some places, but where it was good they dried it.

After this, they called a potlatch and exhibited before the people's eyes what had been killing their relatives. Now, not just anyone could use the rat-skin, only a chief could sit on the monster rat-skin. At the potlatch the people kept saying, 'No cheapskate will sit on it. Only chiefs. Too many people have fallen victim to this rat. Those poor wretches, all killed. That's why only chiefs will sit on it.'

Word spread of this giant rat-skin and a tribe from some distant land wanted it for themselves. These people from another land came and made war over it. Many people died, but the rat-skin was not wrested from them. The chief who used to sit on it was the first to be killed in the war for that rat-skin. Therefore it could not be abandoned. It was of no concern to them how many would perish on its account, or how many would die in the pursuit of that skin. They fought to a finish.

When the battle ended, they took the chief's corpse from among the other dead people and put it inside the rat's tail. Then they wrapped it in the rat-skin and burned it.

(In the old days people didn't bury one another. Whoever died was cremated and his charred remains were gathered in a box.)

Thus they did to their chief's bones. But then the other tribe found out about the box and stole it and packed it up the mountain and threw it in the water.

Then there was another battle, between that other tribe and those whose chief's bones had been thrown into the water. They were all wiped out, except for old men and women and children. They killed all the young men. That's what happened to those whose chief's bones were thrown in the water.

Their children grew up and wanted revenge, but never got revenge. They got wiped out, those whose chief's bones were thrown in the water.

These people were just like each other, though living in a different land. There are people from Sitka living here at Yakutat just like we do. Though they are foreigners, they live harmoniously with us. But these people waged war over that rat-skin, people just like each other. What good is a rat-skin? They did that, though, and nothing more could happen to them, no more wars with anyone. They were wiped out completely.

 **39**

An Expedition to the Pole

ANNIE DILLARD

Born in Pittsburgh and educated in the creative writing program at Hollins College in Virginia, Annie Dillard (1945–   ) has been one of her country's most distinguished authors for nearly two decades. Her first book of prose, Pilgrim at Tinker Creek (Harper & Row, 1974), was awarded the Pulitzer Prize for general non-fiction. Later works have included poetry, literary criticism, familiar essays, and a personal memoir. She lives in Middletown, Connecticut.

This selection, originally published in The Yale Literary Magazine, was included in Teaching a Stone To Talk: Expeditions and Encounters (Harper & Row, 1983). It is in "An Expedition to the Pole" that Annie Dillard observes that the polar explorers sought at the poles not so much material accomplishment and personal fame, but, rather, "the sublime." This quest for vision and epiphany is also evident in the selection here, which is excised from the much longer parent essay that is essential reading for anyone interested in the arctic literary experience.

The Land (from Part III of "An Expedition to the Pole")

Several years ago I visited the high Arctic and saw it: the Arctic Ocean, the Beaufort Sea. The place was Barter Island, inside the Arctic Circle, in the Alaskan Arctic north of the North Slope. I stood on the island's ocean shore and saw what there was to see: a pile of colorless stripes. Through binoculars I could see a bigger pile of colorless stripes.

It seemed reasonable to call the colorless stripe overhead "sky," and reasonable to call the colorless stripe at my feet "ice," for I could see where it began. I could distinguish, that is, my shoes and the black gravel shore, and the nearby frozen ice the wind had smashed ashore. It was this mess of ice—ice breccia, pressure ridges, and standing floes, ice sheets upright, tilted, frozen together and jammed—which extended out to the horizon. No matter how hard I blinked, I could not put a name to any of the other stripes. Which was the horizon? Was I seeing land, or water, or their reflections in low clouds? Was I seeing the famous "water sky," the "frost smoke," or the "ice blink"?

In his old age, James McNeill Whistler used to walk down to the Atlantic shore carrying a few thin planks and his paints. On the planks he painted, day after day, in broad, blurred washes representing sky, water, and shore, three blurry light-filled stripes. These are late Whistlers; I like them very much. In the high Arctic I thought of them, for I seemed to be standing in one of them. If I loosed my eyes from my shoes, the gravel at my feet, or the chaos of ice at the shore, I saw what newborn babies must see: nothing but senseless variations of light on the retinas. The world was a color-field painting wrapped round me at an unknown distance; I hesitated to take a step.

There was, in short, no recognizable three-dimensional space in the Arctic. There was also no time. The sun never set but neither did it appear. The dim round-the-clock light changed haphazardly when the lid of cloud thickened or thinned. Circumstances made the eating of meals random or impossible. I slept when I was tired. When I awoke I walked out into the colorless stripes and the revolving winds, where atmosphere mingled with distance, and where land, ice, and light blurred into a dreamy, freezing vapor which, lacking anything else to do with the stuff, I breathed. Now and then a white bird materialized out of the vapor and screamed. It was, in short, what one might, searching for words, call a beautiful land; it was more beautiful still when the sky cleared and the ice shone in the dark water.

40

The Subsistence Cycle

RICHARD NELSON

 Anthropologist Richard Nelson (1941–   ) received his doctorate from the University of California, Santa Barbara, and has subsequently devoted his life to living with and studying the native peoples of Alaska. He has authored numerous works of cultural anthropology, including Hunters of the Northern Forest (University of Chicago, 1973), which documents the cultural ecology of the Kutchin Indians near Ft. Yukon, Alaska, and Make Prayers to the Raven (University of Chicago, 1983), which examines the boreal lifestyle of the Koyukon Athabaskan Indians of Huslia, Alaska.

In this selection from Make Prayers to the Raven, Nelson describes the close seasonal interaction of the native people of the Koyukon River with their environment. Although the northern forests are an austere realm that provide a meager bounty on which to live, Nelson discovered in his year among the Koyukon how ingeniously the residents have adapted to survive there. He observes also that there is "an alternative view on the nature of nature" in Huslia that "stands outside the established realm of Western science." The Koyukon have inhabited the land for many generations in a state of harmony, and Nelson concludes in his book that there are lessons for modern civilization in the quiet success of their culture: "The fact that Westerners identify this remote country as wilderness reflects their inability to conceive of occupying and utilizing an environment without fundamentally altering its natural state."

"The Subsistence Cycle" from Make Prayers to the Raven: A Koyukon View of the Northern Forest by Richard K. Nelson. Copyright © 1983 by the University of Chicago Press. Reprinted by permission of Richard K. Nelson.

The Subsistence Cycle

Life in a modern Koyukon settlement is patterned around the changing seasons, the natural cycle that is preeminent over all environmental events. Every species of plant and animal in the subarctic forests leads several different lives, each according to the season. Such are the transformations of this world, from the warm, bright, and flowing to the cold, dark, and frozen. Perhaps no creatures are more affected by this cycle than humans, who must respond both to the physical changes and to the permutations of behavior in all other living things as well.

Spring

In a sense the subsistence year begins with spring—the living environment is renewed and the seemingly endless austerity of winter is swept away on a rush of warm. (Incidentally, my dividing the year into four seasons is both a personal choice and a reflection of the modern Koyukon practice.) Spring begins with the long days of April, when snowshoe hares bask in the evening sun atop drifts at the thicket edge, where boys hunt them with light rifles. If the mountain snows have been deep, ptarmigan congregate in lowland thickets, another quarry for hunters seeking fresh meat. Caribou are also hunted in late winter and early spring, before they begin moving north out of the Koyukuk country. This is also the time for beaver trapping, when the cold is losing intensity but the ice remains thick and strong.

The Koyukon people are passionate travelers, and spring is the traditional season for long journeys. The uninterrupted daylight and relative warmth are ideal for wandering afar in search of game and taking trips to neighboring settlements. Occasionally someone chances upon a black bear, still fat after emerging from its den; or a moose may be taken if meat is needed for the breakup season. Prudent villagers also try to cut and haul a good supply of firewood before the snow softens to a quagmire.

As the season progresses, people begin watching for the earliest waterfowl, the white-fronted and Canada geese that land on newly thawed patches in the meadows. By early May the cold breaks, and flights of geese are joined by cranes, swans, ducks, and a host of smaller birds. Robin and blackbird songs drift over the melting snows, a counterpoint to the distant booming of waterfowl hunters' shotguns. Following an old tradition, some people establish spring camps at favored spots among the lakes and meadows, hunting birds, trapping muskrats, and absorbing the season's beauty.

The snow shrinks away quickly in the intense sunshine. Travel becomes difficult, then impossible. The river ice softens, lifts on the rising flood, and is carried away in chaotic floes during the early part of May. Breakup is an exciting and important event, perhaps the most dramatic seasonal transition in interior Alaska. Once the river and lakes are clear, people are again free to travel, this time with outboard-powered boats or small hunting canoes. They take a wide range of game, but waterfowl and muskrats are their primary objectives. Now, in the growing warmth, willow buds burst into new leaves, and summer is on the land.

Summer

Some families celebrate the new season by establishing camps along tributary streams, where they set nets for pike and whitefish and occasionally hunt to provide a taste of fresh meat. Summer may begin with an expedition to a favored grove for house logs, if some family member plans to begin a new home or an addition. Cutting logs and rafting them to the village is a major undertaking, usually done by a fairly large work party.

June becomes warm, then hot. Mosquitoes rise in clouds along the grassy riverbanks. Some men leave the village for wage employment elsewhere in Alaska—to work in canneries, fight forest fires, crew on the river barges, or take construction jobs. The village becomes quiet, and idle sled dogs excavate long, cool burrows to escape the heat.

After mid-June people begin watching the river for signs of the first salmon, which usually arrive near the month's end. Nets are quickly mended and made ready. Boats loaded to the gunwales with gear and supplies pull slowly away from the village, heading for fish camps. The camps are managed principally by women, who do most of the fishing and related work. They are widely scattered along the river, near eddies known for rich catches of salmon.

By early July the drying racks are heavy with split, drying fish, and children jig for whitefish attracted by offal from the cutting tables. Salmon continue running through July, abundantly in some years and poorly in others. With luck the harvest will provide enough cured fish to feed people and sled dogs over the long months of winter.

In August the chum and king salmon runs quickly fade, and a smaller run of silver salmon passes the Koyukuk villages. Fish camps vanish one by one and the racks stand empty for another year. Ambitious people begin cutting firewood from woodlots near the river, hauling the logs home in their boats. Occasionally someone may shoot a few ducks or geese, perhaps even a moose if meat is in short supply; but late summer is mostly a time for waiting. By the end of August, blueberries are ripening in the muskegs, and cranberries will be ready soon afterward. People travel to the richest patches to gather them, always keeping watch for bears after the same delicacy.

Fall

Fall is the most important season for the wild harvest. By early September the sandbar willows are a blaze of brilliant yellow and hunters know that moose are entering the rut. Men, often accompanied by their wives, travel by boat to their favorite hunting areas searching for the largest and fattest bulls. They are easy to hunt at this time because they congregate near the water, and kills can be made where the meat is readily hauled to the boat. Black bears are in peak condition and are sometimes taken too. When the hunt is over, huge quarters of meat are hung in the smokehouses to age, and the freeze soon assures that they will not spoil.

Fishing continues past the end of summer and through the time of freeze-up (in early October). Gill nets remain in the river for sheefish and late salmon and at the mouths of sloughs for pike, whitefish, and burbot. Upper Koyukuk villagers seine prodigious quantities of whitefish just before the river begins to freeze. Afterward, gill nets are set beneath the ice in certain lakes where large, rich whitefish abound. As the lakes close, ducks congregate in the river and hunters in boats try to take a few before they fly away southeast. Soon there is no open water anywhere and travel is impossible until the snow arrives. Night has come again to the northland, and winds whisper mysteriously in the new darkness.

Near the end of October the first serious snowfalls drive black bears into their dens. It is time for the most exciting, dangerous, and prestigious hunt. Men travel widely searching for occupied dens, sometimes going partway inside to shoot the animals. It is a feat of skill and bravery, and the hunters' reward is more than a rich repast of meat. The best parts of these bears are saved for winter potlatches, where the hunters receive praise and the meat is used for spiritual communion with the dead.

The last wage workers usually return home by late fall, anxious to prepare for winter. Once the supply of meat is in everyone waits for the early snows so they can start cutting wood and piling it beside their houses. As soon as the ground is whitened, snow machines and dog teams rush in and out of the village from twilight to twilight. The longest season is about to begin.

Winter

The door of winter closes suddenly with the deepening snows of early November and the onset of intense cold soon afterward. Thick hoarfrost comes as a warning; then the temperature sinks to $-30°$ or $-40°$ [Fahrenheit], perhaps colder. Firewood cutters work to exhaustion in the shortening daylight, building large woodpiles that will free them for the trapping season just ahead. Periodically during the winter they will have to replenish their supply, and on any given day from now until April someone is sure to be at work in the woodyards.

Hunting falls off in winter, especially during the recurrent spells of deep cold. But snares are set for snowshoe hares, grouse are hunted as they feed atop the tall willows on winter evenings, and flocks of ptarmigan that appear late in the season are enthusiastically sought. From time to time families may run short of meat and remedy the problem by finding a moose. Some years, caribou move into the flats or nearby mountains, and hunters search widely for this favored quarry.

But the pervasive winter activity is trapping, which provides fur for personal or commercial uses as well as delicious meat from some species. As with many Koyukon subsistence activities, both men and women participate, although the men dominate those taking place in winter. Trapping gets under way after mid-November, the early season focused on mink, marten, and fox. Lynx, wolverine, otter, and wolf are also taken during the winter. Levels of activity depend on the abundance of each, the weather, and the species that are most common in a person's trapline. Trapping is not just an occupation for some Koyukon people, it is a passion, a reconnection with the freedom of life outdoors in the wild country where they were born.

As winter gradually slopes upward toward spring, trappers shift their efforts to beaver and muskrat. Days lengthen and the sun becomes perceptibly warm. Hunting intensifies as caches run out and people seek fresh meat—moose, caribou, ptarmigan, and other small game. The burden of long confinement is lifted; people visit distant villages and talk about where they will camp in the spring.

Old-timers listen as the distant tapping of hawk owls on tree trunks echoes into the forest. They are "measuring the winter," it is said: If they tap for a long time spring will come late, but if their tapping is short the winter will soon be over.

 **41**

Gather at the River

EDWARD ABBEY

Edward Abbey (1927–1989) authored eighteen books of fiction and non-fiction, and was one of the most influential environmental writers of his time. Although he considered himself chiefly a novelist—his second novel The Brave Cowboy was made into the critically acclaimed film Lonely Are the Brave with actor Kirk Douglas—it is perhaps for his wilderness classic Desert Solitaire and his nature and political essays that he will be remembered. Abbey adopted as his twin maxims "Question Authority" and "Growth is the enemy of progress" and steadfastly resisted the loss of civilization to the forces of development. When Edward Abbey died in March 1989, his body was, according to his instructions, taken into a desert wilderness outside Tucson, Arizona, where it was buried under a pile of rocks known only to a few close friends. There is already a movement to establish a desert wilderness area in his name.

In this selection, originally published in Outside magazine and later included in Beyond the Wall (Holt Rinehart Winston, 1984), Abbey describes a rafting trip in the Arctic National Wildlife Refuge. The author's democraticizing humor is present here—he refers to himself mockingly as "the most sissified rugged outdoorsman in the West"—as are the wilderness values to which he committed his life. On the bush flight back to Barter Island he sees a herd of 40,000 caribou—the last great migratory herd of ungulates in the northern hemisphere:

> Well, I'm thinking, now I'm satisfied, now I've seen it, the secret of the essence of the riddle of the Spirit of the Arctic—the flowering of life, of life wild, free, and abundant, in the midst of the hardest, cruelest land on the northern half of Earth.

July 2

John and Mark catch a big char and a small grayling for breakfast. A fine kettle of fish.

We go for a walk up the Velvet Valley, through the willows, through the muskeg, up onto the tundra, deep into the valley. Flowers everywhere, each flower concealing a knot of mosquitoes, but we're accustomed to the little shitheads by now; they don't bother us. We rub on the bug juice and let the insects dance and hover—patterns of organic energy made visible—in futile molecular orbits one inch from the skin. Like the flies in Australia the mosquitoes here become simply part of the atmosphere, the décor, the ambience. We ignore them.

A ram watches us from a high point of rock; his flock grazes above. Mark kneels by a mountain stream trying to photograph the cross-hatched ripples of converging currents. Dana glasses the high ridges for bear, shotgun at his side. John is fishing back at the river. Mike, Maureen and Ginger are eating cheese and crackers and identifying the many flowers (with the help of a guidebook) that I have not mentioned. I sit on the grass scribbling these notes, with a clump of Siberian asters fluttering at my elbow.

Alaska is not, as the state license plate asserts, "The Last Frontier." Alaska is the final big bite on the American table, where there is never quite enough to go around. "We're here for the megabucks," said a construction worker in the Bunkhouse at Kaktovik, "and nothing else." At the bunkhouse the room and board costs $150 per day, on the monthly rate, but a cook can earn $10,000 a month. Others much more. Alaska is where a man feels free to destroy an entire valley by placer mining, as I could see from the air over Fairbanks, in order to extract one peanut butter jar full of gold dust. Flying from Barter Island to the Kongakut, pilot Gil Zemansky showed me the vast spread of unspoiled coastal plain where Arco, Chevron, and others plan oil and gas exploration in the near future, using D-7 bulldozers pulling sledges, thus invading the caribou calving grounds and tearing up the tundra and foothills of the Arctic Wildlife Refuge, last great genuine wilderness area left in the fifty United States. Under the heavy thumb of James Watt [Secretary of the Interior during Ronald Reagan's first term], the Fish and Wildlife Service apparently has no choice but to knuckle under to the demands of the oil industry. In southeast Alaska the industrial tree farmers who now run the U. S. Forest Service are allowing the logging companies to clearcut and decimate vast areas of the Tongass National Forest, home of our national bird, the bald eagle, and officially, ostensibly, the legal property of the American public—all of us. With Dracula placed in charge of the blood bank (as Congressman Morris Udall has said), Alaska, like the rest of our public domain, has been strapped down and laid open to the lust and greed of the international corporations. "Last Frontier"? Not exactly: Anchorage, Fairbanks, and outposts like Barter Island, with their glass-and-aluminum office buildings, their air-lift pre-fab fiberboard hovels for the natives and the workers, their compounds of elaborate and destructive machinery, exhibit merely the latest development in the planetary expansion of space-age sleaze—not a frontier but a high-technology slum. For Americans, Alaska is the last pork chop.

What then is a frontier? The frontier, in my view, is that forgotten country where men and women live with and by and for the land, in self-reliant communities of mutual aid, in a spirit of independence, magnanimity and trust. (As Henry Thoreau once said.) A few people, but not many—few of the natives and even less of the whites—still attempt to inhabit Alaska in such a manner. The majority, it appears, or at least the majority of the vocal and powerful, are here for the profits. For the megabucks.

July 3

Down the river, through the portal of the mountains into the foothills, approaching the coastal plain, we float northward in our little air-filled boats. Seeing that I have come back to life, the literary natives on shipboard badger me with bookish questions. I am happy to oblige.

What's the best book about Alaska. The best book about the North, I say is *The Call of the Wild*. In the words of a critic, Jack London captures there the essence of the mythos of the wilderness. No, she says, I mean about Alaska? *Winter News*, I say, by John Haines—pure poetry; and by "pure" I mean poetry about ordinary things, about the great weather, about daily living experience, as opposed to technical poetry, which is concerned mainly with prosody, with technique (one of my favorite lectures). Don't lecture me, she says, I'm talking about prose—about books in prose. (I sense a trap about to snap.) What's the best prose book about Alaska? I pause for a moment, pretending to reflect and say *Going to Extremes* by Joe McGinniss. A brilliant book. Mandatory for anyone who wants a sense of what contemporary life in Alaska is like. My opinion does not set well with the locals. No! they say. McGinniss writes only about the sensational. Alaska is a sensational place, I reply. He's a scandalmonger, they say. Alaska is a scandalous place, I say; McGinniss tells the truth. How much time have you spent in Alaska? they want to know. About four weeks, all told, I answer. They smile in scorn. Four weeks of observation, I explain, is better than a lifetime of day-dreaming. What about *Coming into the Country?* someone asks. I had to admit that I had started on that book but never finished it. More questions. I say, since I left Cherry Tree down in Tennessee, this is the first time I've been warm. McPhee, I explain, is a first-rate reporter, but too mild, too nice, too cautious—no point of view. You like Robert Service? I love him. But, says my first inquisitor, I don't think you really love Alaska, do you? The most attractive feature of Alaska, I say, is its small, insignificant human population, thanks to the miserable climate. Thanks a lot, she says. I like the mountains, the glaciers, the wildlife, and the roominess, I hasten to add—or I would if the bugs would stop crowding me. I think you are a geographical chauvinist, she says; a spatial bigot. Special? Spatial. Well, I confess, I'll admit I've lived too long in the Southwest; I should have saved that for last. Then what are you doing in Alaska? she says.

Me?

You.

Slumming, I explain.

Quiet, whispers Mark, resting on the oars. Look over there.

We look where he points. Three wolves are watching us from another bar beside the river, less than a hundred feet away. Three great gray shaggy wolves, backlit by the low sun, staring at us. Silently we drift closer. Gently, Mark pulls the boat onto the gravel, where it stops. Don't get out, Mark whispers. The wolves watch, the cameras come out, the wolves start to move away into the willow thicket and toward the open tundra. A whistle stops the last one as it climbs the bank. I stare at the wolf through my binoculars, the wolf stares at me; for one, still, frozen sacred moment I see the wild green fire in its eyes. Then it shrugs, moves, vanishes.

We drift on, silently, down the clear gray waters. After a while my friend says to me, When's the last time you saw something like that in Arizona? In your whole crowded, polluted Southwest?

Me?

You.

Moi?

Vous.

Another pause. Never did, I say.

You ought to be ashamed of yourself.

I am.

You ought to take back everything you've said.

I take it all back. (But, I think, all the same . . .)

Now the river tangles itself into a dozen different channels, all shallow. The main channel runs straight into a jungle of willow. We unload the boats, portage them and our gear around the obstruction. As I'm lugging two ten-gallon ammo cans across the damp silt I see a pair of tracks coming toward me. Big feet with claw marks longer than my fingers. The feet are not so long as mine but they are twice as wide. Double wides, size 10-EEEE. I stop and look around through the silence and the emptiness.

Old Ephraim, where are you?

He does not appear.

We go on. We camp for the day and the daytime night at what Mark calls Buena Vista—a grand view upriver of the Portal, Wicked Witch Mountain, the hanging glaciers of the high peaks beyond. Charbroiled char for supper. A female char, and Mark has saved the pinkish mass of hard roe for possible use as bait. "Ever eat fish eggs?" I ask him.

"I ate caviar once," he says.

"Only once?"

"Once was enough."

I'm inclined to agree; once was enough for me too. Caviar is cold, salty, slimy stuff—tastes like fish eggs. As Shakespeare says, caviar is for the general; let him eat it.

John and I go for a long walk into the hills, over the spongy tundra, taking one of the shotguns with us. Peacock can face his bear with only a camera; I want firepower. As we walk uphill toward the sun we see the mosquitoes waiting for us, about two and a half billion of them hovering in place above the field, the little wings and bodies glowing in the sunlight. "It looks like a zone defense," John says. But they part before us, lackadaisical atoms unable to make up their pinpoint minds, yielding before our scent and our more concentrated nodules of organic energy, as Alan Watts would say.

John is a quiet fellow, likable, attractive despite his Yasser Arafat-type beard. He tells me a little about life in Whittier, Alaska. To get to his classroom in winter he walks from his bachelor apartment in a dormitory through an underground tunnel to the adjacent but separate school building. The wind outside, he says, would knock you down; when there is no wind the snow comes up to your armpits. Yet Whittier is in the far south of central Alaska—the balmy part. (You have to be balmy to live there.) When the one road out of town is closed he buckles on touring skis and glides five miles over the pass to the railway station for a ride to the heart of Anchorage. He likes his life in Whittier. (He says.) Likes his students, the bright and lively Indian kids. Doesn't mind the isolation— he's a reader of books. Is fond of snow, ice, wind, mountains, the soft summer—bugs and icicles both. "How long do you plan to stay there?" I ask him.

"Oh, another year, maybe two."

"Then where?"

"Oh . . . back to the other world."

**42**

Yukon-Charley:
The Shape of Wilderness

BARRY LOPEZ

Barry Lopez (1945–   ) *was born in Port Chester, New York, and since the late 1960s has made his home in a small town in Oregon. His works, which include* Of Wolves and Men *(Scribner's, 1975) and* Arctic Dreams *(Scribner's, 1986) have won numerous honors, including an Award in Literature from the American Academy and Institute of Arts and Letters, the American Book Award, and the John Burroughs Medal. This selection, part of an essay that first appeared in* Wilderness *magazine in 1982, narrates a trip the author and a companion made down the Yukon River in east-central Alaska. Once an active mining region, the area has been protected since 1980 as the Yukon-Charley Rivers National Preserve. Some local residents still pursue a subsistence life-style based on fishing, trapping, and hunting, activities permitted in a national preserve. Lopez is captivated by the quiet, unpretentious beauty of the Yukon-Charley, which may not be the "Valhalla of Denali National Park" or possess "the Cambrian silence of Grand Canyon," but which has, as the author so eloquently relates, its own kind of magnificence.*

Barry Lopez, excerpted from "Yukon-Charley: The Shape of Wilderness" in *Crossing Open Ground*. Copyright © 1988 Barry Holstun Lopez. Reprinted with the permission of Charles Scribner's Sons, an imprint of Macmillan Publishing Company.

I know that cocoon feeling, wearing wool socks, long underwear, jeans, hip boots, several shirts, a down vest and windbreaker. Sitting motionless in the box of the nineteen-foot Grumman as it cuts cold water transparent as glass, I imagine I can pull my skin back from the innermost wall of fabric, pretend that I have found, by some inexplicable and private adventure, the tunnel to a strange window: I look out on what the map calls the Eastern Intermontane Plateau physiographic province, deep in Alaska's gut. Some of the peaks in the distance have no names; the water of the Charley River rides like glycerin up my fingers and over my palm, feels frigid against my wrist.

Behind us, eight miles to the east, the Charley enters the upper Yukon. Sixty miles to the north, the Yukon will pass the town of Circle, from where we have come. Another sixty miles farther on, at Fort Yukon, the Porcupine will come in. Then the Yukon will turn sharply southwest and line out a thousand riverine miles to Norton Sound and the Bering Sea. From this cartographer's sense of isolation, as though I had vibrissae or other antennae extended, I surface, aware we will hit the gravel bar ahead, haul out, and build a fire to cook, to dry socks soaked in leaky boots.

I look, as if drawn by puppet strings, to find a bald eagle dipping its hunting arc over us. Working the river. It breaks away and heads north and west into low mountains. The bow of the canoe rides up hard, rattling over the stones.

It is hours between such noises.

On shore we find again what we have known with such pleasure for days—signs of animals. Fresh moose tracks, much older bear tracks, and the bones of a grayling from some animal's meal. With 10 × 40 Leitz glasses, elbows pressed to my knees, I can see back down the river: warbonnet heads of red-breasted mergansers, long-necked pintails, the green bandit masks of male widgeon, and white, quarter-moon slashes on the faces of male blue-winged teal. Some of the birds are so far away I have to guess.

Our trip had begun that morning from a base camp on a gravel bar in the middle of the Yukon at the mouth of the Charley. The Charley's luminous black surface, crinkling in the wind, foundered in the silt-laden, war-horse current of the larger river, as far as a Dakota wheat field, a bold child slipping into a twilight clearing.

The first morning in camp on the Yukon we found fresh grizzly tracks only twenty feet from the tent, an errand that, thankfully, hadn't included us. In the benign light of an arctic summer—the two of us stood about, waking up with mugs of coffee, our shoulders to a cool wind—a beaver arrived. Huge, he slacked his stroke, circling back in the leaden sweep of the river, slapped his tail twice and moved on, his head riding the current like the bow bumper of a tugboat. I watched a marsh hawk alone far to the west, a harrier, unload itself repeatedly against the wind in somersaults and chandelles and remembered the erroneous summary of the field guide: ". . . the flight low, languid, and gliding." He flew as if his name were unrecorded.

That morning, too, as I pulled on my boots, a wolverine walked into camp, looked us over, stabbing the air with his nose to confirm what he saw: dead end. Bob and I stood up, as though someone important had walked in, his arrival as unexpected as the smell of cinnamon.

The Charley and the Yukon, the beaver, the widgeon, the grizzly, lie within a federal preserve, created by emergency presidential order under provisions of the Antiquities Act and designated Yukon-Charley Rivers National Preserve on December 2, 1980. Among the reasons for this laying by: an exemplary weaving of interior Alaska flora and fauna. Untouched by Ice Age glaciation, the land has a high potential as a reservoir for undisturbed early aboriginal sites. The area is rich in fur-trapping and gold-mining history. And it offers protection for an entire watershed, that of the Charley, and for peregrine falcons, who nest on the high bluffs that rise along this part of the upper Yukon.

The landscape itself, however, the pattern of birch and spruce and creeks spreading over the hills and up into the steep mountains where sheep dwell, shows no sign of the designation. There are no green park buildings, no managers, campfire circles or roads. Instead there is the trace evidence of thirty or so people living here, placer miners and subsistence trappers whose predecessors have been in the vicinity for more than eight years. Their cabins are spotted every six or seven miles along the Yukon; the colored floats on gill nets bob close by on the khaki-brown surface of the river—salmon nets, winter food for their dogs. At Coal Creek and Woodchopper Creek, the two working mines, crude landing strips have been bulldozed near a few buildings; the mills and the rest of the improbable heavy machinery were brought into the country by barge. Supplies come to this part of the river now by skiff, canoe, dogsled, or snow machine, depending on the season and one's circumstances, down from the roadhead at Eagle, 105 miles above the mouth of the Charley, or up from Circle.

Until someone forces them to change their way of life, to give all this up and quit the country, the Yukon-Charley Rivers National Preserve will, in residents' minds, remain little more than a colored panel on someone else's map. The formal setting aside of this land, in fact, represents to them an incomplete understanding of the country.

When we shoved off from camp that morning on the Yukon we took most of our gear in the canoe with us, a nuisance, but a necessary precaution against bears, who might shred it or drag it off into the river.

The sight of the broad back of the Yukon in mid-June triggers a memory of the Nile or the Amazon; but breakup ice is piled in shattered rafts the size of freight cars along the shores. The banks have been deeply gouged, the bark scraped from trees to reveal gleaming yellow-white flesh beneath. Silt boils against the canoe, a white noise that is with us until we cross half a mile of open water and hit the Charley. Its transparent flow, turned against the downstream bank of the bigger river, narrows to nothing after a thousand yards, absorbed.

The mouth of the Charley—its name oddly prosaic, a miner's notion, fitting the human history of the region—is a good place to fish for pike or burbot. (We bait a trotline for burbot, a freshwater cod that looks like a catfish. We will check it on the way out.) The flats of the river's floodplain, several square miles, are dense with an even growth of willow, six to eight feet high. The undersides of the long, narrow leaves are a lighter shade of green than that above; their constant movement, a synaptic fury in the wind, makes them seem all the more luminous. Moose are bedded down among them, beyond the reach of our senses. Their tracks say so.

The river's banks, flooded with an aureate storm light underneath banks of nimbus cloud, are bright enough to astonish us—or me at least. My companion's attention is divided—the direction of the canoe, the stream of clues that engage a wildlife biologist: the height at which these willows have been browsed, the number of raven nests in that cliff, a torn primary feather which reaches us like a dry leaf on the surface of the water. Canada goose.

What is stunning about the river's banks on this particular stormy afternoon is not the vegetation (the willow, alder, birch, black cotton-wood, and spruce are common enough) but its *presentation*. The wind, like some energetic dealer in rare fabrics, folds back branches and ruffles the underside of leaves to show the pattern—the shorter willows forward; the birch, taller, set farther back on the hills. The soft green furze of budding alder heightens the contrast between gray-green willow stems and white birch bark. All of its rhythmic in the wind, each species bending as its diameter, its surface area, the strength of its fibers dictate. Behind this, a backdrop of hills: open country recovering from an old fire, dark islands of spruce in an ocean of labrador tea, lowbush cran-berry, fireweed, and wild primrose, each species of leaf the invention of a different green: lime, moss, forest, jade. This is not to mention the steel gray of the clouds, the balmy arctic temperature, our clear suspension in the canoe over the stony floor of the river, the ground-in dirt of my hands, the flutelike notes of Swainson's thrush, or anything else that informs the scene.

A local trapper advised us against the Charley. Too common, too bleak. Try the Kandick, he said, farther up the Yukon. I did not see a way in the conversation—it was too short, too direct—to convey my pleasure before mere color, the artifices of the wind. My companion and I exchanged a discreet shrug as we left the man's cabin. Differing views of what will excite the traveler.

At Bonanza Creek, while our socks dried by the fire, we fished for arctic grayling. Our plan had been to go twenty-five or thirty miles farther up the Charley, to where mountains rise precipitously on both sides and we might see Dall sheep with their lambs, or even spot a new species of butterfly (a lepidopterist in Fairbanks, learning of our destination, had urged a collecting kit on each of us). We abandoned the plan. Mosquitoes got to us as the river narrowed, and it was a banner year for them. Step a few feet into the bush and hundreds were on you. Insect repellant only kept them from biting—and they quickly found an un-sprayed spot where cloth hugged skin close enough to let them drive home, so often the inside of a thigh. Nothing to be done about their whining madly in the ears, clogging the throat, clouding one's vision.

The memory of our windswept campsite on the Yukon, far from shore, a gravel bar without vegetation and so mosquito-free, passed wordlessly between us. We put on dry socks, cleaned two grayling, folded our 1:250,000 physiographic maps, and swung the Grumman downriver.

**43**

Cape Prince of Wales, Alaska: A Suite

JOHN MORGAN

John Morgan (1943–   ) studied poetry at Harvard
under the Pulitzer-Prize winning poet Robert Lowell
and was awarded the Roger Conant Hatch Prize for lyric
poetry. He has received the Academy of American Poets' Prize at the
Iowa Writers' Workshop and has won the Discovery Award of the New
York Poetry Center. His books of poetry include The Bone-Duster
(Quarterly Review of Literature, 1980), The Arctic Herd (University of
Alabama Press, 1984) and Walking Past Midnight (University of Alabama Press, 1989). He has taught at the University of Alaska since 1976.

In this poem John Morgan writes of one of the most remote locations
in Alaska, if not in the world—Wales, Alaska—a village which occupies
the point in the United States closest to the Soviet Union. Elsewhere he
has observed of this harsh polar world that "in fact not winter but
summer is the alien season here." John Morgan portrays in this poem a
native culture in upheaval. There is a bathtub in a B. I. A. house with no
plumbing, a current catalog from Sears only thirty miles from the
Russian border, a D. E. W. radar installation above a whaling community that has existed along the coast since before European civilization
began. He takes a whale vertebra with him back to the interior, a
powerful symbol evoking the travail and splendor of the land of the
Eskimo.

Dead Walrus on the Beach

The Cessna that flew me in
skimming the coast
banked around those
rocky points of land and
moved in close
where a dead one was
its flesh thrown up
by the sea. We'd
hoped for tusks
but this bulk without a head
a white suffused with brown
too much to move, too dead
to eat—what's to be
done with it?
         Like a compact
car, you can't tell
front from back. Seagulls
probe for entry
into its rotting entrails
and I am appalled by the smell.

Zip Code

At Wales, to the west of the weather
the islands crowd toward tomorrow.
My Eskimo host, the
postmaster, sports a digital
watch and smokes as he talks:
"I collect records. You
pick up the phone, call
Anchorage and have the
albums you want within six days."
At the tarpaper shack

where he works an arrow on the wall
pointing west says, "Russia
30 Miles." He wears a
wispy beard, a black moustache,
black shoulder-length hair like me:
Wales, Alaska—99783.

Subsistence

Seal for dinner, and after
when cranes in a lopsided "V"
honk over, someone
runs outside and takes a shot.

B.I.A. Housing

Eight calenders on the walls, no
plumbing. The bathtub stocked
with laundry, Pampers, a rusted
two-gallon can, towels, rags, Friskies,
and that fancy oval makeup box:
"Cardin." Here you sit
on the plastic "Honey-pot" above
a disposable plastic bag; but
there are amenities: two stoves
in the kitchen, radio,
CB. For reading, *National
Geographic, Ski-Mobile, Newsweek,*
or the current catalog from Sears.
Outside, the kids play soccer,
basketball, climb on the
roofs. Inside, the Eagles gloat
"The Greeks Don't Want No
Freaks" on the hi-fi.

A Village Littered with Bones

Walrus, whale, and seal
vertebrae and ribs—bones of all
sizes going back

to the sand. 130 people
on a spit of land
in an arctic sea: how
elemental it must
be when winter closes in.
But August's dull, a rainy
fall. Come January: dogsleds,
skiing, skating, snow-
machines. Chop a hole
in the ice and drop
a line. Vent
a snow-tunnel out to the street.
No fragile enterprise
under cold, shifting skies: snow
is the Eskimo's element.

Neighbors: Gossip

In the next town, Shish-
maref, some sixty miles off
you hear they bought a truck, paid
double the purchase price
to ship it in. Then
just last week the son
of the village mayor
who didn't know about gears crashed
into the town hall—bad luck.
This winter flying up
to Shish from Nome, Walter's
cousin went down in the hills: half
a dozen people killed, never
found her body or her
baby's. There's a lady
in that town, dug in the
mound behind the village, found
carved fossil ivory
worth fifty thousand bucks.

Privilege

I find my moods are
jagged as the rocks. Today I climb
through tundra to the ridge

two hours toward the sun. A blessing
on you snowbirds,
arctic hare. There
on a farther ridge—radar—
a disc of silver rivaling the
sun, staring at its double
like a loaded gun across the strait.
On a boulder I sit and muse.
Away to the north a lagoon
lies flat and gray. Those
water-borne cliffs to the west:
Siberia. Awed by this place
the top of my head comes loose
and tears assault my eyes. Hairy
with impending ice-ages
I see the past arriving at
our shore: mammoths, mastodons,
and man. All
times are crowded into this
small village, its
magic, my privilege.

To Fish Camp

I stand by a tractor
hitched to a flat-bed
truck. On it a boat
and in the boat brown
plastic bags full of gear.
Four people sit on the bags,
two wearing holstered guns
and one of them is White:
someone who stayed. A large tan
dog is hoisted up
shivering with excitement
at his luck
as they drive off to camp.

What to Bring Away?

I can name it: behind
the Weyapuks' house, discarded

among sand-grass, a large
whale vertebra from that
bowhead they got last spring.
It must be
twenty inches across the beam,
a rich and creamy brown and
nobody seems to claim it.

The Frame

Next day, wind and mist.
I lug my suitcase, sleeping
bag, my whale bone
to the air-strip. I seem
to need another hand
for this. Alone in the sheet-metal
hanger I stand and wait
listening through fog
for the buzz of my plane
two hours late. I love it
here but I can't stay.
My trip takes on a frame.
I feel it going deeper
like a dream, its
salt in my pores. Flo Weyapuk said
when I asked about that
bone, a bit puzzled, a bit
amused: "You found it. It's yours."

 **44**

This Tangled Brilliance

DAVID RAINS WALLACE

The author of eight works of natural history and one of fiction, David Rains Wallace (1945–   ) has, in the words of author John Muste, established himself "firmly in the front rank of naturalist writers." Twice the winner of the Commonwealth Club of California's Silver Medal for Literature, Wallace also holds the John Burroughs Medal for Nature Writing, awarded for The Klamath Knot (Sierra Club, 1983). Wallace was born in Virginia and educated at Wesleyan University and Mills College. His articles and essays have appeared regularly in Sierra, Wilderness, The New York Times Book Review, and other national periodicals. The editor of this book had the pleasure of accompanying Mr. Wallace on a vigorous day hike in Denali National Park on June 10, 1989, and can attest to the fact that he is a tireless bon vivant on the long march and can spot grizzly bears at distances of up to one mile. He lives in Berkeley, California.

"This Tangled Brilliance," the title echoing Darwin's image of "this tangled bank" in the last paragraph of The Origin of Species (London, 1859), is an acutely observant portrait of nature along the coast of southeastern Alaska. The author brings all of his descriptive skills to bear in this piece, and artfully excludes any human references—save the jet contrail—from this pellucidly clear picture of wild nature.

Summer sunsets last much of the night on the fjords of southeastern Alaska. The sun does not stay up all night, as it does above the Arctic Circle, but darkness is very late in descending.

A little shoreline meadow on Stephens Passage glowed in the slanting sunlight of a late afternoon in July. The wet climate and long days had packed the slope between the salt water of the passage and the trees of Tongass National Forest with oversized cow parsnips, dandelions, and ferns. Pale paintbrush, a wildflower whose greenish-yellow bracts are barely tinged with the scarlet of its mountain relatives, grew several feet tall. The dark purple blossoms of Indian rice (so called for the masses of small, edible tubers at its roots) stood out like dark stars against this tangled brilliance.

The shade of the forest's Sitka spruce, western hemlock, and alder seemed very dark in contrast to the meadow, but there were flowers there too—orderly beds of white clintonia and spiky devil's club. A small porcupine was climbing one of the alders. When it reached a height to its liking, it pulled a leafy branch to its mouth with its forepaws. The hairs on its forehead drooped and nodded as it munched the leaves. Its footprints in the soft earth at the base of the tree resembled a human baby's.

The meadow was rich in odors as the afternoon breezes stirred the air. The forest exhaled dim odors of mold and spruce gum that mingled with spicy meadow herb fragrances and fishy, rocky smells from the shore. The tide was out, and the sea smells were accentuated by piles of damp seaweed and the decomposing remains of a harbor seal.

The meadow overlooked a small cove, a crescent of sand and granite boulders overgrown with rockweed and red algae. Both ends of the crescent were walled with steeply upended rock strata from which the tides had eroded the boulders. Little tide-pools lay in the crevices—reminders that the sea had released the rocks only temporarily. Shore crabs with neat, white leg-joints sidled about in the pools, and tiny yellow blennies—fish especially adapted to life in tidepools—hid in the rockweed. They were slender as eels and so well camouflaged that only their movements revealed them.

Another species of blenny that lived in the tidepools had evolved a very different camouflage strategy. They resembled the members of a large mussel colony, being exactly the right dark blue color when they lay in the shadows of the colony (although they were light green in sunlight), and having on their bodies blotches of bone white that perfectly mimicked the barnacles growing on the mussels. They are aggressive fish, chasing their companions about their small niche and rising to the surface at every falling speck. Soon they would have to retire deeper into the mussel beds, however; the tide was beginning to come in, bringing larger predators.

The tide came in gently because the cove was screened from the open Pacific by the massive bulk of Admiralty Island, visible a few miles across Stephens Passage. As the tide slowly rose in the cove, the snow cornices on Admiralty's distant peaks became tinged with orange. The island became a backdrop for a crowded stage as dozens of shoreline creatures came out for the evening feeding period.

A flock of gulls circled above a school of fish, and a bald eagle flew past them toward its nest in a spruce just north of the cove. The eagle whistled and chattered like an overgrown songbird as it wheeled about the untidy platform of sticks built halfway up the tree. Just off the cove a guillemot in black and white summer plumage stretched its wings, then dove underwater. Two gray-headed arctic loons sat placidly on the surface.

A humpback whale spouted in the deep water. The sound of its exhalation reached the cove several seconds after the white spume and dark back had subsided into the quiet water. The little guillemot surfaced. Gull cries drifted across the water. On the shore, a strangely bedraggled red squirrel ran along one of the big drift logs that separated the meadow from the beach. It passed this way most evenings. When it reached the end of the log, it followed a well-beaten trail back into the trees.

The light on the meadow and its surrounding trees grew intense as the sun sank toward the Admiralty peaks. A blue-needled spruce sapling seemed to crackle with electricity at the top of the meadow. The granite boulders on the shore took on an orange glow, and the snowfields on Admiralty began to turn pink. A raven croaked in the trees.

Three whales surfaced in quick succession. One of them held its flukes in the air for a long moment before sliding ponderously out of sight. The gull flock had drifted westward, and two eagles appeared to prowl along its edges. One of the eagles swooped and stole a fish from a gull, then fled in the direction of the nest north of the cove. Three gulls pursued a little way, screeching in annoyance, then gave up and flew eastward over the meadow. There was a rocky inlet in that direction where tired gulls could rest.

The gentle rise of the tide had been accelerating, and all at once the rockweed that had been drying in the sun was waving underwater. At the same time, the sun began to leave the cove. The light weakened and faded first on the sand and granite, then on the meadow. It lingered on the trees, though, and clouds of excited midges danced in its brilliance. The air grew cooler, and a breeze arose to ruffle the newly risen water. It carried a salty smell deep into the trees.

There was an abrupt fading out of the light. Shadows crept to the treetops in a few minutes. The sun had set on the cove, although it still shone full on the mountains of the Glass Peninsula of Admiralty Island. The circling gulls appeared black against the illuminated peaks. The bald eagle that remained was distinguishable from the gulls by its longer, slower-moving wings.

The breeze died down, and the water of Stephens Passage became very smooth, mirroring the orange of the sky and the silver of the peaks. Sounds were emphatic in the stillness. A squirrel scolded in the trees. A fish jumped, then jumped again. A boat passed along the shore, heading north to Juneau. After it was out of sight, its wake splashed into the cove, tossing tufts of salt rush that grew at the water's edge. Even the rustle of a vole running through the meadow seemed loud. It was getting chilly, and no insect calls masked the other sounds.

The bald eagle left the gull flock and headed for the nest. Larger size and harsher cries identified it as the female of the pair. The chatter of the circling gulls sounded clearly over a mile of water. Two ravens flew over the cove, calling softly to one another. Their calls were so precisely enunciated and inflected that they might have been conversing.

"Kah. Koo-ah pah."

"Kapa. Koo-ra ka."

The shadows reached timberline on the Admiralty peaks, intensifying the contrast of forest and snowfield. The sky was red at the horizon, and the water paled from silver to platinum. The darkening had slowed considerably, however, and the rosy light stayed on the mountaintops a long time. Small clouds appeared, also rose-colored, and drifted eastward above the peaks.

A whale reared its bulk halfway out of the passage, making an explosive sound as it toppled back into the quiet water.

"Whump!"

The harsh cry of the female eagle came from the nest. The male eagle was flying over the cove at that moment, and he turned his head to glance back at his mate before veering across the water toward the gulls. A pair of guillemots fluttered along the shore and landed in the cove. The dove-sized, penguinlike birds rested on the water for a moment, ducking their heads with quick, rhythmic movements as though to make sure their feathers were fully waterproofed. Then they dived underwater in search of fish.

Colors shifted again as the light faded from the highest peaks. The little clouds on the horizon darkened to purple, the mountains to blue, and the water reflected them to green. For a moment, a jet climbing from Juneau caught the sunlight, and it left an indigo vapor trail across the sky. Away from the green land shadows, the passage waters glowed a very faint orange.

The final descent of the sun affected the gulls. They stopped fishing and began to circle upward in a column that soon rose high above the peaks. The male eagle remained among them, which seemed a not-altogether intelligent thing to do since there were no more fish to steal. Gulls swooped at him from time to time, but he merely ducked away. Perhaps he simply enjoyed being part of the ascending throng.

Suddenly the entire southwestern sky turned bright coral except for the dark seam of the jet vapor trail. Two swallows flitted past the cove, and one of the guillemots rose from the water and flew after them. The white of the guillemots' wings was still discernible, but the trees around the cove and the outline of the distant mountains were becoming vague. The pink sky faded to dull violet as suddenly as it had flared up.

The breeze came up again, raising leaden swells along the shoreline of the cove. A mink emerged from the forest and loped down to the water's edge, making tiny scampering sounds on the sand, driftwood, and stones as it hurried along. It didn't pause to look about or even sniff the ground. Like the red squirrel, the mink had a habit of passing this way at a certain time of evening. It followed the same well-beaten trail back into the forest. It was a diminutive predator, and seemed hardly larger than the squirrel.

The alder trees tossed in the breeze, but the spruces and hemlocks only stirred stiffly and sighed. Grunts and crunching sounds from one alder indicated that the small porcupine was still feeding, oblivious of the gathering darkness. Darkness was welcome to the deer mice that lived in the forest; the meadow's edge resounded with patterings and bumps as they emerged to look for seeds and berries.

A buoy lit up across the passage. The water was dim and gray now, a gulf broken only occasionally by the fluke of a spouting whale. The whales' ponderous breathing sounded close in the dimness, as though the great animals were rising just outside the cove.

The tide was in. It covered the sand beach completely, and its wavelets lapped at the driftwood logs. The sloping garden of wild-flowers was a vague, greenish mass beneath the black of the trees. Some buzzing creature, sphinx moth or hummingbird, paused above a lacy cow-parsnip umbel for a moment.

The seam of the vapor trail was reversed—a pale streak against the dark sky. Directly above the cove, the first small star began to shine. It was past midnight.

 **45**

Haida Hunters and Legend of the Two Fin Killer Whale
(told in Haida)

GEORGE HAMILTON,
collected by VESTA JOHNSON and
translated into English
by ERMA LAWRENCE

George Hamilton, a Haida Indian from Craig, Alaska, died in 1984 at the age of 101. The Haida, together with the Tlingit Indians, historically were present throughout the many islands and mainland of southeastern Alaska. They are perhaps best known for their elaborately carved cedar totem poles, freestanding wood sculptures used for ceremonial purposes throughout their homeland. Both the Haida and the Tlingit made their livings primarily from the sea, and early Russian explorers were often met by large numbers of their dugout war canoes. The Tlingit and Haida felt a special kinship with various animals—including the raven and the bear—as well as the more prominent sea mammals, as is evidenced here as fishermen come back transformed, in a process resembling that which informs Ovid's Metamorphoses, as killer whales.

"Haida Hunters and Legend of the Two Fin Killer Whale," "Shag and the Raven," and "Story of the Double Fin Killer Whale" reprinted with permission from Erma Lawrence.

Right below Howcan, there's a little village they call "K'wii Gandlaas." Our uncles used to live there. The schooners would come there and they would go up North to go hunting. Haidas were good hunters so they would take them clear up to the Bering Sea. They would be gone for nine months. After that they would come back. They would bring back blankets, and food. That's all they got paid. When our uncles went back up there, I don't remember their names, one of them said, "If we don't come back, we will come back as Killer Whales, but we will have two fins, it will be us," they said.

Sure enough, late in the fall they were lost at sea and never found. During the winter, some children while playing outdoors became very excited. They saw Killer Whales with two fins. Everyone ran outside to see it, as the two fin Killer Whales circled around in the bay. That's how we claim the Killer Whale with two fins.

 **46**

Two Great
Polar Bear Hunters

ALOYSIUS PIKONGANNA

King Island, located in the Bering Straits midway between Alaska and Siberia, is inhabited by a small permanent population of Inupiat Eskimos. These residents
rely on marine resources, including bowhead and beluga whales,
walrus, migratory birds, and seals, to sustain themselves. In this story
Aloysius Pikonganna (1909–1986) evokes the mysterious spirit of the
arctic wilderness in the form of an immense polar bear hunted by two
King Islanders on the ice pack.

"Two Great Polar Bear Hunters" and "The Cormorant Hunters" reprinted with
permission of Gabriel Payenna, Chief, King Island Native Community, Nome, Alaska.

Avuk was along when the men went out hunting on the ice; Kuguk had started out earlier. At King Island we'd go out hunting on the ice before daybreak. That is how they used to be.

Near Land's End Avuk went down and left the shore ice, walking out onto the pack ice. Earlier, someone had gone down onto the pack ice before him. But what was that? There he saw large tracks, the large tracks of a polar bear. [Land's End is a high cliff on the east side of King Island.]

"Oh dear!" he thought. "That man who set off earlier is all alone." Following his tracks, he started after him.

He set off. The other man had started walking in the right direction; he had walked down onto the ice in front of King Island. Then, when it had gotten lighter—coils of sealskin rope are big and round and can be worn here around the neck—Avuk took off his coil of sealskin rope and placed it down on that polar bear's tracks. The coil fit inside. He knew, therefore, that it was a very large polar bear.

Avuk spent all day following the tracks. He tried not to catch up to the two who were ahead of him and tried not to be seen by them either. It was his idea to take his time tracking them. Only after going far out from shore, from a large ice pan he climbed to the top of a tall ice pile. Down there! Way down below two forms stood out in the middle of an ice pan. The tracks led to them. He went to where they were.

Both of them were completely exhausted. Not far from the man, the polar bear lay completely exhausted. And there was the man, lying flat on his face. (They say of them that they were foaming at the mouth.) Bubbles and froth had come out of that man, until his head was covered. From there Avuk went over to the polar bear, which was in the same condition. They had both become exhausted these two—the polar bear and the person—at the same time.

When he went over to the polar bear from there, Kuguk's companion [Avuk] said to him, "Come on now, stand up! Put a cut in at least. Then I will kill it." [To cut one's prey is to declare ownership.]

"No, I am unable to do it. You go ahead and kill it; I am unable."

This is the way it happened; they were like people quarreling. He didn't want to do it, the one who had been following the animal all day. Then, when it was clear that the other man was unable to do it, Avuk killed it himself. The two of them cut a piece from its rump. It is said that Kuguk was amazed by the size of it. (Both of them were very large men.) He cut off the bear's head.

He set the head right down in front of him. He was a big man and must have had very long legs. Like this it is said, he set down in front of him what could only have been a very large head. (I am a small person.) It was this big. He was able to grab the ears, it is said, only if he stretched. That is how large the polar bear was.

Kuguk said to the other man, "Let us take this head back with us." He was utterly amazed by its size.

"Definitely not," said the one who had followed him. "No." It would take up all the space for the meat. He [Kuguk] wanted to bring it back so that it could be seen by people for a long time. Then they got their bearings and checked the weather and their location, since night was coming on. Far behind was King Island; they were "giving it a drink"!

Those that go far out on the sea are said to be "giving King Island a drink," for in the distance are seen the two peaks with the gap between them, far above the shore of the island, and when the sea appears to be at the level of this low spot between the peaks, it is said of those who see King Island this way that they have "given it a drink."

Despite everything, the two men started back when they were ready. After a while night fell, but it was still possible to see. They hadn't been traveling long. Then, from the west came a call.* "Oh my!" Kuguk said to his companion. "Oh my! We are not the only ones to have night fall upon us!" The other agreed. Although it did not sound to him like a human, he agreed. They continued to pull their catch along behind them.

As they pulled it along, Kuguk kept turning to look back in different directions. There it was, the thing they thought they had heard. A giant polar bear was walking along. Its snout just touched the ground below as it walked along. Then, it is said, when it reached the trail they had made as they pulled their catch behind them, it rolled over on its back and lay there. There it was lying on its back, and then it headed east toward Twin Peaks on the mainland. Then it was gone, that one!

From a distance, not far away, it made the call they had heard before. They found out later that this giant polar bear was not to be killed. But even so, it is said, Kuguk said to his companion "Shouldn't we try to get that one?" His companion said he did not want to do it, lest they get hurt. Perhaps they would have been able to kill it as the first man had suggested. "He might hurt us," the other had said. [Aloysius Pikonganna laughs.]

* [The call sounded like that of a hunter who has made a kill.]

47

The Cormorant Hunters

FRANK ELLANA

In this selection Frank Ellana (1904–   ), a King Island Eskimo, tells of a different kind of wilderness—the wild reaches of the human heart—in a tale of infidelity and murder that could have been taken from Greek mythology of drama, so intensely tragic is it.

Reprinted by permission of Gabriel Payenna, Chief, King Island Native Community, Nome, Alaska.

There were a husband and wife, the two of them, one fall. In those days, people used to go to get cormorants from the northeast point of the island, northeast of Putu [Putu is a large cavity in the cliffs along the eastern shore of King Island], from the cliff there. It is a very steep cliff. The base of it is not bad, though; it has a place where you can walk.

The top part is very steep, and the base has a place that can be walked on. The cormorants would sleep, with their big long necks thrust under their wings.

In the fall, then, when the sea was rough and the north wind was blowing strong, the two people climbed up, up to the northeast point of the island at night.

While the birds were asleep, the man tied a length of yearling walrus rope to himself. A person would wind it around his own waist here, and would lower himself down the face of the cliff. Another person would not lower him, because if the rope rubbed it could be heard by the birds. He would lower himself, after removing his mukluks.

When he reached those sleeping cormorants, he pressed down on one, along its neck, and when it began to kick, he yanked it out.

Killing them one after another, this is how they hunted cormorants. When there are ten of them, they are very heavy, when a person tries to climb back up with them. They hunted even at night, those people of long ago.

The husband and wife went to the cliffs. Then, leaving his wife behind, the husband went down. He went down! The sea was very rough down there, at the foot of the land. He fell. When he fell, he began to whirl the walrus hide rope around in the air. Making the rope go around like this, whirling it around, he came to a stop. By whirling it around, he began to move upward. He went upward. Perhaps the wind helped him, for it was very windy. He went up, whirling his rope around, through the air, over toward Qulaġuq, the pinnacle of rock that rises above the cavity Putu; right above it is Qulaġuq. He landed on the tip of it. Coming up from the cliffs far down below. He landed there and came to rest. It is precarious and dangerous, that Qulaġuq. When he could find no way down, he attached that walrus hide rope, since there was a place to tie it. He went down using that rope.

Then he went home. He made it home suspecting nothing—made it to his walrus-skin-covered house there; when he arrived he started down toward the door. He went in. There was his wife up above, with her exchange husband. This wife of his, by untying him, had caused her husband to fall. Her exchange husband was up there, and his wife. When he spotted the two of them, he just stood there. The other man was unsure of what to do and wished to go out, her exchange husband. He thought about going out head first [King Island houses had a small, narrow door about three feet high which a person could not walk through upright. The bottom of the doorway was at about the level of a person's knees]. He'd get stabbed by the one out there! He thought about going out feet first. He'd get stabbed! Then, after thinking it over, he gave up. "Well, let him get me, that one out there," he thought. Feet first, he cautiously started out. When would the knife strike him?

Without being struck, he got through the doorway. He stood up. With his back turned, the cormorant hunter just stood there. The other man went down to the outer door and left. The cormorant hunter did nothing to his wife. All winter long, he gathered animal hides, he gathered walrus rawhide rope, he gathered hides. He never showed any ill will toward his wife.

When spring came and the ground had thawed, inviting all the King Islanders, he led them up the island. Over there, to Naniurait [Naniurait is a flat rock on the east side of the crest of King Island. It is surrounded by rock on two sides and has a sheer drop on another side]. Behind the outcroppings of rock known as Siukazuit, he stopped with them. He cut up the hides, and the couple cut lengths of rope and passed them out to the King Islanders. When they were through, the people started to dance. After they had danced on and on, he began to taunt and poke at his wife with his drumstick. His wife did not respond. He continued to taunt and poke at her, and when his drumstick broke, he used his drum. He broke his drum on his wife. When he had broken it, he began to beat her. He beat her to death. When she was dead, he threw rocks at her. Whatever rocks he could manage, he threw at her. Finally the woman could no longer be seen, because the rocks had covered her. When he had finished with her and she could no longer be seen, with a cry of victory, he ran down to the sheer cliff at Naniurait. Beneath those outcroppings of jagged rock, Siukazuit, there is a sheer drop, like this. Running down with a cry of victory, when he reached the edge, he leapt down.

There is said to be a rock there which comes to a point like this. He landed on it between his legs. With his legs spread—that rock was there—he was split in two. The man is said to have been split in two.

Having taken revenge for having been made to fall back then, he was avenged, and then he took his own life.

It was a terrible thing they did, that couple, those two.

**48**

Ragged Ear of Sable Pass

JOHN A. MURRAY

It was my great pleasure to be able to spend a portion of the summer of 1989 photographing and videotaping grizzly bears in Denali National Park. This essay, a chapter from a work in progress on Denali National Park, relates my experiences with Ragged Ear, a twelve-year-old female grizzly bear whose home range is centered on Sable Pass. Her story—gleaned from the field notebooks in which I recorded daily observations—tells much about the difficulties the bears face as they try to survive and reproduce in interior Alaska, about some of the surprising truths that contradict the myths that have accreted around the species, and also about the value of our national parks, sanctuaries where animals such as the grizzly bear have been given the same rights to exist as people—a remarkable change, considering all that has come before, and one rich in hope for the future of civilization and of nature.

I first saw Ragged Ear, one of only four radio-collared grizzly bears in Denali National Park, three days before the end of May. She was digging for peavine roots (*Hedysarum alpinum americanum*) on a gravelbar of the East Fork of the Toklat River, just below Ade Murie's old wolf study cabin. Her three new cubs were playing 'King of the Mountain' on top of what had recently been a bull caribou. It was snowing lightly—not unusual for May so near the Arctic Circle—and the wind was blowing cold from the glaciers of the Alaskan Range just upstream. The snow was still deep in the highlands, but on the valley floors the overflow ice had largely melted, and it was here the grizzly bears had come to replenish their depleted body fat before the country greened up. Unlike the other bears who had recently emerged from the long sleep, Ragged Ear would not be shedding in the weeks to come—lactating females have so little energy they can not afford the cost of a new fur coat until late in the season. She was, frankly, in poor condition. Even at a distance, her once magnificent blond fur had the matted, unkempt appearance of a wet head of hair that has been slept on. There is no more stressful time in the life of a grizzly than the spring, and the nutritional difficulties of this period are only compounded by the presence of three actively nursing cubs.

I watched her through the viewfinder of a long-lens camera as she tore up the sand and gravel to reach the coarse roots, alternately using her formidable claws like rakes and shovels. The caribou remains had fed wolves, eagles, ravens, and a wolverine before she arrived and had provided her with little sustenance. The three cubs, each a shade of charcoal with the natural white collars that make them easier for their mothers to locate, wrestled and boxed with the boundless energy that is always in such marked contrast to the sober demeanor of their hard-working single parents. These dominance games would prepare them well for the complicated social hierarchy in which they would exist as adults. Occasionally, Ragged Ear would find a patch of over-wintered crowberries (*Empetrum nigrum*) or bearberries (*Arctostaphylus rubra* and *alpina*) and she would eat these wizened but nutritious black and red berries with greater relish than the gnarled woody peavine roots. The cow caribou and their spring calves grazing on the nearby hills Ragged Ear ignored, as she did the moose calves that were almost certainly lingering about the river with their mothers, for most of these miniature thoroughbreds were now a week or more old and could outrun her, if not accidentally surprised at close quarters.

After about an hour of rooting around, Ragged Ear suddenly raised her head in that alert purposeful manner that means a bear is about to travel. She loped playfully the one hundred yards to the river, tossing her head back and forth as she looked over her shoulder, and the three cubs tumbled eagerly behind their mother, looking for new adventure under every rock and completely unaware of what was to come. When Ragged Ear reached the river bank—here the water deepened in a narrow channel—the trio of furry musketeers sniffed once or twice timidly, and then backed off a respectable distance into the alders. Their mother turned to them, open-mouthed and panting from the run, and cocked her head several times, as if to encourage them to follow her. With that she plunged into the current and swam slowly across, with only the very top of her massive head—the crown, the ears, and the dark muzzle—visible in the white-water. When she got to the other side, she shook the water off in great shimmering curtains, rose up on her hind feet to get a better view, and woofed sternly for the cubs to follow.

Two of the four-month-old, fifteen-pound cubs dutifully obeyed their mother's order and jumped into the flood. They were immediately swept away from view like children's toy boats made from birch bark. Ragged Ear was beside herself with fear, and frantically raced up and down the opposite bank, woofing loudly and searching the rapids for her cubs. Finally the tough little grizzlies surfaced and with determined amphibious effort made it to the far bank, where they scampered onto terra firma as if the devil himself was nipping at their hind quarters. Here they were greeted with slobbering bear kisses, as their relieved mother thoroughly warmed them from head to trembling tail with her large red tongue. Assured the first two were now secure, Ragged Ear woofed to the last cub, the runt of the litter, and this cub, after much Hamlet-like pacing and several false starts, finally jumped in and was very nearly drowned—several times I thought it was a complete goner—before it joined the rest of the family. The four soggy bears then trotted up a wide moose trail into the dense swale of willow and alder that surround the Murie cabin. I remember hoping that Professor Fred Dean, who frequently stays there while studying grizzlies, did not have his back to the river, for a ravenously hungry Ragged Ear and her mischievous fold were headed that way in a great hurry.

The next time I saw Ragged Ear, in mid-June, most of the grizzlies in Denali National Park had moved out of the river bottoms into the low, moist passes of the Outer Range—what Ade Murie called the Sheep Hills—where the grass (*Arctagrostis latifolium*), horsetail (*Equisetum arvense*), and saxifrage (*Boykinia richardsonii*) had begun to green up on the south-facing slopes. Here the famished bears were able to secure a reliable source of early summer food, as the crude protein levels in the plentiful young leaves of these and other alpine plants are suprisingly high. Like many other grizzlies, Ragged Ear spent entire days grazing over the lush pastures of Sable Pass with a seemingly inexhaustible appetite. Her steady, bovine-like chomping at the grass reminded me of the dairy cow farm in southwestern Ohio where I often roamed as a boy with my plant presses and collecting jars, dreaming of natural history expeditions to far-off Alaska. At that time a star-nosed mole captured alive for my private zoo had approximately the same excitement value as filming the great white bears on the barren grounds.

The smallest of the three cubs—the Prince of Denmark—was now back in the food chain somewhere, and in his absence the other two grizzlies were maturing rapidly on their mother's rich milk. Every few hours either Ragged Ear would flop over on her back, inviting the cubs to nurse with a wave of one of her giant paws, or the cubs would become so much of a nuisance, hungrily nosing her body, that she would be compelled to nurse them. In just a matter of three or four minutes the tenacious feeders would drain her six mammaries, and would soon fall asleep on their mother's stomach, dreaming such dreams as little bears dream. After awhile Ragged Ear would slowly rise, gently letting the sleeping cubs slide off into the grass, and would begin grazing again. Once while the two cubs were playing on a nearby snowfield—grizzly bear cubs like nothing more than glissading and frolicking on snow—Ragged Ear assumed the nursing position, and when the preoccupied cubs delayed in coming to her, she cuffed each one lightly on the head, for she was a very strict disciplinarian. Whenever they were punished—and always it was for a good reason—the cubs would literally fall over each other in attempting to get back in their mother's good graces. After sufficient whining and fawning about her head, she would finally give them each a welcome lick on the nose, after which they would go about their play with renewed confidence and vigor.

Ragged Ear was very solicitous of the safety of her cubs and was constantly vigilant for danger—in the form of grizzly bears, wolves, golden eagles, and other predators. She was noticeably uneasy whenever she was in some low-lying area on Sable Pass that did not afford a good view of the surrounding terrain. For that reason, I rarely saw her as relaxed as some of the other adult bears, particularly those sows whose cubs were in their third summer and who were at a distance sometimes indistinguishable in size from their mother. A group composed of one adult sow and her three subadult cubs can easily intimidate a sow with two spring cubs. Once, though, when Ragged Ear had climbed a distant knoll to escape the mosquitoes, I did see her playing with abandon, for the salience offered a commanding prospect of Sable Pass, and she could keep an eye on the other bear families as she joined her two cubs in repeatedly sliding down a long snowfield on her back, side, stomach, and, most comically, on her head. Regardless of the circumstances, each night around ten-thirty P.M.—which is a full two hours before sunset at the latitude of the Park in mid-June—Ragged Ear would lead her family to the safety of a remote outcropping on Sable Mountain. She would remain in this rocky fortress—I called it "The Cliff House"—throughout the night as wolf packs—hunting for hungry pups back at the den—and boar grizzlies—restless in the height of the bear breeding season—crossed the wide, windy expanse of Sable Pass in their nightly wanderings.

One evening in mid-July I was on Sable Pass videotaping Ragged Ear as she fed on the sourdock leaves (*Rumex arcticus*) and mountain sorrel (*Oxyria digyna*) that were then well developed. Suddenly an arctic ground squirrel darted out from an alpine willow where it had been hiding—apparently the tension had been finally too much for it to take—and an unsuccessful chase ensued as Ragged Ear attempted to capture the animal, a food item that grizzlies savor as much as people relish delicatessen sandwiches. After futiley digging at the burrow entrance, Ragged Ear bawled loudly in frustration—she was, I had previously noted, much more vocal than other grizzlies. Unbeknownst to either of us, the largest female grizzly bear on Sable Pass—Queen Isabella (named for her royal bearing)—and her two-year-old son Columbus (named for his sometimes annoying curiosity around people)—were just over the hill. Queen Isabella was so large that she had the "look" of a coastal brown bear, which because of their rich environment are several times larger than inland grizzlies. When Queen Isabella heard Ragged Ear, she charged over the hill, moaning and gnashing her teeth, and then began walking stiffly in profile to show her great size. Columbus imitated every movement of his mother's aggressive display. Ragged Ear wasted no time in leaving the area and galloped—slowing every thirty yards to let her out-of-breath cubs catch up—for half a mile over the tundra, until she reached the secure heights of Sable Mountain.

I became quite curious about Ragged Ear after this—she was the only radio-collared bear I had seen in Denali—and made arrangements with Joe Van Horn and Dave Albert, two bear biologists at the Park, to review her file at Park Headquarters. I learned there that she had first been darted—anesthetized with a rifle-fired syringe—after an incident on June 5, 1984, in which she had acquired some food from backpackers on Tattler Creek, which drains east from Sable Mountain. Equipped with a radio-collar, she had then been closely monitered and periodically put through "aversive-conditioning," an educational process in which firecrackers were set off and plastic bullets were fired into her side when she approached rangers camped in the backcountry. She was—based on a tooth sample—seven years old in 1984, had never born cubs, which is not unusual in the depauperate interior of Alaska, and was a normal sized bear: about 300 pounds, a thirty-inch shoulder height, a head fifteen inches long and twenty-seven inches around, a total body length of just over six feet, a stomach girth of fifty inches, a hind foot eleven inches in length, and foreclaws three inches in length. On June 6, 1986, she treed a photographer in Igloo Creek and was put through aversive-conditioning again. On June 5, 1987, park researcher Brad Shultes, flying in a Supercub, saw Ragged Ear mating with another bear on Tributary

Creek, which drains west from Sable Mountain. Rick McIntyre, a park naturalist, subsequently told me that she had born three cubs in 1988, but that all three had been killed—possibly by a boar grizzly—and that after going into heat and mating again (possibly with the same boar) she had produced the three cubs I had seen in late May on the East Fork. Rick told a funny story about how Ragged Ear had brazenly led her cubs over the East Fork bridge one day in June, much to the amazement of those who had to stop their vehicles for the family to safely cross. Bill McDonald, a patrol ranger for the Sable Pass area, also mentioned to me that Ragged Ear (he called her Bear Number 102, as she was known to park officials) had been down in the Igloo Creek Campground in July and that he was concerned for her future. After that incident, park personnel watched her as closely as possible, but there were no further developments.

Early one August evening I found Ragged Ear and her two cubs—now quite a bit larger than in May—at the bottom of Igloo Canyon, feeding in a patch of nearly ripened soapberries (*Sheperdia canadensis*). After awhile her two cubs wandered down the hill. When they saw me they stopped, glared, and stuck their lower jaws out in such a way that their lower canines protruded out over their upper lips—like a vampire in reverse. After boldly making these "frightening" faces, they returned to their mother—a good distance up the hill—and I watched her carefully for any signs of irritation—yawning, drooling, panting—but there were none. Ragged Ear was accustomed to my presence—I believe bears can distinguish among people as easily as other animals can, and that, if anything, we underestimate their memories, as well as their capacity to feel pain. Although she was an insecure animal near the bottom of the hierarchy around Sable Pass, she seemed to tolerate my presence, so long as I was predictable—I never moved—and maintained a respectful distance, which I always did. After several minutes of berry-eating—grizzlies have the same penchant for sweets that people do—Ragged Ear froze, as did her cubs. They either heard or smelled something that was not to their liking, for in the next instant all three turned as if they were one animal and loped up the hillside toward the safety of Cathedral Mountain. Not long after that, Queen Isabella and Columbus—they seemed to become fatter each time I saw them—lumbered heavily into the soapberry patch. Once again the huge dominant sow had displaced the much smaller sow from a prime feeding area.

I had just begun to photograph Queen Isabella and Columbus when, in the corner of my left eye, a whitish-colored wolf suddenly appeared about twenty feet away. She was aware of the fact that Queen Isabella and Columbus were in the soapberry patch—the bears were oblivious to her arrival—but was hesitant to pass by so near the bears. I should say that wolves in general avoid grizzlies, but that on July 23, 1989, a pack of twelve wolves from the East Fork Pack attacked a grizzly bear family on the west side of Sable Pass and killed two yearling grizzlies before the mother and one cub escaped. The wolves were last seen carrying grizzly bear body parts back to their den. Grizzlies have little tolerance for wolves, particularly if cubs are involved. The wolf looked directly at me—as if assessing my intentions—and, after a moment of thought, continued on her route, which led her directly between me and the two bears. I took photographs of her as she passed by—body tense, ears back, eyes half-closed, and tail between her legs—and when she was a short distance to my right, the wind, which was coming down the canyon, brought her scent to the berry patch. Queen Isabella instantly woofed an alarm to her wandering cub. Columbus scrambled over to his mother and the two stood rigidly together, sniffing the air. So distraught were they at this sudden intruder that they descended the hill and disappeared into the dense brush of Igloo Creek, where they could mount an effective defense in the event a wolf pack was deploying for attack. The last I saw them—in a clearing near Igloo Creek—they were headed downstream toward Igloo Mountain.

I settled back after this and continued to watch Ragged Ear as she climbed Cathedral Mountain and noted on a hand-drawn sketch where she dug out an arctic ground squirrel and where she excavated a night bed on a secluded slope. The next afternoon, when she was at the bottom of the canyon feeding on berries, I hiked up to her bedding location, using my sketch as a map, and took photographs and measurements. The bed—shaped like a bathtub—was approximately four feet long and two feet wide and one foot deep, and was lined with reindeer moss and her own blond fur, which smelled something like an old blanket left out in the weather for a few days. I took some of the dense fur in my hand— golden and soft as lamb's wool—and wondered what kind of warm little booties my wife could knit for our new baby boy with yarn pulled from it. After some thought, though, I left it, deciding that it was dangerous to smell like a female grizzly bear; not to mention the fact that it is inadvisable to remove nutrients from a park ecosystem. There were large berry-filled scat piles all around the bed, probably marking ownership in the event any other bears wandered by. The nearby dig site was an astonishing piece of heavy field work—an entire subterranean squirrel house had been ripped unceremoniously from the earth—and the residents were nowhere to be seen. As I photographed the 360° view from the bed, I noticed seven Dall sheep milling around the base of Igloo Mountain. After what seemed like a silent conference among the leaders, they crossed Igloo Creek at a run, trotted through the soapberry patch, and climbed right past me—one small ram, four ewes, and two lambs—on their way to the rocky pinnacles above. A double rainbow forming on the edge of a black storm cloud behind summer-green Igloo Mountain made the scene all that more beautiful.

That evening I returned to the soapberry patch after observing Ragged Ear upstream on Igloo Creek and was surprised to see a backpacker setting up camp on the knoll where Ragged Ear had established her bed. I hiked up a short distance and caught the backpacker's attention and he hiked down. After exchanging friendly introductions— he was nineteen-year-old Greg Simonette, a freshman at Saint Cloud State College in Minnesota working for the summer at the Denali Hotel— I explained the situation and he expressed relief. Greg had seen the dig site, the bed, and the scat piles, but had not known what to make of them. He told me he was a biology major and was planning to transfer to the university where I teach. Ragged Ear was at that moment a quarter of a mile upstream and headed toward the soapberry patch. We talked about bears and after a short time Ragged Ear appeared in an upstream meadow, loping toward the berry patch. Greg began looking around nervously for a tree to climb, but the nearest sizeable spruce were a considerable distance away. Ragged Ear entered some tall brush and the young man's nervousness increased to a mild panic, but I assured him we were in no danger. "She will come out on that knoll above the berry patch in less than ten minutes," I said, and within that time she did. That was enough for Greg Simonette—he began walking east out of the canyon toward Igloo Mountain, which was in his camping permit area. After he left I realized that he was walking in the general direction where I had last seen Queen Isabella and Columbus headed the night before. The mercy of nature, I suppose, is that we are not permitted to see what is ahead of us on the trail.

I was back on Ragged Ear's range recently—it is late August as I write this—and saw some other bears, but not the blond sow with the torn ear and the two ring-necked cubs. I know she is up there, of course, but it is a big country. I will look for her again over Labor Day when I gather some of those wild blueberries that are still as sweet as August but have a hint of frosted tartness in the pulp. Perhaps I will see Ragged Ear then. I will certainly be looking for bears, not only because they will be sharing the hillsides with me and should always be treated with respect, but also because I have learned that bear-watching, above all, restores the sense of wonder we had as children, and that one day of watching a grizzly in the wild can almost wholly reverse the folklore of a lifetime. And if I do not see her and the others, I will look for them again after the northern lights have come and gone, for the long days of late May next year will find me back down on the East Fork where this season began, and where the Denali spring will begin when Ursa Major has been cast asunder and Polaris is no longer the North Star.

Further Reading

Abbey, Edward. *Beyond the Wall, Essays from the Outside*. New York: Holt, Rinehart and Winston, 1984.

Alexander, Mary, Gertrude Analoak, and Margaret Seeganna, eds. *Ugiuvang-Miut Quliapyuit, King Island Tales*. Fairbanks: Alaska Native Language Center and University of Alaska Press, 1988.

Allen, Henry T. *Report of an Expedition to the Copper, Tanana, and Koyukuk Rivers in the Territory of Alaska in the Year 1885*. Washington, D.C.: Government Printing Office, 1887.

Anderson, Jean, and Elyse Guttenberg. *Inroads: An Anthology Celebrating Alaska's Twenty-seven Fellowship Writers*. Fairbanks: Alaska State Council on the Arts and University of Alaska Press, 1988.

Beach, Rex. *Personal Exposures*. New York: Harper & Row, 1940.

Beaman, Libby. *Libby, the Sketches, Letters and Journals of Libby Beaman, Recorded in the Pribilof Islands 1879–1880*. Tulsa: Council Oak, 1987.

Belcher, Edward. *Narrative of the Voyage of H.M.S. Sulphur During the Years 1836–1842*. London, 1843.

Bohn, Dave. *Glacier Bay: The Land and the Silence*. Sam Francisco: Sierra Club, 1967.

Bohn, Dave. *Backcountry Journal: Reminiscences of a Wilderness Photographer*. Santa Barbara: Capra Press, 1974.

Bohn, Dave. *Rambles Through an Alaskan Wild: Katmai and the Valley of the Smokes*. Santa Barbara: Capra Press, 1979.

Brody, Hugh. *Maps and Dreams*. New York: Random House, 1979.

Brooks, Alfred Hulse. *Blazing Alaska's Trails*. Fairbanks: University of Alaska Press, 1953.

Brooks, Paul. *Roadless Area*. New York: Alfred Knopf, 1964.

Brooks, Paul. *The Pursuit of Wilderness*. Boston: Houghton Mifflin, 1971.

Brooks, Paul. *Speaking for Nature*. San Francisco: Sierra Club, 1980.

Broughton, William R. *Voyage of Discovery to the North Pacific Ocean and Round the World*. London, 1804.

Brower, Kenneth. *Earth and the Great Weather: The Brooks Range*. San Francisco: Friends of the Earth, 1973.

Buchanan, James. *Sketches of the History, Manners, and Customs of the North American Indians*. London, 1824.

Burney, James. *A Chronological History of Northeastern Voyages of Discovery, and of the Early Eastern Navigations of the Russians*. London, 1819.

Campbell, Archibald. *Voyage Round the World, From 1808–1812*. Edinburgh, 1816.

Caras, Roger. *Monarch of Deadman Bay: The Life and Death of a Kodiak Bear*. Boston: Little Brown, 1969.

Carey, Alan. *In the Path of the Grizzly*. Flagstaff: Northland, 1987.

Carrighar, Sally. *Icebound Summer*. New York: Alfred Knopf, 1958.

Chamisso, Adelbert Von. *Reise um die Welt mit der Romanzoffischen Entedeckungs Expedition in den Jahren 1815–1818, auf der Brig Rurik, Captain Otto Von Kotzebue*. Leipzig, 1836.

Chevigny, Hector. *Russian America*. Portland: Binford and Mort, 1965.

Chorus, Louis. *Voyage Pittoresque Autour du Monde*. Paris, 1822.

Coates, Ken S. and William R. Morrison. *Land of the Midnight Sun: A History of the Yukon*. Edmonton: Hurtig, 1988.

Cook, James. *Voyage to the Pacific Ocean in the Years 1776–1780*. London, 1782.

Cooper, David J. *Brooks Range Passage*. Seattle: Mountaineers, 1982.

Coxe, William. *Account of the Russian Discoveries Between Asia and America*. London, 1780.

Crisler, Lois. *Arctic Wild*. New York: Harper & Row, 1958.

Curtis, Edward S., "The Rush to the Klondike over the Mountain Passes," *The Century Magazine* vol. LV, no. 5 (March 1898): 692–97.

Dall, William Healy. *Alaska and Its Resources*. Boston, 1870.

Davidson, George. *Coast Pilot of Alaska: Southern Boundary to Cook's Inlet*. Washington, 1869.

Dawson, George. *The Yukon Territory. Narrative of an Exploration Made in 1887 in the Yukon District*. London, 1898.

Dean, David M. *Breaking Trail: Hudson Stuck of Texas and Alaska*. Athens: Ohio University Press, 1988.

Delisle de la Croyère, Joseph Nicholas. *Explication de la Carte Des Nouvelles Découvertes au Nord*. Paris, 1752.

Denali National Park General Management Plan and Wilderness Suitability Review. Washington, D.C.: Government Printing Office, 1986.

De Mofras, Duflot. *Voyage Autour du Monde 1841–1842*. Paris, 1845.

Denys, M. Ferdinand. *Les Californies, L'Oregon, et les Possessions Russes en L'Amérique les Iles Noutka et de la Reine Charlotte*. Paris, 1849.

Dillard, Annie. *Teaching a Stone to Talk: Expeditions and Encounters*. New York: Harper & Row, 1983.

Dixon, George and Nathaniel Portlock. *Voyage Round the World, but more Particularly to the Northwest Coast of North America*. London, 1789.

Douglas, William O. *My Wilderness: The Pacific West*. New York: Doubleday, 1960.

Dunn, John. *History of the Oregon Territory and the British North-American Fur Trade*. London, 1844.

Dunn, Robert. *The Shameless Diary of an Explorer*. New York: Outing, 1907.

Espinosa, Don Josef. *Memorias Sobre las Observaciones Astronomicas por los Navigantes Españoles*. Madrid, 1809.

Findlay, A. G. *Directory for the Navigation of the Pacific Ocean*. London, 1851.

Fleurieu, C. P., Claret de. *Voyage Autour du Monde Pendant les Années 1790–1792*. Paris, 1794.

Forster, John Reinhold. *Geschicten der Reisen Seit Cook auf Den N. W. und N. O. Küsten von Amerika*. Berlin, 1791.

Fowles, John. *The Tree*. San Francisco: Ecco Press, 1979.

Franklin, John. *Narrative of a Second Expedition to the Shores of the Polar Sea, from 1825 to 1827*. London, 1828.

Glacken, Clarence J. *Traces on the Rhodian Shore: Nature and Culture in Western Thought from Ancient Times to the End of the Eighteenth Century*. Berkeley: University of California, 1967.

Glenn, Robert. *The Tongass.* New York: Aperture, 1986.

Goetzmann, William H., and Kay Sloan. *Looking Far North, the Harriman Expedition to Alaska, 1899.* New York: Viking, 1982.

Goetzmann, William H. *New Lands, New Men: America and the Second Great Age of Discovery.* New York: Viking, 1986.

Gough, Barry M. *To the Pacific and Arctic with Beecher: The Journal of Lt. George Peard of H.M.S. "Blossom" 1825–1828.* Cambridge: Hakluyt Society, 1973.

Greely, Adolphus W. *Three Years of Arctic Service: An Account of the Lady Franklin Bay Expedition of 1881–1884 and the Attainment of the Farthest North.* New York, 1886.

Greenhow, Robert. *Memoir, Historical and Political, on the Northwest Coast of North America and the Adjacent Territories.* Washington, 1840.

Grewingk, C. Von. *Beiträge zur Kenntniss der Orographischen und Geognostischen Beschaffenheit der Nordwest-Küste Amerikas mit den Anliegenden Inseln.* St. Petersburg, 1850.

Gruening, Ernest. *An Alaskan Reader: 1867–1967.* New York: Meredith, 1967.

Haines, John. *Living off the Country: Essays on Poetry and Place.* Ann Arbor: University of Michigan Press, 1981.

Haines, John. *Other Days: Selections from a Work in Progress.* Port Townsend, Wash.: Graywolf, 1981.

Haines, John. *The Stars, the Snow, the Fire.* Port Townsend, Wash.: Greywolf, 1989.

Halpern, Daniel. *On Nature: Nature, Landscape, and Natural History.* San Francisco: North Point, 1986.

Hartwig, John. *The Polar World: Arctic and Antarctic Regions.* London, 1869.

Healy, M. A. *Cruise of the Steamer Corwin in 1884.* Washington, 1885.

Higginson, Ella. *Alaska, The Great Country.* New York: Macmillan, 1908.

Hirschmann, Fred. *Lake Clark Country.* Anchorage: Alaska Geographic Society, 1985.

Hoagland, Edward. *Notes from the Century Before: A Journal of British Columbia.* New York: Random House, 1969.

Holthaus, Gary, Nora Dauenhauer, and Richard Dauenhauer. "Alaska Native Writers, Storytellers and Orators," *Alaska Quarterly Review.* Vol. IV, nos. 3 & 4 (1986): see esp. p.34 for "Haida Hunters and Legend of the Two Fin Killer Whale."

Holthaus, Gary, and Robert Hedin. *Alaska: Reflections on Land and Spirit.* Tucson: University of Arizona, 1989.

Hooper, W. H. *Ten Months among the Tents of the Tuski, with Incidents of an Arctic Boat Expedition in Search of Sir John Franklin, as Far East as the Mackenzie River and Cape Bathurst.* London, 1853.

Hopkins, David., et al. *Paleoecology of Beringea.* New York: Academic, 1982.

Hoshino, Michio. *Grizzly.* San Francisco: Chronicle, 1986.

Hoshino, Michio. *Moose.* San Francisco: Chronicle, 1987.

Humboldt, Alexander von. *Essai Politique sur le Royaume de Lau Nouvelle Espagne.* Paris. 1811.

Huth, Hans. *Nature and the American Mind.* Lincoln: University of Nebraska, 1957.

Jetté, Julius. "Riddles of the Ten'a Indians." *Anthropos* (1913). 8: 181–201, 630–51.

Kent, Rockwell. *Wilderness: A Journal of Quiet Adventure in Alaska.* New York: Putnam's, 1920.

Kesselheim, Alan S. *Water and Sky: Reflections of a Northern Year.* Golden: Fulcrum, 1989.

Kotzebue, Otto von. *Voyage of Discovery into the South Sea and Behring* [sic] *Straits, for the Purpose of Exploring a Northeast Passage, in 1815–1818.* Weimar and London, 1821.

Kraus, Michael E. *In Honor of Eyak: The Art of Anna Nelson Harry.* Fairbanks: University of Alaska, 1982.

Krusenstern, Admiral von. *Hydrographic Memoirs and Charts of the North Pacific.* Leipzig, 1819.

Krusenstern, Admiral von. *Voyage to the Russian American Colonies, 1803 to 1806.* St. Petersburg, 1812.

Kurten, Bjorn, and Elaine Anderson. *Pleistocene Mammals of North America.* New York: Columbia University Press, 1980.

Lamb, May Wynne. *Life in Alaska: The Reminiscences of a Kansas Woman, 1916–1919.* Lincoln: University of Nebraska, 1988.

Langsdorf, G. H. von. *Voyages and Travels, 1803 to 1807.* London, 1813.

La Perouse, Jean Francois de Galooup. *Voyage Around the World.* London, 1799.

Lasareff, M. P. *Voyage of the Sloop-of-war Ladoga, 1822–1824.* St. Petersburg, 1832.

Lebrun, M. *Abrégé de tous les Voyages au Pole Nord.* Paris, 18-?.

Lesseps, M. de. *Journal Historique de Voyage de M. De. Lesseps.* Paris, 1790.

Lisiansky, Urey. *Voyage Round the World in the Ship Neva.* London, 1814.

Litke, Frederic. *Voyage Autour du Monde sur la Corvette Seniavine, dans les Annees 1826–1829.* Paris, 1835; reprinted and translated by The Limestone Press, Kingston, Canada, 1987.

London, Jack. *The Call of the Wild.* New York: Macmillan, 1904.

London, Jack. *White Fang.* New York: Macmillan, 1906.

London, Jack. *Love of Life, and Other Stories.* New York: Macmillan, 1906.

Lopez, Barry. *Of Wolves and Men.* New York: Scribner's, 1978.

Lopez, Barry. *Arctic Dreams.* New York: Scribner's, 1986.

Lopez, Barry. *Crossing Open Ground.* New York: Scribner's, 1988.

Lyon, Thomas J., ed. *A Literary History of the American West.* Ft. Worth: Texas Christian University, 1987.

Lyon, Thomas J., ed. *This Incomperable Lande: A Book of American Nature Writing.* Boston: Houghton Mifflin, 1989.

Mackenzie, Alexander. *Voyage from Montreal over the Continent of North America to the Frozen and Pacific Oceans, in the Years 1780–1793.* London, 1801.

Marshall, Robert. *Arctic Village.* New York: Smith and Haas, 1932.

Marshall, Robert. *Arctic Wilderness.* Berkeley: University of California, 1956.

McCandless, Robert G. *Yukon Wildlife: A Social History* [includes "Here I Am Yet!" by Johny Jack in Appendix]. Edmonton: University of Alberta, 1985.

McCormick, John. *Reclaiming Paradise: The Global Environmental Movement.* Bloomington: Indiana University, 1989.

McCracken, Harold, "The Alaskan Grizzly," *Field and Stream,* 1941.

McIntyre, Rick. *Denali National Park.* Santa Barbara: Sequoi, 1986.

McPhee, John. *Coming into the Country.* New York: Farrar, Straus & Giroux, 1977.

Mech, L. David. *The Arctic Wolf*. Stillwater, Minn.: Voyageur, 1987.

Mech, Carl Heinrich. *Siberia and Northwestern America 1788–1792*. Kingston, Canada: The Limestone Press, 1980.

Merriam, C. Hart, ed. *Harriman Alaska Expedition*, 13 vols. New York: Doubleday, Page and Company, and Washington, D.C.: Smithsonian Institution, 1901–1914.

Merton, Thomas. *Thomas Merton in Alaska: The Alaskan Conferences, Journals, and Letters*. New York: New Directions, 1989.

Milton, John. *Nameless Valleys, Shining Mountains*. New York: Meredith, 1970.

Mirsky, Jeannette. *To the Arctic!: The Story of Northern Exploration from Earliest Times to the Present*. Chicago: University of Chicago, 1970.

Mitchell, Lee Clark. *Witnesses to a Vanishing America: The Nineteenth Century Response*. Princeton: Princeton University, 1981.

Morgan, John. *The Arctic Herd*. University: University of Alabama, 1985.

Morison, Samuel Eliot. *The European Discovery of America: The Northern Voyages, A.D. 500–1600*. New York: Oxford University Press, 1971.

Mountifield, David. *A History of Polar Exploration*. New York: Dial, 1974.

Mueller, Gerhard Friedrich. *Voyages from Asia to America*. London, 1761.

Murie, Adolph. *The Wolves of Mount McKinley*. U.S. National Park Service, Fauna Series, no. 5. Washington: U.S. Government, 1944; Seattle: University of Washington Press, 1985.

Murie, Adolph. *A Naturalist in Alaska*. New York: Devin-Adair, 1961.

Murie, Adolph. *The Grizzlies of Mount McKinley*. Scientific Monograph Series, no. 14, Washington: U.S. Government, 1981; Seattle: University of Washington Press, 1981.

Murie, Margaret. *Two in the Far North*. New York: Alfred Knopf, 1962.

Murie, Olaus. *Journeys to the Far North*. Palo Alto: The Wilderness Society and American West Publishing, 1973.

Muir, John. *Travels in Alaska*. Boston: Houghton Mifflin, 1915.

Muir, John, John Burroughs, et al. *The Harriman Expedition, 1899*, partial reprint. New York: Dover, 1986.

Murray, Alexander Hunter. *Journal of the Yukon 1847–1848*. Ottawa: Government Printing Bureau, 1910.

Nansen, Fridtjof. *Farthest North, Being the Record of Exploration of the Ship "Fram" 1893–96 and of a Fifteen Months Sleigh Journey by Dr. Nansen and Lt. Johnson, with an Appendix by Otto Sverdrup, Capt. of the "Fram."* New York, 1898.

Nash, Roderick. *Wilderness and the American Mind*. New Haven: Yale University, 1967.

Naske, Claus and Herman E. Slotnick. *Alaska: A History of the 49th State*. Norman: University of Oklahoma, 1987.

Neatby, L. H. *In Quest of the Northwest Passage*. New York: Thomas Y. Crowell, 1958.

Neatby, L. H. *Conquest of the Last Frontier*. Athens: Ohio University Press, 1966.

Nelson, Richard. *Hunters of the Northern Ice*. Chicago: University of Chicago, 1969.

Nelson, Richard. *Hunters of the Northern Forest*. Chicago: University of Chicago, 1973.

Nelson, Richard. *Make Prayers to the Raven: A Koyukon View of the Northern Forest*. Chicago: University of Chicago: 1986.

Nelson, Richard. *The Island Within*. San Francisco: North Point, 1989.

Newcomb, Raymond Lee, ed. *Our Lost Explorers: The Narrative of the "Jeanette" Arctic Expedition as Related by the Survivors and Last Journals of Lieutenant De Long*. Hartford and San Francisco, 1884.

Nordenskiöld, A. E. *Voyage of the Vega Around Asia and Europe*. London, 1881.

Olson, Sigurd. *Runes of the North*. New York: Knopf, 1963.

Pallas, P. S. *Nordische Beiträge zur Physikalischen und Geographischen Erdund Völkerbeschreibung, Naturgeschichte, und Oekonomie*. Leipzig, 1781.

Parry, Ann. *Parry of the Arctic: The Life Story of Admiral Sir Edward Parry, 1790–1855*. London: Chatto & Windus, 1963.

Parry, William. *Journal of a Voyage*. London: John Murray, 1821.

Pearson, Grant. *My Life of High Adventure*. New York: Ballantine Books, 1962.

Peary, Robert E. *Northward over the Great Ice*. London, 1898.

Peary, Robert E. *The North Pole*. New York: Frederick Stokes, 1910.

Petermann, A. *Notes on the Telegraph Exploration in Alaska*. Gotha, 1869.

Phipps, Constantine John. *Voyage Toward the North Pole*. London, 1774.

Proenneke, Richard. *One Man's Wilderness: An Alaskan Odyssey*. Anchorage: Alaska Northwest Publishing, 1973.

Portlock, Nathaniel. *Voyage Around the World*. London, 1789.

Pruitt, William O. *Animals of the North*. New York: Harper & Row, 1967.

Quammen, David. *Natural Acts: A Sidelong View of Science & Nature*. New York: Schocken, 1985.

Ramsey, Cynthia Ross, et al. *Alaska's Magnificent Parklands*. Washington: National Geographic Society, 1984.

Rasmussen, Knud. *The Report of the Fifth Thule Expedition 1921–24, the Danish Expedition to Arctic North America*. 12 vols. Copenhagen, Gyldendalske Boghandel, 1929.

Rennike, Jeff. *River Days: Travels on Western Rivers*. Golden: Fulcrum, 1987.

Rennike, Jeff. *Bears of Alaska*. Boulder: Roberts Rinehart, 1987.

Richardson, John. *The Polar Regions*. Edinburgh, 1861.

Roberts, David. *The Mountain of My Fear*. New York: Vanguard, 1968.

Roberts, David. *Deborah: A Wilderness Narrative*. New York: Vanguard, 1970.

Rocquefeuil, Camille de. *Journal d'un Voyage Autour du Monde Pendent les Années 1816–1819*. Paris, 1823.

Ross, John. *Narrative of a Second Voyage in Search of a Northwest Passage*. London, 1835.

Saur, Martin. *An Account of a Geographical and Astronomical Expedition to the Northern Parts of Russia, by Commodore Joseph Billings, in the Years 1785–1794*. London, 1802.

Scoresby, W., Jr. *Account of the Arctic Regions, and History and Description of the Northern Whale Fishery*. Edinburgh, 1820.

Schemelin. *Diary of the First Russian Circumnavigation of the World*. St. Petersburg, 1816–1818.

Scherman, Katharine. *Spring on an Arctic Island*. Boston: Little Brown, 1956.

Schwatka, Frederick. *Report of a Military Reconnaissance in Alaska, Made in 1883*. Washington, 1885.

Schwatka, Frederick. *Along Alaska's Great River*. Chicago: George M. Hill, 1900.

Seemann, Berthold. *Narrative of the Voyage of H.M.S. Herald, 1845–1851*. London, 1853.

Service, Robert. *The Spell of the Yukon*. New York: Dutton, 1907.

Seton, Ernest Thompson. *The Arctic Prairies*. New York: Scribner's, 1911.

Seton, Ernest Thompson. *Lives of Game Animals*. 4 vols. Garden City, N.Y.: Doubleday, Doran, 1929.

Shabelsky, Achille. *Voyage aux Colonies Russes de L'Amérique Pendent les Annees 1821–1823*. St. Petersburg, 1826.

Sheldon, Charles. *The Wilderness of the Upper Yukon: A Hunter's Explorations for Wild Sheep in Sub-Arctic Mountains*. New York: Scribner's, 1911.

Sheldon, Charles. *The Wilderness of the North Pacific Coast Islands*. New York: Scribner's, 1912.

Sheldon, Charles. *The Wilderness of Denali: Explorations of a Hunter-Naturalist in Northern Alaska*. New York: Scribner's, 1930.

Shelikoff, Gregorie. *Ereste und Zweite Resie Von Ochotsk in Siberian Durch Den Östlichen Ocean Nach den Kusten Von America in den Jahren 1783–1789, aus dem Russischen Übersetzt Von J. J. Logan*. St. Petersburg, 1793.

Sherwood, Morgan. *Exploration of Alaska, 1865–1900*. New Haven: Yale University, 1965.

Simpson, Thomas. *Narrative of the Discoveries on the North Coast of America, Effected by the Officers of the Hudson's Bay Company, During the Years 1836–1839*. London, 1843.

Simpson, George. *Narrative of a Voyage Around the World During the Years 1841–1842*. London, 1847.

Sokoloff, A. P. *Narrative of Chirikoff's Voyage*. St. Petersburg, 1849.

Staehlin, J. von. *Account of the New Northern Archipelago, Lately Discovered by the Russians*. London, 1774.

Staender, Vivian and Gil. *Our Arctic Year*. Anchorage: Alaska Northwest Publishing Company, 1983.

Stefansson, Vilhjalmur. *My Life with the Eskimo*. New York: Harper, 1912.

Stefansson, Vilhjalmur. *The Friendly Arctic*. New York: MacMillan, 1921.

Stefansson, Vilhjalmur. *Hunters of the Great North*. New York: Harcourt, 1922.

Steller, Georg Wilhelm. *Journal of a Voyage with Bering, 1741–1742*. ed. O. W. Frost. Stanford: Stanford University Press, 1987.

Steller, Georg Wilhelm. *Beschreibung von dem Lande Kamchatka*. Frankfurt and Leipzig, 1744.

Stuck, Hudson. *The Ascent of Denali (Mount McKinley)*. New York: Scribner's, 1914.

Stuck, Hudson. *Ten Thousand Miles with a Dog Sled*. New York: Scribner's, 1916.

Sumner, Charles. *Speech of the Honorable Charles Sumner on the Cession of Russian America to the United States*. Washington: U.S. House of Representatives, September, 1867.

Udall, Stewart. *The Quiet Crisis*. New York: Avon, 1963.

Vancouver, George. *Voyage of Discovery to the North Pacific Ocean in the Year 1790–1792*. London, 1798.

Vancouver, George. *Voyage to the North Pacific Ocean*. London, 1801.

Venianimov, Innocentius. *Notes on the Unalashaka District*. St. Petersburg, 1840; reprinted and translated by The Limestone Press, Kingston, Canada, 1986.

Wallace, David Rains. *The Untamed Garden and Other Personal Essays*. Columbus: Ohio State University Press, 1986.

Watkins, T. H. *Vanishing Arctic*. New York: Aperture, 1987.

Weeden, Robert. *Alaska: Promises to Keep*. Boston: Houghton Mifflin, 1978.

Whymper, Frederick. *Travel and Adventure in the Territory of Alaska*. London: John Murray, 1868.

Wickersham, James. *Old Yukon Tales, Trails and Trials*. St. Paul: West Publishing Company, 1938.

Wilkes, Charles. *Narrative of the United States Exploring Expedition During the Years 1838–1842*. Philadelphia, 1844.

Wrangell, Ferdinand von. Russian America Statistical and Ethnographic Information. St. Petersburg, 1839; reprinted and translated by the Limestone Press, Kingston, Canada, 1986.

Wright, Billie. *Four Seasons North: A Journal of Life in the Alaskan Wilderness*. New York: Harper and Row, 1973.

Wright, Sam. *Koviashuvik, A Time and Place of Joy*. San Francisco: Sierra Club, 1989.

Zagoskin, L. *Travels on Foot, and Description of the Russian Possessions in America, from 1842–1844*. St. Petersburg, 1847.

Index

Abbey, Edward, 4, 7, 8, 12, 13, 15, 189, 263*ff.*
Abrams, M. H., 9
Addison, Joseph, 9
Adirondack Park, 172
Africa, 15
Akiak Island (Alaska), 160
Alaska Commercial Company, 91, 98, 102
Alaska Range, 109–12, 153–58, 161
Alatna River (Alaska), 232–40
Aleut (Native American People), 22, 100, 248
Aleutian Islands, 26, 40, 77, 189
Alexander Archipelago, 14, 104–7
Algae, 59
Allaket (Alaska), 232
Allen, Henry T., 3, 7, 90, 91, 109*ff.*
Allen, Jesse, 173
Alternative perspectives on nature, 10–11
Amchitka (Alaska), 189
American Fur Company, 86
Anaktuvuk Pass (Alaska), 232
Anchorage, 34, 91, 227, 230
Andes Mountains, vii
Antaeus, 17
Arctic National Wildlife Refuge (ANWR), 189, 213–20, 263–68
Arrigetch Creek (Alaska), 232, 239–40
Athabaskan (Native American people), vii, 3, 16. *See also* Jetté, Father Julius; Nelson, Richard
Atlantic Richfield Company, 91
Atlin (British Columbia), 242
Attu Island (Alaska), 91, 99, 243
Austin, Mary, 132
Avacha Bay, 32

Baffin Bay (Canada), 61
Bald eagle, 60, 203, 271, 287

Banner Creek (Alaska), 194
Baranov (Russian trader), 66
Barrow (Alaska), 91
Barter Island (Alaska), 255, 264, 266
Bartlett Cove (Alaska), 208
Beaman, Libby, 4, 8, 9, 12, 64, 91, 97*ff.*
Bear, black, 81, 96, 229
  Glacier Bear, 249, 259, 261, 290
Bear, brown (grizzly), 7, 11, 12, 14, 81, 132, 134, 135–44, 143–47, 151, 210, 214, 220, 223, 238, 267–68, 271–72, 284, 301–9
Bear, polar, 169, 293–96
Bearberry, 303
Beaufort Sea (Alaska), 255
Beaver, 72, 81, 151, 219, 243–45, 262
Bering, Vitus, 22, 23, 26
Bering Sea, 54, 97–102, 157, 161, 220
Bering Straits, 34, 56–62
Berrigan, Phil, 228
Beston, Henry, 4
Bettles (Alaska), 173, 233
Bierdstadt, Albert, 14
Bishop Museum, 94
Bison, 72
Black Fox Creek (Yukon Territory), 203
Blanc, Mount (Switzerland), vii
Blueberries, 36, 82, 175, 237, 238, 309
Bohn, Dave, 8, 205*ff.*
Boone and Crockett Club, 136
Boreal Mountain (Alaska), 177, 178
Boswell, James, 15
Brooks Range (Alaska), 91, 171–77, 213–20, 231–40, 263–68
Brower, Dave, 214, 218
Brower, Kenneth, 4, 8, 189, 213*ff.*
Bryant, William Cullen, 5
Burroughs, John, 5, 14, 117–20*ff.*, 182

Cape Kronotski (Alaska), 32
Cape Navarin (Alaska), 25
Caribou, 72, 81, 167, 168, 214, 220, 259, 264, 303
Cascade Mountains (Washington), 217
Chase, Fanny, 98
Chamisso, Adelbert Von. See Von Chamisso, Adelbert
Chena River (Alaska), vii
Chilkoot Pass (Yukon Territory), 91
Chugach Bay (Alaska), 72, 228
Chugach State Park (Alaska), 189
Chulitna River (Alaska), 157
Cistercian Order, 226
Clear River (Alaska), 173
Cloudberry, 82
Coleridge, Samuel T., 10
Colville River (Alaska), 145
Cook, James, 7, 23, 34ff.
Cooper, Dave, 8, 231ff.
Copper River (Alaska), 69–73, 90, 91, 110–12, 228
Cordova (Alaska), 230, 248
Cormorant, 297–300
Coyote, 229
Crab, 41
Cranberry, wild, 82, 261, 273
Criticism, Literary, of Arctic-American nature writing, 12–14
Crowberry, 303
Currants, 36
Curtis, Edward, 118

Dall, William Henry, 90, 93ff., 118
Dampier, William, 28, 32
Darwin, Charles, 58, 122
Dawson (Yukon Territory), 91
Dean, Fred, 304
Delta Junction (Alaska), 191
Denali (Mt. McKinley), vii, 5, 127–29, 136, 151, 153–58
Denali National Park (formerly Mt. McKinley National Park), 135–41, 153–58, 181–86, 302–9
Dillard, Annie, 5, 6, 8, 9, 12, 13, 14, 15, 16, 253ff.
Dinesen, Isak, 132
Dunn, Robert, 6, 8, 120ff.
Dillingham (Alaska), 227

Elk (Wapiti), 72
Ellana, Frank, 297ff.
Emerson, Ralph Waldo, 4
Estonia (Baltic Republic), 70
Exxon Valdez (oil tanker), 44, 189

Eyak (Native American people), 230, 247–52

Familiar essay, in nature writing, 9, 10
Fifth Thule Expedition, 7, 165–70
Foraker, Mt. (Alaska), 156
Fort Yukon (Alaska), 23, 85–87, 258
Fox, 72, 81, 151, 183, 194
Franklin, John, 23
Frigid Crags (Alaska), 177
Fuji, Mt. (Japan), vii
Fur seals, 63–67, 97–102

Gates of the Arctic (mountain in Alaska), 177
Gates of the Arctic National Park, 4, 172, 232
Geese, 87, 88, 151, 203, 259
Genres, in Arctic-American nature writing
  familiar essay, 9–10
  individual adventure narratives, 7–8
  official expedition narratives, 7–8
  personal journal, 8
  poetry and fiction, 10
  scientific report, 8
Germany, 40
Glacier Bay (Alaska), 5, 117–20, 205–11
Goetzmann, William, 34
Gold, 127–29
Grand Canyon, 104
Gray, Elizabeth, 11
Grayling, 277
Greenland, 28
Grinnel, George, 118, 136
Ground squirrel, 139, 146, 305
Grouse, 82, 262
Gruening, Ernest, 227
Gustavus Peninsula (Alaska), 117–20

Haida (Native American people), vii, 10, 289–91
Haines, John, 4, 12, 13, 15, 188, 191ff., 266
Hamilton, George, 10, 289ff.
Hare, snowshoe, 121–25, 151, 167, 194, 243
Harper, Arthur, 154
Harper, Walter, 154
Harriman Expedition, 117–20
Harry, Anna, 10, 12, 247ff.
Harvard University, 91, 276
Harvey, Kenneth, 173
Hetch Hetchy (California), 104
Higginson, Ella, 7, 12, 14, 131ff.
Horsetail, 304
Horton River (Canada), 144, 146
Huckleberries, 36

Hudson's Bay Company, 23, 50, 86–89, 96
Huslia (Alaska), 258

Igloo Canyon (Alaska), 307, 308
Igloo Mountain (Alaska), 308
Iliamna, Lake (Alaska), 227
Illinois, 114
Inupiat Eskimo, 294

Jack, Johnny Taku, 241*ff.*
Japan, vii, 91, 243
Japan current, 99
Jetté, Father Julius, 3, 11, 149*ff.*
Johnson, Ernie, 173
Johnson, Samuel, 9
Juneau, 229, 230, 287

Kaktovik (Alaska), 265
Kamchatka (Siberia), 27, 59, 99
Kansas, 5, 160
Karstens, Harry, 154
Kenai (Alaska), vii, 72, 91
Kentucky, 226, 230
Ketchikan (Alaska), vii, 81
Kilimanjaro (Africa), vii
King Island Eskimo, 10, 293–300
Kiska Island (Alaska), 91
Kluane National Park (Canada), 91
Kodiak Island (Alaska), 189, 222, 230
Kolodny, Annette, 11
Kotzebue (Alaska), 6
Kotzebue, Otto Von. *See* Von Kotzebue, Otto
Koyukon Athabaskan people, 16, 149–51, 257–62
Koyukuk River (Alaska), 90, 110–12, 171–79, 260
Kraus, Michael, 248
Kuskokwim River (Alaska), 156, 159–64

Lake Clark (Alaska), 221–24
Lamb, May Wynne, 4, 8, 12, 159*ff.*
Last Lake (Alaska), 215
Lichen, 217, 239
Linnaeus, Carl, 14
Literary style, of Arctic-American nature writing, 14
Litke, Frederick, 16, 23, 63*ff.*
Lituya Bay (Alaska), 208
London, Jack, 10, 11, 91, 121–25*ff.*, 266, 274
Loon, Arctic, 217, 286
Lopez, Barry, 8, 9, 11, 12, 14, 15, 16, 144, 269–74
Lyon, Thomas, 16, 232
Lynx, 96, 194, 245, 262

Mackenzie, Alexander, 49–52*ff.*
Mackenzie River (Yukon Territory), 49–52, 96
Malespina, Alexandro, 23
Mammoth, 280
Marmot, 72, 262
Marshall, Robert, viii, 5, 7, 8, 171*ff.*
Marten, pine, 72, 194
Mastodon, 195, 280
Matanuska (Alaska), 230
McGinnis, Joe, 13, 266
McKinley, Mt. (Alaska). *See* Denali
McPhee, John, 266
Merchant, Carolyn, 11
Merck, Carl, 6, 37*ff.*, 59
Merton, Thomas, 5, 7, 8, 154, 225*ff.*
Mice, deer, 288
Milton, John, 189, 214
Mink, 243, 262, 288
Mombasa, 132
Moose, 137, 175, 176, 178, 194, 215, 260, 262, 271, 303
Moran, Thomas, 14
Morgan, John, 5, 10, 275*ff.*
Mosquitoes, 137, 199–205, 239, 260, 265, 274, 305
Muir, John, 5, 14, 91, 103*ff.*, 118, 208
Murie, Adolph, 3, 8, 16, 181*ff.*
Murie, Margaret, ix, 2, 4, 5, 8, 12, 197–203*ff.*
Murie, Olaus, 3, 182, 197–203
Murray, Alexander, 4, 14, 91, 103–7*ff.*, 118, 208
Murray, John A., 301*ff.*
Musk-ox, 72, 96, 169

Nelson, Richard, 8, 12, 80, 150, 257*ff.*
New Mexico, 230
Northwest Fur Company, 50
Northwest Passage, 23
Northwest Territories, 50, 144
Norton Bay (Alaska), 81
Nulato (Alaska), 80–83

Octopus, 41
Old Crow River (Yukon Territory), 198–203
Osgood, Wilfred, 136
Otter, river, 82, 243
Otter, sea, 63–67
Ovid, 290
Owl, snowy, viii, 151, 262

Pallas (German naturalist), 5, 59
Pascal, Blaise, 16
Peacock, Doug, 268
Pearson, Steve, 189, 214

Peary, Robert, 144
Peavine, wild, 303
Pierce, Richard, 40
Pikongonna, Aloysius, 293*ff.*
Pliny the Elder, 58
Polaris (North Star), 309
Porcupine, 72, 286, 288
Porcupine River (Alaska), 96, 198–203
Post, Wiley, 91
Pribilof Islands (Alaska), 8, 63–67, 75, 97–102
Prince William Sound (Alaska), 14, 44, 46, 134, 189
Prishvin, Mikhail, 80
Proenneke, Richard, 7, 8, 9, 192, 221*ff.*
Ptarmigan, 82, 138, 151, 259
Puget Sound (Washington), 105

Queen Charlotte Islands (Canada), vii, 132

Rasmussen, Knud, 7, 10, 11, 165*ff.*
Raven, common, 210, 258, 286, 290
Raspberry, wild, 36
Reindeer, 72
Redoubt, Mount (Alaska), 227
Red River (Minnesota), 86
Richardson (Alaska), 193
Richardson, John, 85–89
Roethke, Theodore, 5
Rogers, Will, 91
Romantzoff Range (Alaska), 96
Roosevelt, Theodore, 136
Rose, wild, 82
Rousseau, Jean-Jacques, 17
Rungius, Carl, 136, 140
Russian Geographic Society, 70

Sable Pass (Alaska), 301–9
Saint Elias, Mount (Alaska), vii, 71
Saint Ferdinand Island (Alaska), 32
Saint George Island (Alaska), 66–67
Saint Lawrence Island (Alaska), 53–56
Saint Paul Island (Alaska), 66–67*ff.*
Salmon, 71–72, 91, 112, 260, 261, 272
San Francisco, 23, 112, 122
Savage River (Alaska), 185
Saxifrage, 304
Schwatka, Frederick, 7, 91, 113–16*ff.*
Scotland, 50, 104
Sea lion, 63–67
Seals, 97–102, 278, 285
Sea otter, 63–67, 74–77
Sequoia National Park, 104
Service, Robert, 12
Seton, Ernest Thompson, 118

Seward (Alaska), 189
Sheenjek Valley (Alaska), 213–20
Sheep, Dall, 72, 214, 220, 221–24
Sheldon, Robert, 7, 11, 12, 14, 135*ff.*, 222
Siberia, 23, 40, 54, 70, 74, 227, 254
Sitka (Alaska), 23, 70, 72, 91, 105
Skagway (Yukon Territory), 91
Sloth, 195
Soapberry, 307
Sorrel, mountain, 306
Sourdock, 306
Sourdough Expedition, 91
Squirrel, red, 137, 194, 287, 288
Stefansson, Vilhjamur, 7, 143
Steller, Georg, 6, 8, 11, 12, 14, 22, 25*ff.*, 58, 59
Steller's sea cow, 25–32
Stuck, Hudson, 8, 153*ff.*
Susitna River (Alaska), 6, 127–29
Swallows, 72
Swans, 82, 87–89
Swift, Jonathan, 248

Taku Inlet (Alaska), 130–34
Tanana River (Alaska), 90, 91, 110–12, 156, 192–95
Tattler Creek (Alaska), 306
Tenderfoot Creek (Alaska), 194
Thailand, 226
Themes, in Arctic-American nature writing
    achievement, 6–7
    communion, 5–6
    in general, 3–4
    self-reliance, 4–5
Thoreau, Henry David, 4, 192
Tlingit (Native American people), vii, 11, 229, 242, 290
Toklat, East Fork (Alaska), 182–88, 301–3
Tongass National Forest, 260, 285
Trapping, fur, 191–96, 241–45, 272
Tributary Creek (Alaska), 307

Udall, Morris, 226
Udall, Stewart, viii
Unalashka (Alaska), 23, 37–42, 63, 74
Universalgeschichte, 16
Ursa Major, 309

Valdez (Alaska), 189, 228
Vancouver, George, 14, 23, 43*ff.*
Van Horn, Joe, 306
Velvet Valley (Alaska), 265
Venianimov, Ivan, 23, 73*ff.*
Victoria Island (Canada), 147
Violets, bog, 217

Voltaire, François, 10
Von Chamisso, Aldelbert, 6, 57ff.
Von Kotzebue, Otto, 6, 23, 53ff., 58

Wagner Institute of Science, 94
Wallace, David Rains, 5, 9, 16, 104, 188, 283ff.
Walrus, 170, 277, 278, 299
Wang Wei, 166
Weasel, 151
Weltanschaunng, 16
West Indies, 216
Western Union Expedition, 23, 91
Whale, 276, 278, 281, 286, 289–91, 294
Whitefish, 260
White Mountains (Alaska), vii
Whistler, James M., 255
Wiseman (Alaska), 173
Whittier (Alaska), 268

Whitehorse (Yukon Territory), 189
Williams, Ambrose, 216
Wolf, 72, 81, 91, 181–86, 214, 220, 229, 262, 267, 303, 307
Wolverine, 72, 262, 272, 303
Wordsworth, Dorothy, 8
Wordsworth, William, 9, 10, 166
Wrangell, Ferdinand, 23, 69ff.

Yakutat Mountains (Alaska), 71
Yakutat (Alaska), 229, 248
Yukon-Charley National Preserve (Alaska), 269–74
Yukon River, viii, 9, 81–83, 86–89, 94–97, 111, 113–16, 156, 157

Zagoskin, L. A., 79ff.
Zemansky, Gil, 265